64-5 1640 ÷ E. a. & Lond. —

66-8 *independent* +74, 86, 87, 92-3, 127, 136
133.
75sqq Land
226 *communism*

79-80 E. of Pembroke

89-90 *Solutamum* +102-3-4, 108
100+ N. Italy — Lucca fishing-vipund
126
Bik - Kellon-Cone
Jordan 4 vols.

About the volume:

This study provides the most comprehensive treatment to date of the exiled Calvinist communities who settled in southern England in general, and in London in particular, during the second half of the sixteenth century. Not only does it locate the foreign Reformed churches within their continental and English religious context, but it also analyses their relationship with the Church of England and English Puritans in the late sixteenth and early seventeenth centuries. Furthermore it offers a new insight into the role and significance of immigrant Calvinist merchants in London, not only for their own communities, but for the economic and cultural life of their hosts.

It also contains chapters on the educational concerns of these communities, such as schooling and university education, in which the Dutch and Walloon churches played a prominent part by directing English students to the newly-founded University of Leiden, which by the early seventeenth century had becomed renowned as the greatest Reformed seat of learning.

It will be invaluable to historians interested in the religious, social, economic and cultural impact of the Calvinist refugee communities on the rapidly changing nation that was Tudor and Stuart England.

About the author:

Ole Peter Grell is a Wellcome Trust Fellow at the Cambridge Wellcome Unit for the History of Medicine and an affiliated lecturer at the Faculty of History, University of Cambridge.

Calvinist Exiles in Tudor and Stuart England

For my parents

Calvinist Exiles in Tudor and Stuart England

OLE PETER GRELL

SCOLAR PRESS

Published by
SCOLAR PRESS
Gower House
Croft Road
Aldershot
Hants GU11 3HR
England

Ashgate Publishing Company
Old Post Road
Brookfield
Vermont 05036-9704
USA

British Library Cataloguing in Publication Data

Grell, Ole Peter
    Calvinist Exiles in Tudor and Stuart England.
    1. Calvinists—England—History—16th century. 2. Calvinists—
    England—History—17th century. 3. Dutch—England—History—
    16th century. 4. Dutch—England—History—17th century. 5.
    England—Church history—16th century. 6. England—Church
    history—17th century.
    I. Title.
    942'.0088242

    ISBN 1-85928-340-3

Library of Congress Cataloging-in-Publication Data

Grell, Ole Peter.
    Calvinist exiles in Tudor and Stuart England/Ole Peter Grell.
        p.   cm.
    Some of the essays were previously published in various other
    publications.
    Includes index.
    ISBN 1-85928-340-3 (cloth)
        1. Reformed (Reformed Church)—England—History—16th century.
    2. Dutch—England—History—16th century. 3. Immigrants—England
    —History—16th century. 4. England—Church History—16th century.
    I. Title.
    BX9458.G7G74 1997
    305.6'42042'09031—dc20
                                                            96-27875
                                                            CIP

ISBN 1 85928 340 3
Printed on acid free paper
Typeset in Sabon by Manton Typesetters, 5-7 Eastfield Road, Louth, Lincolnshire, LN11 7AJ and printed in Great Britain by The Ipswich Book Company Ltd., Suffolk

Contents

Tables

Figures

Preface

Historical interest in the exiled, Reformed communities that settled in England in the reigns of Edward VI and Elizabeth has proliferated since the late 1980s and the publication of Andrew Pettegree's study, *Foreign Protestant Communities in Sixteenth-Century London* (1986) and my own, *Dutch Calvinists in Early Stuart London* (1989). It has recently resulted in the publication in 1993 of a major volume of important source-material, consisting of the consistory records of the Dutch community in London in the Elizabethan period, and the completion of no less than four doctoral dissertations from 1992 onwards, while more are in the pipeline. After the attention given to the larger and more influential stranger communities in the capital the focus has now gradually expanded to include provincial communities in places such as Sandwich, Norwich and Southampton.[1]

Accordingly, it seems an appropriate time to bring together some of the articles concerned with different aspects of the history of the Dutch and Walloon exiles in Elizabethan and Stuart England which I have published over the last ten years in a variety of Dutch and English publications. Of the 11 chapters included in this volume nine have appeared before in different journals and edited volumes. They are reprinted here in a more or less unchanged form, apart from the correction of a few factual errors and the necessary adjustment of the notes.

Chapter 1, 'A new home or a temporary abode? Dutch and Walloon exiles in England', appears here for the first time, as does Chapter 8, 'Tribute and triumph: Dutch pageants and Stuart coronations'. Chapter 2, 'The French and Dutch congregations in London in the early seventeenth century' was first published in *Proceedings of the Huguenot Society*, XXIV, 1987; Chapter 3, 'A friendship turned sour: Puritans and Dutch Calvinists in East Anglia, 1603–1660', was originally published in E. S. Leedham-Green (ed.), *Religious Dissent in East Anglia*, Cambridge, 1991; Chapter 4, 'From uniformity to tolerance: the effects on the Dutch church in London of reverse patterns in English church policy, 1634–1647', first appeared in *Nederlands Archief voor Kerkgeschiedenis*, 66, 1986; Chapter 5, 'Merchants and ministers: the foundations of international Calvinism', was first included in A. Pettegree et al. (eds), *Calvinism in Europe, 1540–1620*, Cambridge, 1994; Chapter 6, 'From persecution to integration: the decline of the Anglo-Dutch communities in England, 1648–1702', appeared in O. P. Grell et al. (eds), *From Persecution to Toleration: The Glorious Revolution and Religion in England*, Oxford, 1991, for the first time; Chapter 7, 'The schooling of the Dutch Calvinist community in London, 1550–1650', was first published in *De zeventiende Eeuw*, 2-2, 1986; Chapter 9, 'Calvinist *agape* or Godly dining club?', was originally printed in *Nederlands Archief voor Kerkgeschiedenis*, 68, 1988; Chapter 10, 'Plague in Elizabethan and Stuart London: the Dutch response', first appeared in *Medical History*, 34, 1990; Chapter 11, 'The attraction of Leiden University for English students of medicine and theology, 1590–1642', was first published in C. C. Barfoot and R. Todd (eds), *The Great Emporium: The Low Countries as a cultural crossroads in the Renaissance and the eighteenth century*, Amsterdam, 1992.

Most of the research for this book was done while I held fellowships from the Carlsberg Foundation in Copenhagen and the Wellcome Trust in London and I should like to express my gratitude to these foundations. Without their support none of this would have been possible.

Over the years I have benefited from the opportunity to discuss my work with friends and colleagues, among them especially Professor Jan van den Berg and Professor Paul Hoftijzer, Leiden, Professor Jonathan Israel, London, Dr Alastair Duke, Southampton, Dr Andrew Pettegree, St Andrews, Dr Edward Chaney, Oxford, and Mr Jeremy Maule, Cambridge and last, but not least, my colleague at the Wellcome Unit for the History of Medicine at the University of Cambridge, Dr Andrew Cunningham.

Ole Peter Grell
Cambridge

Note

1. See A.J. Jelsma and O. Boersma (eds), *Acta van het consistorie van de Nederlandse gemeente te Londen 1569–1585*, Rijks Geschiedkundige Publicatiën, Kleine Serie 76, The Hague 1993; O. Boersma, *Vluchtig Voorbeeld. De nederlandse, franse en italiaanse vluchtelingenkerken in londen, 1568–1585*, The Hague 1994; M. F. Backhouse, *The Flemish and Walloon Communities at Sandwich during the Reign of Elizabeth I (1561–1603)*, 3 vols, University of Southampton Ph.D. 1992; R. Esser, *Niederländische Exulanten den späten 16. und frühen 17. Jahrhunderts. Die Norwicher Fremdengemeinden*, University of Cologne, doctoral dissertation 1993; forthcoming in Historische Forschungen, 55, *Niederländische Exulanten in England des 16. und frühen 17. Jahrhunderts*, Berlin 1996; A. Spicer, *The French Speaking Reformed Community and their Church in Southampton, 1567–c. 1620*, University of Southampton Ph.D. 1995.

CHAPTER ONE

A new home or a temporary abode? Dutch and Walloon exiles in England

For the Reformed diaspora of the sixteenth century, southern England in general and London in particular played a unique part in offering refuge to Calvinist exiles for more than a century. London's and England's popularity among Dutch and Walloon Protestants leaving the Spanish Netherlands, and Huguenots fleeing France, was only matched or temporarily exceeded by that of Geneva for evangelical, French and Italian refugees, and by that of Emden for Dutch and Walloon exiles, and then only for a few decades around the middle of the sixteenth century.[1]

The foundation of the stranger churches in London in 1550 under their own superintendent, the Polish reformer, Johannes a Lasco, had been encouraged by leading figures within the English government and the Church of England who wanted to carry the English Reformation further. The exiles were supported not only by leading evangelicals within the Church of England, such as Bishop John Hooper, but also by Archbishop Cranmer who saw the example of the exiled, Reformed communities not only as a potentially beneficial example for the English church, but also as serving to prevent the spread of Anabaptism among the immigrants themselves, but perhaps more importantly from them to the English host population.[2]

Following the brief Catholic interlude during the reign of Mary, when more than 200 members of the London Dutch community sought temporary refuge in Emden, the accession of Elizabeth in 1559 encouraged the strangers to seek to re-establish their churches in London. Initially the negotiations between leaders of the community and Elizabeth's chief adviser, Sir William Cecil, were far from promising, but eventually the stranger churches were allowed to resume their services. However, the total independence of the Church of England granted them in 1550 was no longer on offer from the English government. The foreign communities were allowed to retain their own discipline, but were placed under the jurisdiction of the bishop of London. That this, in the first instance, turned out to be Edmund Grindal who was positively inclined towards the refugees, having himself spent years in exile under Mary, undoubtedly made this restriction easier to accept for the strangers. For the English government the attraction of the exiles was no longer their Reformed religion and discipline, but rather the economic potential of their community, consisting of highly skilled craftsmen and merchants who might help transfer important skills which could prove beneficial to the English economy.[3]

This economic rationale, which after some hesitation had convinced Elizabeth and her chief ministers to encourage the resettlement of the Dutch and Walloon immigrants in London, quickly led to a close co-operation between the leaders of the Reformed churches in London and the English government in establishing new communities of godly immigrants in a number of provincial towns in southern England during the 1560s. Most of these towns had witnessed a rapid economic and demographic decline during the sixteenth century and were keen to receive an injection of highly skilled craftsmen who might help invigorate the local economy. Thus, the Dutch community in Austin Friars in London were instrumental in establishing communities in Sandwich (1561) and Maidstone (1567), and undoubtedly assisted in the creation of the Dutch and Walloon communities in Norwich (1565) and Colchester (1568–69).[4]

Considering the dramatic increase in the number of refugees who arrived from the Netherlands in the wake of the failed attempt of a Reformed reformation during the so-called Wonderyear of 1566,[5] which was further accelerated by the violent repression of Protestantism by the Duke of Alvà and his Council of Troubles between 1567 and 1572,[6] this was evidently a sensible solution for the Elizabethan government, as well as for the foreign churches in London. It took the pressure off the capital where the arrival, especially after 1567, of considerable numbers of refugee craftsmen in particular might easily unsettle the often volatile native population of apprentices and craftsmen in the City and generate xenophobia towards the stranger churches in particular. Similarly, it lightened the financial burden for the stranger churches in the capital, who often struggled to find enough capital to assist the many, often destitute, new arrivals from the southern Netherlands.

For the Elizabethan authorities it remained a problem throughout most of the Queen's reign to balance the perceived economic benefit from this Calvinist immigration with the worries it produced in the host population, especially in London. Periodically strong popular fears were voiced to the effect that the capital was being swamped with waves of new refugees who would undercut the livelihoods of the native population by taking over their work at lower rates. Throughout her reign it remained an essential part of the Queen's strategy to try to contain such escalating xenophobia within the host population by ordering returns of aliens to be compiled in the capital. This was done, more often than not to dispel the hysterically inflated figures concerning the size of the alien population in the capital which circulated at intervals. Simultaneously, of course, these returns compiled by the individual aldermen or their deputies in the wards, provided Elizabeth with a realistic assessment of the number of aliens within the City, their abode and occupation. Discretion was a major concern for the Elizabethan administration when returns were ordered. At each occasion, in 1568, in 1582–83 and finally in 1593, the Privy Council emphasized that the greatest care should be taken when the information was collated. This should be done to prevent general xenophobia and individual troublemakers within the host population from taking action against the immigrants in order that the refugee communities should not be caused unnecessary anxiety.[7] Undoubtedly popular perception in London was strongly influenced by the considerable number of immigrants who arrived after Alva's anti-Protestant campaign had commenced in 1567. If numbers were, indeed, high only a fraction appears to have stayed on in London. A fair number, encouraged by the English authorities and the leaders of the stranger churches in London, left to join the provincial Dutch/ Walloon communities in southeast England, while others quickly returned to the Continent, initially to join the immigrant comunities in Germany, but later after the start of the Dutch Revolt in 1572 to settle in the rebellious provinces of Holland and Zeeland.

From the outset the emigration from The Netherlands was complex, not only in motivation – being religious, as well as economic – but also in terms of destination. The refugees were constantly on the move. Initially they found safe havens in Emden, London and southern Germany. Most of these places were in both communication and traffic excellently placed for retaining close contacts with family and friends in The Netherlands. Obviously with the optimism surrounding the events leading to the Wonderyear of 1566 many refugees wanted and were able to return quickly to their country or region of origin, only to seek renewed exile either in the cities which had previously given them refuge or in some of the other major centres for the Reformed exodus, when the Wonderyear proved a failure. Once more the revolt in 1572 encouraged re-emigration, while the Pacification of Ghent in 1576 prompted a large scale return initially to the northern provinces of Holland and Zeeland in particular and somewhat later, from 1580 onwards, to the southern provinces where the returning exiles joined the semi-clandestine churches 'under the cross', especially in the cities of Antwerp, Bruges, Ghent and Brussels. Meanwhile a stream of Reformed refugees were fleeing France as a consequence of the St Bartholomew Massacre (1572), often joining the exiled communities established by their French-speaking, Walloon co-religionists in Germany and England.

Finally, the fall of Antwerp in 1585 and the other major cities in the southern Netherlands once more caused new waves of religious refugees to leave these areas. It has been estimated that half the population of Antwerp, around 38,000 people, left the city within four years of its surrender to the Duke of Parma, Alexander Farnese.[8] This time, however, the majority settled in the rebellious United Provinces, even if considerable numbers reached both England and Germany. Gradually, however, the exiled communities in Germany and England saw members return to the Dutch Republic, especially after 1590 when Philip II of Spain lifted the embargo against Dutch shipping and goods to the Iberian Peninsula while simultaneously changing his military strategy in The Netherlands away from the costly offensive warfare of the 1580s towards a cheaper defensive policy which made it possible for him to intervene in the Wars of Religion in France. The Dutch took full advantage of this opportunity and recaptured a considerable amount of territory from the Spaniards, including the cities of Deventer and Zutphen in 1591, securing the borders of the young Republic, opening up routes between Germany and Holland, while blockading the Flemish coast. This all served to enhance the growing economic preponderance and mercantile strength of the Dutch Republic, which in turn encouraged many emigrant merchants, who had previously settled in Germany and England, to return to the Netherlands.[9]

Obviously, an accurate estimate of the size of this emigration is extremely difficult to make, bearing in mind the complex web of emigration and re-emigration which often continued for generations and did not end until the first decades of the seventeenth century.[10] Combining data from the research of Geoffrey Parker and J. Briels, Jonathan Israel has recently estimated the first major wave of Reformed emigrants to leave the Netherlands in the period 1567–72 to have comprised around 60,000 people, while the second wave, post-1585, may have consisted of 100,000 or even as many as 150,000 people.[11] Undoubtedly Israel is correct when concluding that these two waves were among the four great west European migrations of the early modern period and that the largest of them all was the migration from the southern Netherlands which followed the fall of Antwerp in 1585. However, allowances have to be made for the effects of the continued re-emigration of the period. It strikes me as being highly likely that a large proportion of the first wave of 60,000 is included in the post-1585 figure of between 100,000 and 150,000, thus having been counted at least twice. A more cautious figure for the whole period 1567–90 would probably put the number of emigrants closer to 100,000 rather than 200,000. That however, still remains an impressive figure.

Recent estimates assume that 10,000 of these refugees had found refuge in London by 1590. Considering that the returns of 1593 list around 7,000 aliens in the capital the 10,000 may well be close to the true figure, at a time when the extensive re-emigration of the 1590s to the provinces of Holland and Zeeland had yet to begin.[12] Furthermore, it is evident that the alien Reformed communities in the City were seriously boosted in the wake of the Duke of Alva's repression which began in 1567. For England as a whole, a rough estimate would suggest that the number of Reformed, Dutch, Walloon and French refugees peaked in the late 1580s, reaching nearly 20,000 people.[13] In purely numerical terms this was an impressive figure constituting close to a fifth of the total emigration from the Netherlands. However, the size of the immigrant population in England fluctuated widely in the late sixteenth century and may have declined rapidly during the 1590s when the economic and political fortune of the United Provinces, as already mentioned, improved dramatically, while the deteriorating economic climate in England saw a growing hostility towards the immigrants not only within the host population but also within local government and Parliament.[14]

By the early seventeenth century the immigrant population in England remained much more stable. Those Reformed exiles who wanted to return to the Netherlands had left by then and, until the 1620s, only a trickle of new refugees arrived. Then a number of Huguenots sought refuge as a consequence of the renewed Religious Wars in France. Consequently, the Dutch-speaking communities and churches shrank slowly but gradually during the first decades of the seventeenth century, losing members who were often second- or third-generation Netherlanders born in England to their host community.

Not all Dutch and Walloon immigrants took up membership of the foreign Reformed churches in England. A fair number only attended the services as visitors – passanten – while some would have stayed clear of the churches and their discipline altogether, for either religious or social reasons. The tendency to stay outside the confines of the foreign churches would undoubtedly have been less pronounced outside London in the smaller provincial towns where it would have been difficult for the exiles to exist without membership of the churches. The percentage of the immigrants who took up membership of the foreign Reformed churches appears to have grown over time from around 50 per cent in the 1560s to around 80 per cent towards the end of Elizabeth's reign. The fact that the stranger churches to an increasing extent also dealt with purely lay matters towards the end of the sixteenth century, negotiating with local authorities, companies, guilds and so on, in order to protect the interests and livelihood of their members, would have made them increasingly attractive to most Dutch and Walloon immigrants. The success of the Dutch Revolt and the establishment of a network of Reformed churches in the provinces of Holland and Zeeland in particular would simultaneously have served to remove the perceived risk entailed in membership of one of the exiled churches for the many immigrants who continued to maintain close contacts with the Netherlands.[15]

However, even for those Reformed immigrants who made England their permanent home, many, especially within the merchant elite which came to dominate these refugee communities and churches towards the end of the sixteenth century, retained close family contacts and business interests in the Netherlands. Evidence from the Dutch community in London would suggest that post-1585 and the fall of Antwerp, the focus of these contacts shifted away from the cities of the southern Netherlands, which by then seemed irrevocably lost to the Spaniards, and from where most of the Dutch and Walloon exiles in London originated, to the province of Zeeland, and the city of Middelburg in particular, which proved especially popular as a new place of residence for many of the refugees from Brabant and Flanders.[16]

A few examples of how this immigration worked in practice might help to clarify the nature of this Reformed exodus and also help explain why the foreign Reformed churches in England managed to retain members who in many instances were children if not grandchildren born to the original immigrants. The experience of the learned merchant Johan Radermacher (see Figure 1.1) is undoubtedly representative of a large number of Reformed refugees. Radermacher, who was born into a patrician family from Aachen in 1538, appears to have spent his early years in London, where his parents seem to have settled shortly before the foundation of the stranger churches in 1550. When Radermacher's father died in 1554, the sixteen-year-old Johan was apprenticed to the wealthy Antwerp merchant Aegidius Hooftman, with whom his family might already have been associated, since both families originated from the Aachen region. The reign of Mary and the Catholic reaction which followed may well have encouraged the Radermachers to seek an apprenticeship for Johan among co-religionists back on the Continent rather than to let him stay in London.[17] Five years later, undoubtedly enticed by Elizabeth's succession, Johan Radermacher returned to London where he may well have acted as a representative for the firm of Hooftman. He was actively involved in once more securing the use of the church of Austin Friars for the Dutch community in London in connection with the stranger churches' refoundation in 1560. Accordingly, a year later Radermacher was elected deacon to the London Dutch church, a capacity in which he served for

1.1   Johan Radermacher (1607). Engraving by Johan Dircksz van Campen

five years until the Wonderyear of 1566 encouraged him to return to
Antwerp. The disappointed expectations which accompanied the

collapse of the Wonderyear must have encouraged him to return to London in 1567 this time as the official representative or factor of the merchant-house of Hooftman. On his return he joined the small Italian church in London, where his friend, the Dutch historian Emanuel van Meteren, had become a member following the strife surrounding the ministry of Adriaan van Haemstede which had split the Dutch community in London in the early 1560s. It was probably no coincidence that Radermacher became an elder to the London Dutch church in 1571 at the same time as Van Meteren was finally reconciled with the community in Austin Friars and rejoined the church. Bearing in mind that he had felt unable to serve the Italian church in any formal capacity only three years earlier, pointing to his many business obligations, it is amazing that Radermacher felt able to take on the much greater responsibilities of an eldership in Austin Friars. His brief membership of the Italian church may well have been a religious and political move intended to force the Dutch church to heal the split which had occurred in the 1560s and initiate the reconciliation which eventually happened in 1571. There are no indications that Radermacher's financial and commercial engagement had changed or that his association with Aegidius Hooftman had weakened by 1571. If anything, it was strengthened in 1571 when Johan Radermacher formalized his ties with the Hooftman family by marrying a niece of Aegidius Hooftman, Johanna Racket, who over the years bore him no less than 12 children.[18]

For the next nine years Radermacher dilligently served the Dutch church in London as an elder, until he re-emigrated to Antwerp in December 1580.[19] During the last year of his eldership Radermacher seems to have spent a considerable time in Antwerp possibly preparing his return to that city.[20] The positive religious and economic climate which followed the Pacification of Ghent in 1576 and which had seen a rapid expansion of the semi-clandestine Reformed churches in the southern Netherlands, may well have encouraged Radermacher to return to Antwerp, as may of course the declining health of his boss, Aegidius Hooftman, who died in 1581 shortly after Radermacher's return. By 15 July 1581 Radermacher had exchanged his London eldership for an Antwerp one. He played an active part in the Reformed community in Antwerp until the city's surrender to Alexander Farnese in 1585. His standing in Antwerp must have been considerable since he was heavily involved in the negotiations which led to the city's surrender. He was awarded a gift by the city for an agreement which allowed those Protestants within the city who refused to convert to Catholicism, four years to leave Antwerp.[21]

Radermacher himself returned to his birthplace Aachen, where he was elected an elder to the Dutch Reformed church in 1589. His importance was not only acknowledged within the exiled, Reformed community, but also in Aachen as such where he was made 'Weinmeister' in 1598 shortly before the city's return to the Catholic fold forced him to find a new refuge in Hamburg. His stay here proved short and within a year or two he settled in Middelburg in Zeeland, where he was elected an elder in 1602 and lived until his death in 1617. Thus Radermacher's active involvement in the Reformed Dutch churches spanned more than 40 years and comprised four elderships in London, Antwerp, Aachen and Middelburg respectively, reflecting the ever-changing pattern of emigration and re-emigration which characterized these exiled Reformed communities from around the middle of the sixteenth until the first years of the seventeenth century. In spite of having left the Dutch church in London in 1580 Radermacher maintained close relations with the leaders of this community with whom he corresponded regularly. Social and religious experiences such as his served to create a network of godly, Reformed merchants and ministers spread across Germany, southern England and the United Provinces.[22]

While the case of Radermacher can be seen as typical of the significant number of Reformed immigrants whose residence in England proved temporary, the experience of William Courten and his family offers an excellent example of those who stayed and made England their home.

William Courten and his wife Margaret Cassier (see Figures 1.2 and 1.3) fled their home town of Menen, near Kortrijk in Flanders, in 1568 and sought refuge in London together with their daughter Margaret and possibly an apprentice, Matthias Boudaen from Antwerp, who 16 years later married Margaret in London.[23] Menen had been a centre for Reformed Protestantism during the Wonderyear in 1566, but the repression initiated by the Duke of Alva in 1567 led to mass emigration from the town primarily to England.[24] Courten, who must have been a wealthy cloth manufacturer and merchant before he left for London, celebrated his successful flight from Menen by having a large silver drinking-cup made which carried an inscription, telling us that he had been imprisoned by Alva's Council of Troubles on 2 March 1568, but thanks to God's Providence, in the form of a helping hand from his wife, he had managed to escape from prison three weeks later (see Figures 1.4 and 1.5).

The Courten family quickly re-established the family firm in London and continued to trade successfully in the specialized, luxury end of the cloth trade, such as silks and fine linen, in which the highly skilled immigrant craftsmen were dominant. Likewise, they became active members of the Dutch church in London where William Courten became a deacon in 1574 eventually succeeding to the eldership 12 years later.[25]

1.2   William Courten (1575). Painting. Artist unknown. Southern Netherlands
school

A son, the later Sir William Courten, was born in London in 1572
and another son, Peter, was born ten years later. At an early age both
brothers were dispatched to learn the ropes of the trade and to repre-

1.3 Margaret Cassier (1616). Painting. Artist unknown. Northern Netherlands school

sent the family firm at important trade centres in northern Europe. William took up residence in Haarlem in the United Provinces from where he did not return to London until the turn of the century, having

1.4   William Courten's silver drinking-cup (*c.* 1567). Height 16 cm

by then made an excellent match, in financial terms at least, by marry-ing the deaf and dumb daughter of the wealthy Haarlem merchant, Peter Cromling. According to contemporary rumours the Cromling daughter came with an impressive dowry of £60,000. Some years later William's younger brother, Peter Courten, left for Cologne to represent the firm there. Meanwhile their sister, Margaret, who at the age of 20 had married Matthias Boudaen, gave birth to at least five children from 1584 to 1599; of these, the first three were baptized in the Dutch church in London, while Pieter Boudaen (Courten), born in 1594, and Anna Boudaen (Courten) (see Figure 1.6), born in 1599, were both born in Rotterdam.[26] Their father, Matthias Boudaen, appears to have

1.5 William Courten's silver drinking-cup (c. 1567). Inside of cup, diameter 16 cm

died around the turn of the century, followed closely by the death of his father-in-law, William Courten, senior.

In 1606 the family firm of Courten witnessed a major transformation as a consequence of these recent deaths. In May 1606, Margaret, the widowed sister of William and Peter Courten (see Figure 1.7), married the merchant John de Moncy, a fellow exile from Flanders, and shortly

1.6 Anna Boudaen Courten (1619). Painted by Salomon Mesdach in Middelburg

afterwards Moncy entered into a formal business partnership with his brothers-in-law, taking a 25 per cent interest in the firm of Courten.[27] By then Peter Courten may well have taken up residence in Middelburg

1.7 Margaret Courten (1625). Painted by Salomon Mesdach in Middelburg

to look after the firm's interest in the Netherlands. The choice of Middelburg was an obvious one for exiles who originated from the southern Netherlands. Together with Leiden and Haarlem, Middelburg was undoubtedly the city in the United Provinces which benefited most from the immigration of Reformed merchants and craftsmen from the south. In 1576 Middelburg had a population of 7,000 people, but thanks to immigration this had more than quadrupled less than 50 years later, reaching 30,000 in 1622.[28] Bearing in mind that by far the greater number of the deacons and elders, who served the Dutch community in London in the late sixteenth and early seventeenth centuries, originated from the southern Netherlands, especially from the larger cities such as Antwerp and Ghent, it is not surprising that Middelburg came to play such an important role for the Dutch community in London, especially from the 1590s onwards when the dominance of the 'rich traders' – the capital intensive market in luxury items – by the young Dutch Republic had become evident to contemporaries.[29]

Being a partner in the wealthy merchant house of Courten, Peter Courten (see Figure 1.8) quickly rose to prominence in Middelburg and in 1615 he was elected an elder of the Reformed church in the city for the first time – a post of trust and influence to which he was regularly re-elected every four years until his death.[30] Sir Peter Courten died without issue in 1630 and left his considerable estate, estimated to be worth £100,000 at the time of his death, in the hands of his nephew, Peter Boudaen Courten. Considering his active involvement in the merchant house of Courten, Peter Boudaen Courten may well have resided with his uncle in Middelburg until he married Catharina Fourmenois in 1618. A few years later, in 1621, he was elected a deacon to the Reformed church in Middelburg and within three years of Sir Peter Courten's death he had succeeded his uncle as an elder to the Reformed community in the city.[31]

The merchant house of Courten was one of the wealthiest firms trading out of London in the reigns of James I and Charles I. It has been estimated that Sir William Courten personally forwarded loans to King James and King Charles of more than £18,000 and £16,000 respectively, while far greater loans provided for the crown, close to the value of £200,000, were provided by the firm of Courten in partnership with one of its closest collaborators, Sir Paul Pindar.[32] It was undoubtedly in recognition of these services that James knighted the brothers Peter and William Courten in 1622–23.

The house of Courten was not only engaged in the European trade in general, and in trade in Portugal and Spain in particular, but was also heavily involved in trade in Guinea and the West Indies and, from 1635, it began interloping the English East India Company in trade with Goa, Malabar, China and Japan. At its peak, the firm is supposed to have owned around 20 large ships and employed around 5,000 sailors and to have been a major force in the herring fisheries around Britain while simultaneously acting as one of the major banking and insurance houses

1.8 Sir Peter Courten (1617). Painted by Salomon Mesdach in Middelburg

in the City.[33] By the time of Sir William Courten's death in 1636 there were, however, already strong indications that the firm was seriously overextended even if it relied for extra capital and investment on a number of wealthy English and Anglo-Dutch merchants. By then, many of the loans the house of Courten had provided for the Crown and others were no longer recoverable, and the bankruptcy which eventually engulfed the second Sir William Courten in 1642 was predictable.

The first Sir William Courten had followed in the footsteps of his father as an active member of the Dutch Reformed church in Austin Friars, where he remained one of the community's major financial backers from the beginning of the seventeenth century until his death in 1636.[34] However, he showed no inclination to succeed his father within the church's leadership. Thus he declined to take up the eldership he was elected to in 1628. His many business affairs may well have prevented him from accepting the eldership, but he might also have felt that the family was already doing its bit in that respect through his brother-in-law, John de Moncy. Moncy had already taken his place among the leadership of the Dutch Reformed community in London in 1612 when he was elected a deacon, eventually being promoted to the eldership in 1621. He served the community uninterrupted until his death in 1632, being among other things heavily engaged in the collections in England for Calvinist refugee ministers from the two German Palatinates during the Thirty Years War.[35]

In this major relief operation for fellow-Calvinists on the Continent, which was to continue for nearly 20 years, John de Moncy was joined by another two elders and colleagues from the consistory of the London Dutch church, John la Motte and Dirick Hoste.[36]

Like Moncy, John la Motte (see Figure 1.9) originated from Ypres, from where his father Francis had fled to Colchester in 1563–64 and where John was born on 1 May 1577.[37] By the second decade of the seventeenth century La Motte had become a successful merchant and it was during this period that he moved from Colchester to London. He is recorded as residing in the parish of St Bartholomew by the Exchange in 1615. By 1618 he lived in Broad Street and was a freeman of the Company of Weavers. Initially he must have joined his local parish church; after having served as a constable in 1619, he became a church warden in 1621. Three years later, however, he was elected an elder of the Dutch Reformed church in the city, unusually without having served the community as a deacon prior to his election.[38] That year he also married one of the wealthiest women members of the Dutch church in London, Elizabeth van Poele, the widow of the former Clerk of the Signet, Sir Levinius Munck, who had died in 1623 leaving his widow an estate estimated to be worth close to £40,000.[39] His business acumen

1.9 John la Motte (1655). Engraving by Faithorne

combined with his financially astute marriages guaranteed that La Motte belonged to the merchant elite, not only within the Dutch community but within the wider London merchant fraternity. That his abilities were highly thought of can be seen from the fact that he was elected Upper Bailiff of the Weavers' Company in 1629.[40]

However, it was his piety and godliness which particularly impressed many of his contemporaries. Samuel Clarke included him in his lives of pious men and women of the age. According to him La Motte:

> For the nourishment and increase of Piety in his Soul, and main-
> taining Communion with God, he was constant and dilligent in
> attendance upon the publick Ordinance and means of Grace, not
> only in the Dutch Church, whereof he was made a member, but
> also in the Parish Church wherein his habitation was, and wherein
> were several Lectures, which he frequented, as I myself observed,
> who was his near Neighbour for many years.[41]

Through his daughter's marriage to Maurice Abbot, John la Motte was
linked to one of the leading Calvinist/Puritan merchant families in the
City. It was most likely through his son-in-law's father, Sir Maurice
Abbot, who was an active member of the vestry of St Stephen's Coleman
Street and sponsor of the minister John Goodwin, that La Motte got to
know Goodwin who dedicated one of his early works, *Christ's Approbation to Marie's Choice*, to him.[42]

In his funeral sermon for John la Motte Fulke Bellers rightly emphasized La Motte's deep involvement in charitable causes, especially those
which sought to relieve the sufferings of fellow-refugee Calvinists:

> And how real his piety and acquaintance with God was, appeared
> sufficiently, as by many other discoveries, so also by those streams
> of true Christian *charity* which uncessantly issued from him, and
> made him not only willing and ready to impart and communicate
> liberally in that kind himself, but also to solicite and stir up others
> perpetually, *setting* all (as it were) on *fire of compassion* that came
> neer him, especially where and whensoever any publick calamity
> befell the people and Church of God.[43]

In spite of his deep involvement with the Dutch church in London and
his activities on behalf of fellow Reformed refugees abroad, John la
Motte continued his work within the Company of Weavers and his
local English community. He continued to attend his parish church, and
was elected a governor of Bridewell Hospital. Consequently he became
the first member of Austin Friars to be elected an Alderman in 1648.[44]

Every year he celebrated the anniversary of Queen Elizabeth's coronation by inviting friends to his house

> and put them in mind of the great *Mercy of God* shewed to
> England on that day, by quenching the fires in Smith field, and
> continuing the *Gospel* ever since, for so many years among us,
> even *beyond the number of years recorded in Scripture, of an
> uninterrupted prosperous estate of the Church*; and then, as also
> on his *Birth-day*, and other joyfull occasions of friends, meeting at
> his house he would often say he had desired their company, *to eat
> bread with them before the Lord* (as *Jethro* and *Moses* did) in
> remembrance of such and such signal *Mercies* and *Deliverances*,
> whereof *his memory was a living Chronicle*, especially of those
> grand Deliverances both before and since the *Reformation*, from
> under the great sufferings and bloody *Persecutions* in France, and

the *Low Countries*, whereof he would often discourse in so punctuall and feeling manner, as if he had been an eye-witness, yea a sharer in them, taking many arguments thence of encouraging himself and others to be still *mindfull* of them in bonds and miseries, as being themselves in the body; saying, why, their case might have been ours, or may yet, who knows?[45]

Among John la Motte's many business ventures was a stake in the East India association organized by Sir William Courten and licensed in 1635 to compete with the English East India Company which had hitherto held a monopoly on this trade.[46] In this venture he was joined by a group of prominent elders and deacons from the Dutch community in London, such as Joos Godschalck, Walrave Lodewyck, Jan Ruyshout, Nicolas Corselis, Adam Lawrence, and Dirick Hoste, of whom no less than three were already active within the English East India Company.[47] Together with William Courten these Dutch merchants collaborated closely with a group of new, English merchants in the City, of whom the most prominent was Maurice Thomson. Later in the early 1640s, on behalf of Parliament, Maurice Thomson together with Adam Lawrence, Nicolas Corselis and Dirick Hoste were engaged in raising funds for suffering Irish Protestants in the Holland and Zeeland.[48]

Like William Courten, John de Moncy and John la Motte Dirick Hoste originated from Flanders (see Figure 1.10). His father, Jacques Hoste, appears to have fled Oudenaarde in Flanders for religious reasons in 1568 and subsequently settled in London. Here he married a fellow exile in 1572 and had his first three children baptized in the church of Austin Friars.[49] The Hoste family appears to have been close to the Courtens since William Courten stood godfather at the baptism of the daughter Maria in 1579. Shortly afterwards, however, the Hostes joined many of their co-refugees from the southern Netherlands and left for Middelburg in Zeeland, where Dirick Hoste and his twin brother Jacques were born in 1588. The Hoste family may well have retained some business interests in London, since Dirick had returned to the City by 1607. Six years later, in 1613, Dirick Hoste married Jane van Meteren/Desmaistres (see Figure 1.11), daughter of the wealthy immigrant brewer, James van Meteren, while also being granted denization.[50]

Dirick Hoste seems to have concentrated on overseas trade from the outset. In 1615 he became a member of the English East India Company. At the start of Charles I's reign he also appears to have operated as a member of a group of Dutch and Flemish merchants, who supplied the king of Spain with gunpowder, cordage and iron for his ports in Africa and who received their payment in Brazil wood. These merchants constituted a network with representatives in major European ports, such as Amsterdam, Antwerp, Hamburg and London not to

1.10 Dirick Hoste (1628). Painting by Cornelius Jonson. Private collection; (stolen 1992 – present location unknown)

mention the 'Straits of Venice and Leghorn'.[51] Like so many of his merchant colleagues among the eldership of Austin Friars Dirick Hoste was also active in banking. Among his customers were the Royal physi-

1.11 Jane Desmaistres (1628). Painting by Cornelius Jonson. Private collection; (stolen 1992 – present location unknown)

cian, Sir Theodore de Mayerne, and the Spanish ambassadors to London. That the Spanish customs farmers who financed the Catholic Imperial armies in the Netherlands and in Germany during the Thirty

Years War should have kept their cash on deposit with him is, however, somewhat surprising considering Hoste's strong commitment to the Calvinist cause.[52] Evidently, purely financial motives might occasionally cause Calvinist bankers like Hoste, if not to turn a blind eye, then at least not to enquire too deeply about the possible destination of the money they held and transferred.

Dirick Hoste was elected a deacon to Austin Friars in 1627 and served the Dutch community in this capacity for less than a year before being promoted to the eldership in June 1628.[53] Thus he followed in the footsteps of his father, Jacques Hoste, who had served the Reformed church in Middelburg regularly as an elder between 1597 and 1605.[54] Furthermore, Dirick Hoste was actively involved in at least two of the great collections for persecuted co-religionists of the period. In November 1630 the consistory of Austin Friars delegated the responsibility for the second royal collection in England for Reformed refugees from the German Palatinate to four merchants–elders: Dirick Hoste, John la Motte, John de Moncy and Abraham Beck. Later, in 1643, Dirick Hoste was one of four Commissioners appointed by Parliament to raise funds for persecuted Irish Protestants in the Netherlands. Together with another two elders from the London Dutch community, Nicholas Corselis and Adam Lawrence, and the City radical and colonizer, Maurice Thomson, Hoste was able to extend what had hitherto been a mercantile relationship with Maurice Thomson into the sphere of religion and politics.[55]

For a godly merchant like Dirick Hoste religion, trade and politics could not easily be separated. Thus in 1629 he published an English translation of his friend and consistorial colleague, Jacob Cool's, *Of Death, a true Description*. In the 'Epistele Dedicatorie' to six of his and Cool's English merchant friends, Hoste emphasized the pious conversation they had all benefited from while Cool was alive:

> Yee often haue taken and built your credit on his word, in your bought Wares, which the effect hath confirmed to your profit. Once more beleeue him, and buy these Meditations, on his word, the price is but your acceptance, reading and application. And if thus you will vse, and trie these his last Marchandizes, they will proue vnto you, of infinite worth, and price, for by them you shall obtaine that precarious Pearle and hidden treasure, of which the Gospell mentions.

By using mercantile metaphors Hoste took the opportunity to forcefully recommend Cool's pastoral work on death not only to their mutual friends, but to the wider readership of godly merchants in London, where both he and Jacob Cool would have been well known.[56]

Apart from the individual tales of persecution, exodus and life in exile which the experiences of Johan Radermacher, William Courten

and his family, John de Moncy, John la Motte and Dirick Hoste illustrate, it still remains to determine the general significance of these
examples of merchant immigrants who fled the southern Netherlands in
order to settle in England in the late sixteenth and early seventeenth
centuries.

Merchant families such as these always constituted a minority within
the Dutch and Walloon communities in England. By the beginning of
the seventeenth century only around 25 per cent of the London Dutch
community were classified as merchants, but even so they dominated
the community in nearly every respect. Their influence may well have
been less in the first decades after the stranger churches' re-establishment in 1560, but without them the stranger churches could not have
survived for long. It was their financial clout and organizational skills
which guaranteed that the stranger churches had a long term future.
Without the regular and substantial donations from merchants such as
the Courtens, La Motte and Hoste the necessary sums to provide for the
church and the community would never have been forthcoming, nor
would the organizational skills combined with religious commitment so
necessary for a qualified eldership have been in ready supply.[57] Nor, for
that matter, would the extensive contacts to English central and local
authorities, have existed. In other words, without this Dutch and Walloon
merchant-banking aristocracy, the stranger communities would have
found themselves far more exposed to xenophobic reactions from the
host population in times of crisis.

The example of Johan Radermacher confirms that the emigration of
members of the Reformed faith from the southern Netherlands was not
a simple emigration from one place to another, but more often than not
consisted of a series of movements often stretching over decades.
Radermacher's experience certainly underlines the complexity of this
exodus. Twice Radermacher made his home in London and Antwerp
respectively, only to be forced to return to his birthplace Aachen. From
there he emigrated, again for religious reasons, via Hamburg to
Middelburg, which proved to be the final destination for him and for
many of his co-religionists from the southern Netherlands.

The Courten, La Motte and Hoste families all settled in England.
However, in spite of finding a new and permanent home in England,
they only integrated slowly into their host community. For religious,
cultural and financial reasons the first couple of generations of immigrants tended towards endogamy. Deeply conscious of their Reformed
roots, the cause of their exile, and admired by the Presbyterian/Puritan
opposition within the Church of England, their sense of a specific and
providential identity would have served to reinforce their sense of being
a separate, Dutch-speaking community.[58]

Simultaneously these merchants retained considerable business and property interests in their country of origin, even if by the 1590s most, if not all, of their engagements had shifted away from the southern Netherlands to the United Provinces in the north, where they focused on Middelburg in particular. Peter Courten spent most of his life in Middelburg where he served the Reformed church as an elder and died in 1630. His brother-in-law, John de Moncy, resided in Middelburg for short periods in the early 1630s. Most of Dirick Hoste's family settled in Middelburg and Dirick lived there on and off during the Civil War and Interregnum and he still owned a house in Middelburg at the time of his death. This Middelburg connection is further emphasized by the fact that Dirick Hoste's cousin, Hieronimus Willemsen Aschman, who served Austin Friars as a deacon for most of the second decade of the seventeenth century, later, from 1622, served the Reformed church in Middelburg as a deacon and in the 1630s and 1640s as an elder, eventually became burgomaster of Middelburg.[59]

Thus, in spite of their gradual integration into English society, which accelerated by the third generation, these immigrant merchant families who settled in England made sure that they owned property not only in their new country but also back in their country of origin. Having experienced the turmoil of flight and immigration the need to have an alternative just in case something unexpected happened and their new home proved temporary, must have been paramount. That they should have chosen Middelburg where so many of their friends and family had settled in the wake of their flight from the southern provinces can hardly surprise. Bearing this in mind, the prominence given to Middelburg in the paintings decorating the Triumphal Arch the London Dutch community erected for the coronation of James I in 1604 is perfectly understandable.[60] To many of the merchants of the London Dutch community Middelburg was nothing less than a second home in this period.

Undoubtedly the sixteenth century Netherlandic tradition of such wealthy merchants as Aegidius Hooftman in Antwerp, having their portraits painted, would have inspired these immigrant Calvinist merchants to have their own portraits and those of their wives painted. But the fact that they had been forced into exile might have added further impetus to their choice, providing their families with some sense of identity in the often disorientating world of refugees who had sought shelter in foreign lands.

Disregarding changes in fashion over the period we are concerned with here, some striking differences between the way the original immigrants and their children, and in some cases their grandchildren, had themselves portrayed can be detected. The portraits of the Courten family are particularly revealing in this respect. The portraits of William Courten (1575) (see Figure 1.1) and his wife Margaret Cassier (1616) (see Figure 1.2), painted with an interval of more than 30 years, show us a wealthy, Reformed couple, elegantly but modestly dressed. Little if any lace is worn by either and significantly neither wears jewels or other ornaments. Undoubtedly the self-image which the older Courtens wanted to convey was that of a godly couple. The same image is promoted in the portrait of Johan Radermacher, printed in 1607. Radermacher's attire is similarly low key, while the only ring on his hand is a signet-ring, not a decoration but an essential tool for the man of letters and business. This scholarly orientation of Radermacher is further empha-sized by the presence in the left corner of the portrait of a folio volume on a bookstand, while he holds a smaller volume in his right hand.

By the time the Middelburg painter, Salomon Mesdach, painted the portraits of William and Margaret's children, Sir Peter Courten (1617) (see Figure 1.7) and his sister, Margaret Courten (see Figure 1.6), some significant changes had taken place in the way these Reformed immi-grants wanted themselves to be portrayed. Gone is the former genera-tion's modesty in dress. Black may well remain the dominant colour of their clothes, but the intricacy of patterns and material tell a different story. Thus the clothes worn by Sir Peter Courten are far more elaborate and elegant than those worn by his father. Large and expensive lace-works are incorporated into his collar and cuffs, while he is shown wearing silk stockings and fur-trimmed gloves, not to mention the gold-embroidered belt decorating his waist.[61]

Similar elegance is exhibited by Sir Peter's sister, Margaret, in her portrait. She is shown wearing an elaborate and expensive lace bonnet under her broad-brimmed hat, while her cuffs display similar lace-work to that of her bonnet. But more significantly, Margaret is portrayed wearing a considerable amount of jewellery. It is worn discreetly, but consists of no less than three rings; one is a signet-ring, while the other two are purely decorative, containing different and costly stones. Fur-thermore, Margaret is shown wearing triple-band pearl bracelets and pearl earrings, while inside her ruff-collar a pearl necklace is just visible.[62]

When Salomon Mesdach had painted her daughter Anna Boudaen Courten's portrait six years earlier, the move away from the austere Calvinistic attire of her grandparents, William Courten and Margaret Cassier, had been further emphasized (see Figure 1.6). Even if Anna's dress still remains predominantly black, its elegance, cost and intricate use of a wealth of lace, even in the ruff-collar and inserted in the skirt, demonstrates a distinctive and decisive departure from the way her grandparents would have dressed and expected their offspring to dress. Furthermore, Anna's extensive use of jewellery, some of which is incorporated into her dress, makes that of her mother look positively modest. Another row of pearls is added to her bracelets, thus making a total of four, while large precious stones can be seen in her brooch, earrings and even attached to her hat.

The self-image of a wealthy but godly couple, expressed in the portraits of William Courten and his wife Margaret Cassier, changed in the next generations to one which attached much greater value to temporary wealth and power. It may have been generated in a subtle and understated form, but the message would hardly have been lost on contemporaries. These Calvinist immigrants of the second generation were wordly and self-confident men and women with clear social ambitions and a sense of worth. They saw themselves on a par with the English Puritan gentry into whose families their children often married. This aspiration they, of course, shared with many of their English merchant friends and colleagues in the City of London and like them they acquired what in many cases turned out to be considerable estates in the south of England. Thus, Sir William Courten possessed estates in Northamptonshire which generated around £6,500 annually; John la Motte owned the manors of Ramsey and Brudwell in Essex at the time of his death; and Dirick Hoste owned a substantial country house surrounded by orchards in Mortlake when he proved his will in 1663.[63]

Bearing this in mind, it can be safely concluded that although the second generation of these Reformed, immigrant merchants retained business interests and property in their country of origin, they considered England to be their permanent home. Their economic and social success in their adopted country, which had offered their parents refuge, guaranteed a successful integration of their families into the upper echelons of their host community.

Notes

1. For Geneva, see W. Monter, *Calvin's Geneva*, New York 1967; for Emden, see A. Pettegree, *Emden and the Dutch Revolt. Exile and the Development of Reformed Protestantism*, Oxford 1992; see also below, Chapter 5.
2. For Cranmer's attitude to the stranger churches, see D. MacCullogh, 'Archbishop Cranmer: Concord and Tolerance in a Changing Church' in O. P. Grell and Bob Scribner (eds), *Tolerance and Intolerance in the European Reformation*, Chapter 12, Cambridge University Press 1996; for the foundation of the stranger churches, see A. Pettegree, *Foreign Protestant Communities in Sixteenth-Century London*, Oxford 1986, 23–45.
3. See O. P. Grell, *Dutch Calvinists in Early Stuart London*, Leiden 1989,

11–12. For Edmund Grindal, see P. Collinson, *Archbishop Grindal 1519–1583. The Struggle for a Reformed Church*, London 1979.

4. See below, Chapters 3 and 6.

5. For the 'Wonderyear', see Pettegree, *Emden*, 109–46.

6. For the repression of the Duke of Alva, see J. I. Israel, *The Dutch Republic. Its Rise, Greatness, and Fall 1477–1806*, Oxford 1995, 155–68.

7. Grell, *Dutch Calvinists*, 22–3.

8. J. Briels, *Zuid-Nederlanders in de Republiek 1572–1630*, Sint-Niklaas 1985, 80.

9. J. I. Israel, *Dutch Primacy in World Trade 1585–1740*, Oxford 1989, 38–42; see also Israel, *Dutch Republic*, 330.

10. See below, Chapter 5 and J. Briels, *Zuid-Nederlanders*, 211–28.

11. See Israel, *Dutch Republic*, 160 and 308; see also G. Parker, *The Dutch Republic*, London 1981, 119 and Briels, *Zuid-Nederlanders*, 28, 47, 69–70.

12. For the figure of 10,000, see H. Schilling, *Niederländische Exulanten im 16. Jahrhundert*, Gütersloh 1972, 43. For the returns of 1593, see I. Scouloudi, *Returns of the Strangers in the Metropolis 1593, 1627, 1635, 1639*, Publications of the Huguenot Society, London 1985, 73–5; see also O. Boersma, *Vluchtig Voorbeld, de nederlandse, franse en italiaanse vluchtelingenkerken in londen 1568–1585*, The Hague 1994, 39–40.

13. A reasonably conservative estimate would accept Schilling's figure of 10,000 for London, the second largest community in Norwich probably consisted of between 5,000 and 6,000 exiles; for Norwich, see R. Esser, *Niederländische Exulanten im England des späten 16. und frühen 17. Jahrhunderts. Die Norwicher Fremdengemeinden*, doctoral dissertation, University of Cologne, 1993, 52; Colchester had between 1,500 and 2,000, see below, Chapter 3; while Sandwich may have had around 500, Maidstone around 400, Canterbury around 400, while Southampton and Yarmouth probably no more than around 200 each; for these smaller communities, see below, Chapter 4 and Grell, *Dutch Calvinists*, 83–5.

14. Grell, *Dutch Calvinists*, 21–3.

15. See Boersma, *Vluchtig Voorbeeld*, 39–45.

16. See Grell, *Dutch Calvinists*, 27 and 55. For a discussion of the significance of separate identity and integration, see A. Pettegree, '"Thirty Years On": Progress towards Integration amongst the Immigrant Population of Elizabethan London', in J. Chartres and D. Hey (eds), *English Rural Society 1500–1800*, Cambridge 1990, 297–312 and R. Esser, 'News across the Channel: Contact and Communication between the Dutch and the Walloon Refugees in Norwich and their Families in Flanders 1565–1640', in *Immigrants and Minorities*, 14, 2, 1995, 139–52.

17. Aegidius Hooftman, who died in Antwerp in 1581, was continuously accused of being a heretic and a Calvinist, but is probably best described as a tolerant humanist. Thus, in his will he left 50,000 ducats for the poor in Antwerp, stipulating that the sum should be evenly divided between Protestants and Catholics, see *Antwerpen, verhaal van een metropool, 16de–17de eeuw*, Ghent 1993, 239.

18. See K. Bostoen, 'Kaars en Bril: de oudste Nederlandse Grammatica', *Archief. medelingen van het Koninklijk Zeeuwsch Genootschap der Wetenschappen*, 1984, 2–49, especially 11.

19. See J. H. Hessels (ed.), *Ecclesiae Londino-Batavae Archivum*, 3 vols 4 parts, Cambridge 1887–97, 2, no. 185 and 3, nos 223, 231, 535, 675.

20. *Acta van het consistorie van de Nederlandse gemeente te Londen 1569–1585*, eds A. J. Jelsma and O. Boersma, Rijks Geschiedkundige Publicatiën, Kleine Serie 76, The Hague 1993, nos 2429 and 2517, when he returned important documents to the consistory in London.

21. For this and Radermacher, see below, Chapter 5.

22. See below, Chapter 5.

23. *Acta van het consistorie*, no. 3176. Their engagement was announced in the consistory of the Dutch church in London on 12 December 1583. Evidently the *DNB* is wrong, as is *Biographica Britannica*, when claiming that they were already married in 1568. The daughter Margaret would only have been four years old then having been born in 1564, see *DNB* under Courten; see also *Biographica Britannica*, 6 vols, London 1747–66, 4, 323.

24. See Briels, *Zuid-Nederlanders*, 34.

25. W. J. C. Moens, *The Marriage, Baptismal, and Burial Registers 1571 to 1874 and Monumental Inscriptions, Dutch Reformed Church, Austin Friars*, Lymington 1884, 209 and 211. William Courten, retired as a deacon in April 1585, see *Acta van het consistorie*, no. 3515.

26. In the returns of aliens in 1617 John de Moncy is mentioned as a 'free denizon', living in Love Lane with his wife Margaret and two children born in England, see R. E. G. Kirk and E. F. Kirk (eds), *Returns of Aliens Dwelling in the City and Suburbs of London*, 4 vols, Publications of the Huguenot Society, 10, London 1908, 3, 152. Those two children, the only surviving from her marriage to Matthias Boudaen, can only have been Pieter Boudaen Courten, who was born in 1594 and later settled in Middelburg, eventually to become Director of the Middelburg chamber of the Dutch East India Company, and his sister Anna, born in 1599, whose engagement to Jacob Pergens from Rotterdam was announced in the Dutch church in London in July 1619. Inscriptions on the two paintings by Salomon Mesdach of Anna Boudaen Courten and her brother Peter Boudaen Courten in the Rijksmuseum in Amsterdam give the birthplace for both of them as Rotterdam, see *All the Paintings of the Rijksmusem in Amsterdam. A Completely Illustrated Catalogue*, Amsterdam 1976, nos A2068 and A119. This is confirmed by the denization of Peter Boudaen, dated 3 February 1616, which gives his birthplace as Rotterdam, see W. Page (ed.), *Letters of Denization and Acts of Naturaliztion for Aliens in England, 1603–1700*, Publications of the Huguenot Society, 8, Lymington 1893, 23.

27. John de Moncy had been made a denizen in February 1606 and was later naturalized in July 1610, see Page, *Letters of Denization and Acts of Naturalization*, 15.

28. See Briels, *Zuid-Nederlanders*, 184–9, especially 188–9; see also J. I. Israel, *Dutch Primacy in World Trade, 1585–1740*, Oxford 1990, 35.

29. For the significance of immigrants from the southern Netherlands for the London Dutch community, see Boersma, *Vluchtig Voorbeeld*, 62–6 and Grell, *Dutch Calvinists*, 270–78; for the significance of Middelburg for the Dutch in London during the first decades of the seventeenth century, see 55.

30. F. Nagtglas, *Kerkeraad der Nederduitsch-hervomerde Gemeente te*

Middelburg, Middelburg 1879, 73–4; for the year of Peter Courten's death, see *Biographica Britannica*, 4, 324; the *DNB* mistakenly gives 1631. See *All the Paintings of the Rijksmuseum in Amsterdam*, A913, which gives the right dates of birth and death, but mistakenly gives the name of Peter's brother William Courten. See also note 61 below.

31. See Nagtglas, *Kerkeraad*, 75 and *Biographica Britannica*, 324. See also *All the Paintings of the Rijksmuseum in Amsterdam*, nos A2068 and A2069. Peter Courten married the widowed mother of Catharina Fourmenouis, Hortensia del Prato, who died in 1627, see A910.

32. For the personal loans, see R. Ashton, *The Crown and the Money Market*, Oxford 1960, 20–22; for the collaboration with Sir Paul Pindar, see *Biographica Britannica*, 324–5.

33. See Grell, *Dutch Calvinists*, 72–3 and *Biographica Britannica*, 326; for the interloping of the East India Company, see R. Brenner, *Merchants and Revolution. Commercial Change, Political Conflict, and London's Overseas Traders, 1550–1653*, Cambridge 1993, 170–71.

34. There are numerous donations from Sir William Courten, starting with his first recorded contribution in 1610 of £40 to his last in May 1635 of £20, see Guildhall Library MS 7397/7, fol. 29r and MS 7397/8, fol. 32r.

35. For John de Moncy, see Grell, *Dutch Calvinists*, 187–8 and 264.

36. For the collections for the Palatinate, see Grell, *Dutch Calvinists*, 176–210.

37. These dates are given by Bellers in his funeral sermon for John la Motte, see Fulke Bellers, *Abrahams Interment*, London 1655, fol. Flr. The *DNB* is mistaken when claiming that La Motte was sent to school in Ghent and later to the University of Heidelberg. This John Lamoot, was a son of the former elder to the London Dutch community, Jan Lamot, who had returned to the Netherlands to become a minister in Ysselmonde in 1574, see Grell, *Dutch Calvinists*, 126; age alone would also have excluded John la Motte from being the person referred to in the letter of July 1583 – he would only have been six years old then!

38. Grell, *Dutch Calvinists*, 264. For La Motte's involvement in the affairs of the parish of St Bartholomew by the Exchange, see *DNB*.

39. John la Motte had first married another widow, Anne Tivelin, a Reformed refugee whose parents had settled in Canterbury and who had been married to the merchant David King. Anne and John la Motte's two daughters, Hester and Elizabeth married Sir Thomas Honeywood and Maurice Abbot, son of Sir Maurice Abbot respectively, see Bellers, *Abrahams Interment*, fol. F2r; for La Motte's marriage to Elizabeth van Poele, see Grell, *Dutch Calvinists*, 49.

40. A. Plummer, *The London Weavers' Company 1600–1970*, London 1970, 451.

41. S. Clarke, *The Lives of Sundry Eminent Persons in this later Age*, London 1683, 104.

42. J. Goodwin, *Christ's Approbation of Marie's Choice*, London 1641; see also D.A. Kirby, 'The Radicals of St Stephen's Coleman Street, London, 1624–1642', *The Guildhall Miscellany*, 3, 1970, 98–119, for Goodwin's dedication, see 112. La Motte's other daughter, Hester, married the Puritan Sir Thomas Honeywood of Markshall in Essex. Lady Hester was often joined for days of 'humiliation' and dinners by the Puritan minister, Ralph Josselin of Earls Colne. At such events Josselin occasionally met

her father John la Motte, see A. Macfarlane (ed.), *The Diary of Ralph Josselin, 1616–1683*, Oxford 1991.

43. Bellers, *Abrahams Interment*, F2v–F3r.
44. See Grell, *Dutch Calvinists*, 50, and *DNB*: Among the many charitable bequests in his will La Motte left £25 to fund a regular Sunday lecture in his parish church of St Bartholomew.
45. Bellers, *Abrahams Interment*, F4r–4v. La Motte's godly dinners or commemorative meals seem remarkably similar to the Calvinist *Agape* which was instituted in the London Dutch church in the early 1620s, see below, Chapter 9.
46. Ashton, *Crown and Money Market*, 21–2 and 179; and Brenner, *Merchants and Revolution*, 171–5.
47. See Grell, *Dutch Calvinists*, Appendix 1; for their involvement in interloping the East India trade, see Brenner, *Merchants and Revolution*, 175, 193 and 617.
48. See my forthcoming, 'Godly Charity or Political Aid? Irish Protestants and International Calvinism, 1641–1645', in *The Historical Journal*, 1996.
49. For Jacques Hoste's marriage date and the three baptisms, see Moens, *The Marriage, Baptismal, and Burial Registers*, marriage of Jacob/Jacques Hoste(ns) to Barbara Henricks 30 Nov. 1572; baptism of Abraham 11 Dec. 1575, Jacob 7 July 1577, and Maria 27 Sep. 1579.
50. Kirk, *Returns of Aliens*, 3, 194; see also 153. Dirick Hoste's father-in-law, James van Meteren eventually became Master of the Worshipful Company of Brewers in 1622 and 1627, see Grell, *Dutch Calvinists*, 194. See also 'The Visitation of London Anno Domini 1633, 1634 and 1635', *The Harleian Society*, 15, 1880, 229, 395. Dirick Hoste's year of birth appears from his deposition of March 1627 about a disputed will, where he gives his age as 38, see Hessels, *Ecclesiae*, 3, no. 1865. For the date of Dirick Hoste's wedding, see P.R.O., PROB. 11/310, fol. 36 (will of Dirick Hoste), which gives the date of his engagement inscribed in a gold ring. For the painter Cornelius Jonson, who was born in London to Dutch immigrant parents and later emigrated to Middelburg during the Civil War, see E. Waterhouse, *Painting in Britain 1530 to 1790*, 4th edition, London 1978, 60–62.
51. See *C.S.P. Dom. Charles I*, DXXII, 137 (1625?)
52. *Aubrey's 'Brief Lives'*, (ed.) A. Clark, 2 vols, Oxford 1898, 1, 112–13.
53. Grell, *Dutch Calvinists*, 262.
54. Nagtglas, *Kerkeraad Middelburg*, 71–2.
55. For the second royal collection, see Grell, *Dutch Calvinists*, 194; for the Irish collection, see Grell, 'Godly Charity or Political Aid?'; Hoste appears to have been well connected with influential merchants and politicians in London in the 1640s, see below, Chapter 6.
56. James Cole, Merchant, *Of Death, a True Description: and against it a Good Preparation: together with a Sweet Consolation, for the Surviving Mourners*, London 1629, ('Epistele Dedicatory'). The pamphlet was dedicated to six English merchants, John Milleward, who is described as 'one of the Captaines of this famous Cittie', John Awbrey, Edmond Page, William Gillie, William Middleton and John Bludworth, most of whom, like Hoste, were active within the English East India Company, see T. K. Rabb, *Enterpise & Empire (1575–1630)*, Cambridge, Mass. 1967, 237,

248, 342. It is also noteworthy that Dirick Hoste used the title of merchant for Cool on the front-page of his edition. For Cool, see below, Chapter 5.

57. See Grell, *Dutch Calvinists*, 3–4, 43–53 and 71–4; see also Boersma, *Vluchtig Voorbeeld*, 62–70.

58. For this, see Grell, *Dutch Calvinists, passim,* and below, Chapter 5.

59. For Hieronimus Willemsen Aschman, see Nagtglas, *Kerkeraad Middelburg*, 75–7 and 152. Hoste mentions him as burgomaster in his will proved in March 1663, see P.R.O. PROB 11/310, f. 36. See also Grell, *Dutch Calvinists*, 268 (Jeronymus Willemsen); he is presumably the Jeremy Williams mentioned in 1618 as a denizen born in Zeeland, see Kirk, *Returns of Aliens*, 3, 198.

60. See below, Chapter 8.

61. Considering the dates inscribed on this painting, which are neither the birth- nor death-years of William Courten, but those of his brother, Peter Courten, combined with the fact that Peter Courten resided in Middelburg, where both he and the painter Salomon Mesdach were elected to the eldership of the Reformed church in 1627, this painting must be portraying Peter Courten and not William, as claimed by the catalogue of the Rijksmuseum in Amsterdam. See *All the Paintings of the Rijksmuseum in Amsterdam*, no. A913; for their elderships, see Nagtglas, *Kerkeraad Middelburg*, 74. For the painter, Salomon Mesdach, of whom little is known, see N. Bakker et al., *Masters of Middelburg. Exhibition in the honour of Laurens J. Bol*, Amsterdam 1984, 102–106.

62. For the use of jewellery, see D. Scarisbrick, *Jewellery in Britain 1066–1837*, Norwich 1994; for their use by merchants and citizens, see in particular 73–9. See also D. Scarisbrick, *Tudor and Jacobean Jewellery*, London 1995. For portraiture in England in this period and its dependence on inspiration and painters from the Low Countries, see K. Hearn (ed.), *Dynasties. Painting in Tudor and Jacobean England 1530–1630*, London 1995.

63. For Sir William Courten and John la Motte's estates, see *DNB*; for Dirick Hoste, see P.R.O. PROB 11/310, f. 36.

CHAPTER TWO

The French and Dutch congregations in London in the early seventeenth century

The experiences of the French and Dutch congregations in London under Edward VI and Elizabeth changed radically during the reign of the early Stuarts. From their establishment in 1550, prompted by a desire of leading Protestants within the English government to create a church which could serve as a model for the further Reformation of the Church of England, the alien communities had been supported by succeeding English governments, excluding the brief reign of Mary between 1553 and 1558 which had forced them into exile on the Continent. Elizabeth had welcomed their return in 1560, not as model churches, but as communities which were expected to be beneficial to the English economy. Disregarding government motives, this had meant ultimately that the stranger churches could rely on the support and protection of both Edward VI and Elizabeth.[1]

Government support did not only dwindle under the early Stuarts, but was, on at least two occasions, reversed into policies directed against the French and Dutch congregations which put them under severe strain.

The first incidence of this nature coincided with the depression in the English economy which commenced around 1615 and lasted into the mid-1620s. It was directed against the two congregations' merchant members who were accused in the Star Chamber in 1619 of illegal export of bullion. The second incidence occurred less than 15 years later, in 1634, when the French and Dutch churches found themselves included in the new Archbishop, William Laud's campaign for uniformity within, as well as without the Church of England.

Before giving an account of these two incidents it is, however, necessary to consider the structure and development of the two stranger churches.

The organization and structure of the French and Dutch churches

Historically, the two congregations had more in common than they had separating them. In 1550 they had been established as twin-congregations under a mutual superintendent, Johannes a Lasco, as a separate *corpus corporatum et politicum* outside the Church of England. Initially they had shared the church of Austin Friars until the French church had moved to the chapel of St Anthony in Threadneedle Street during the autumn of 1550.[2] The question of the ownership of Austin Friars later, on occasion, soured the relationship between the two communities.[3] However, it did not prevent co-operation between the churches on all important issues related to their host community. Thus in 1559, one representative from both congregations jointly petitioned Elizabeth for their re-establishment.[4] This was a natural consequence of the fact that most of the members of both churches originated from the southern Netherlands and shared the Reformed faith. The French community consisted almost entirely of Walloons until the St Bartholomew massacre in 1572 brought the first significant number of French refugees to London.[5]

By the beginning of the seventeenth century the membership of the two congregations had changed considerably. It was no longer composed of immigrants solely. Around 40 per cent were by now born in England, being either children or grandchildren of the original refugees.[6] The available evidence indicates that the structure of the membership within the Threadneedle Street congregation would have been close to that of Austin Friars in 1617 when 25 per cent of the Dutch church was classified as merchants and the rest as artisans. This distinction was made according to social rather than occupational considerations. Nearly all the elders and deacons who served the Dutch church during this period belonged to the merchant category.[7]

From the late 1580s neither of the two congregations had received a significant number of new refugee members. Consequently their sizes were declining. While both had peaked with a membership around 1800 in the early 1590s, they probably had less than 1600 members around 1620.[8] This decline continued for the community in Austin Friars during the early seventeenth century. The French church, however, received a new intake of refugees from France, primarily from Normandy in 1621, who had been forced into exile by the beginning of the second phase of the religious wars.[9] Even if the number of refugees was considerably lower than that of the late sixteenth century, it was substantial enough to occasion a royal collection in all parish churches for 'the poor French, Protestant refugees'.[10]

The 1620s saw a steady arrival of new French immigrants in London who gradually began to outnumber the Walloon members of the Threadneedle Street congregation.[11] At the same time the new immigrants served to reinvigorate and boost the size of the French community, making it the largest of the alien churches for the first time. It is, however, dubious whether or not John Bulteel's figures for the mid-1630s, of 840 members for the Dutch church and 1,400 for the French church are valid and immediately comparable.[12] The figure for the Dutch church only included men and women, married couples or single heads of households, but no servants or children.[13] However, the figure of 1,400 for the Threadneedle Street congregation must have included at least some servants and children. Otherwise the difference between the two churches, which had been of more or less the same sizes 15 years earlier, becomes incomprehensible. It would have taken a considerable French immigration into London during the 1620s to have made the church in Threadneedle Street 66 per cent larger than its Dutch sister-congregation around 1635. A difference somewhere between 10–20 per cent seems far more likely.

Both churches employed three ministers concurrently during the early seventeenth century. It was emphasized in the disciplines of the Dutch, as well as of the French, church that the ministers were all equal and 'should not assert priority or dominion over the other'.[14] This equality did not penetrate the economic sphere. By comparison with most of their English colleagues, the Dutch and French ministers were well-paid, even if their salaries differed considerably. In 1610 the two senior Dutch ministers, Johannes Regius and Simon Ruytinck, each received £100 annually whereas their younger colleague, Ambrosius Regemorter, was only paid £60. Around the same time the three ministers to the French church were all paid differently: Aaron Cappell received £96, Nathaniel Marie £84 and the newly employed Abraham Aurelius, £78.[15]

In addition to the three ministers, both congregations had already been served by 12 elders and deacons since the early 1570s. The French church appears to have expanded their number to 13 elders and 13 deacons at the turn of the century.[16] There was a tendency within both communities to move upwards from diaconate to eldership.

Within the Dutch church the elders, once elected, tended to stay in office until old age or illness forced them to retire. This was not the case within the French community. Theoretically, the elders of Austin Friars were elected for a period of two years, but the Corpus Disciplinae of 1609 noted that continuity within the eldership was beneficial to the churches and should be encouraged.[17] Accordingly only 47 men were needed to fill the 12 elderships in Austin Friars between 1603 and 1642, giving an average period of service for each elder of about ten years. Some elders, such as Cornelius Godfrey and Joos Godschalck, held office for an impressive period of 25 years, thereby providing the Dutch congregation with a high degree of continuity and stability.[18]

The discipline of the French churches only stated that 'the number and term of service of the Elders and Deacons shall be left to the discretion of each church'.[19] The 13 elders and 13 deacons in the congregation in Threadneedle Street generally served the community for three years before being discharged, even if a number of examples of both longer and shorter service can be found, as for instance the Englishman, Jean Payne, who only served the congregation as an elder for one year in 1604 or Gideon Delaune, Queen Anne's apothecary, who served the church for four years, between June 1612 and July 1616.[20] In effect this meant that more than double the number of people were needed to fill the elderships within the French community during the early seventeenth century, in spite of several elders serving the church repeatedly. This was the case of Gideon Delaune, the merchants Robert de la Barr and Jean Fortrie, and the wealthy merchant and banker, Philip Burlamachi, who finished his third term as an elder in July 1625, having on that occasion only been able to serve the community for 18 months 'a raison de la access a La Court Roialle'.[21] Thus less cohesion and stability existed within the eldership in Threadneedle Street than within Austin Friars during this period. One might therefore suspect that the initiative within the French consistory rested to a larger degree with the Company of Pastors rather than the elders as was the case within Austin Friars. This would also explain why the Dutch consistory appears to have paid greater attention to economic and political matters.[22] The leadership of the pastors of the French congregation must have been further emphasized through the church's employment of several Reformed theologians of international standing, such as Robert de la Maçon, sieur de la Fontaine, Dr Gilbert Primrose and Ezékiel Marmet.[23]

By the beginning of the seventeenth century both the French and Dutch churches in England had managed to establish a hierarchical Reformed church structure of their own in spite of being under the jurisdiction of the English bishops. Both had opted for the looser structure of the colloquium, rather than the classis, probably in order to cause minimal offence to the English authorities. Their pattern, however, shows some differences. The Dutch churches took the initiative in 1575 when they held their first colloquium, followed by another eight during the reign of Elizabeth. The French did not start until 1581, but then held no less than 17 colloquia between 1581 and 1603. During the early Stuart period the frequency of the French colloquia fell dramatically; between 1604 and 1625 only seven took place, and none was held between 1625 and 1640. The frequency of the Dutch colloquia showed considerably greater constancy. The nine Elizabethan meetings were supplemented by eight in the early Stuart period. The decision of the

Colloquium in 1609 to hold triennial meetings was observed until Archbishop Laud commenced his campaign against the stranger churches in 1634.[24] The tradition of regular colloquia was not resumed until 1641 when the French, as well as the Dutch, congregations met in London and subsequently held a synod of all the foreign communities in England.

This was only the third synod of the alien churches to meet. The first had taken place in March 1604 in order to prepare the petition to James for the renewal of the privileges of the stranger churches. The second synod had been called in order to deal with the threat posed by Archbishop Laud's Injunctions in 1635.[25]

The coetus, the monthly meeting of the foreign churches in London, was the only institution which matched the synod as a policy-making body. It was a considerably older corpus, having already come into existence during the early 1550s, shortly after the official establishment of the churches. It had been formed in order to facilitate maximum co-ordination and agreement between the two communities. During most of the early seventeenth century, the coetus met regularly on the first Tuesday of each month. Periodically it included the small Italian church in the City, but normally consisted of representatives of the Dutch and French communities only.[26] Since 1581 its meetings had been supplemented by regular consultations between the deacons of the French and Dutch congregations. These were held in order to ensure a reasonable measure of co-ordination between the communities in the field of poor relief. The churches wanted to make sure that none of the poor of the Dutch and French nations benefited from the charity of both churches at the same time, and to decide which congregation, if any, was obliged to help distressed strangers who applied for assistance.[27]

The power of the coetus was never particularly well defined and occasionally attempts were made to introduce rules to cover at least part of its activities.[28] It was used as a court of appeal to solve differences between the stranger churches and between their members. However, it was in its dealings with the English authorities that coetus had its greatest importance. It kept records of its meetings similar to the minutes of the consistories of both congregations. Each church was supposed to possess a copy, but only one coetus-book, in the hands of the French church, was in existence around 1612, when Austin Friars made several attempts to acquire a copy in order to facilitate consultations of previous decisions.[29] The fact that the coetus-book for this period cannot be found complicates a reconstruction of coetus' composition and role. Originally it had consisted of all members of the French and Dutch consistories. During the early seventeenth century, attendance had dwindled; consequently in March 1646 the Dutch consistory found it necessary to emphasize that a minimum of six of its elders were required to attend the regular monthly meeting.[30] Coetus was assisted by 12 'hommes politiques' in its dealings with practical and commercial problems concerning members of the two communities. These men were normally recruited from among the merchant strangers. Austin Friars provided eight members of this body, the French church only four. This emphasized the dominance of the Dutch community over the French in economic matters. Among the responsibilities of the 'hommes politiques' were the collections of money needed to obtain the renewal of royal privileges for the churches' artisan members and the annual gift for the new Lord Mayors.[31]

Besides the regular meetings on the first Tuesday of each month, coetus also met when need occurred. These meetings generally took place in conjunction with the weekly consistory meetings, on Thursdays, in Austin Friars or after one of the two Sunday services.[32] There are some indications that the more irregular practice supplanted the regular meetings during the 1630s.[33]

One of the central tasks of coetus was to defend members' privileges. This was especially necessary in the case of the alien artisans who, in times of crisis, were harrassed by informers, City Companies and even local authorities. Evidently a cordial relationship with the Lord Mayors and Aldermen of London was essential to the stranger churches. Every year coetus accordingly greeted the new Lord Mayor; from 1604 a standard formula was used:

> Right Honorable, Wee that Comport here before your honour are some of the Ministers and Elders off the dutch and french Congregations in London. The end is for to performe our duty of Congratulation in the name off our Congregations according to our yearly custome unto your honor Whom itt hath pleased God to call to that great dignitie, honor and authoritie to bee a cheeff Magistrate off this famous citye onder our most gracous King. Wee therefore pray the mightie God in all humilitye to make your honor by vertue off his holy spiritt fitt and sufficient for the full performance off all his dutyes belonging to so great a charge and calling that so by your faithfulnes the glory of God bee advanced and his Church edified. Besides wee beseech your honor according vnto th'example off your predecessors to bee favorable unto us strangers members off the sayd congregations, fledde hether for the truth off the Godspell and charitablye entertained hitherto in this honorable Citye, wee shall bee bound to pray the Lord continually as hitherto wee have done for your honors happy Godly and iust Government.

The new Lord Mayor was then presented with a gift from the stranger churches; during the mid-1620s it consisted – very appropriately, since most of the strangers were employed in the cloth industry – of an

embroidered, damask tablecloth with 24 matching napkins to the impressive value of £30.[34]

Coetus also took care of the stranger churches' relations with the
Church of England. Its members greeted the new bishops of London
and archbishops of Canterbury and congratulated them on their ap-
pointments. A standard formula had also been introduced in 1604 to
greet the new bishops of London.[35] This effort of the French and Dutch
churches was appreciated, even by William Laud, when he was transferred to London in 1628.[36] On these occasions one of the French
ministers acted as spokesman for the churches. Likewise it was also one
of the French ministers who delivered the orations when the stranger
churches greeted the new monarchs.[37] It was obviously not the French
language which granted the ministers in Threadneedle Street precedence
over their Dutch colleagues on these occasions, since the new bishops
were greeted in Latin. The roles allotted to Robert le Maçon, sieur de la
Fontaine, Dr Gilbert Primrose and Ezékiel Marmet appear to have been
based on their positions as Reformed theologians of international standing.[38] Overall the French church seems to have paid greater attention
than the Dutch to liturgical and ceremonial questions during this period. Thus it was the French who raised the issue of holy days and High
Church festivals, such as Easter and Christmas, during the second decade of James's reign. Until around 1614 none of the alien communities
appear to have celebrated these festivals. During that year the Dutch
consistory decided to celebrate holy days which fell on Tuesdays, Wednesdays and Fridays, in the latter two cases the normal Thursday service
would be cancelled. It was argued that this arrangement would prove
beneficial to the poor.[39]

Likewise, in 1616, it was the request of the French church to borrow
the church of Austin Friars to celebrate Communion on Easter Day
which forced the Dutch consistory to adopt this practice. The French
congregation had begun to take Communion during Easter the previous
year in order to please James I who appears to have favoured this
practice. The leaders of Austin Friars found that they could not refuse
the French the use of their church, given that they were not using it
themselves. They feared this might offend the King. In the end the
simplest solution for the Dutch was to celebrate Communion themselves. This decision furnished them with grounds for refusing the French
without falling from favour with James.

Later developments in this area were to show the French church as
highly volatile on this issue. In 1644, during the English Civil War,
which in effect had produced a state of religious tolerance, the colloquium of the French churches decided to abolish all festivals and holy
days. The Dutch churches, however, having introduced this tradition 30

years earlier, preferred to continue a practice which exercised some form of control over the poorer members who might otherwise be tempted to spend their days off in inns and ale houses.[40]

The practical, earthly attitude of the leaders of Austin Friars to matters concerning ceremonies appears occasionally to have offended their French brethren, as well as London Puritans. In December 1614, during a meeting of coetus, the French had pointed out to the Dutch that their habit of enjoying 'long and expensive banquettes' on Sundays was causing offence. The consistory in Austin Friars was imperturbed, simply pointing out to the relevant people that they should finish their meals in time for the service. A couple of years later it was the practice of the wealthy, merchant members of Austin Friars to attend business on the Exchange after Sunday service which aroused criticism from the French and the English. In spite of exhortations from the Dutch consistory, the merchant members continued their practice, 'to the great annoyance of pious Englishmen'.[41] Only in 1626 did Austin Friars appear to have yielded to this type of pressure when they abolished the traditional announcement of forthcoming market-days by the sexton immediately after the sermon.[42]

The Dutch church was not only the more practical and secularly oriented of the two congregations, it was also by far the wealthiest during this period. It was able to give economic assistance to other Reformed communities on a far grander scale than its sister-congregation in Threadneedle Street. Thus in 1623 it collected £154 for the suffering Italian Protestants in Valtellina while the French and Italian churches were only able to collect £60 and £22 respectively.[43]

The economic dominance of the Dutch community over the French was in further evidence in connection with the royal entries into London which normally followed upon the coronation of new monarchs. On these occasions royal processions paraded through the City with great pageantry. At the same time as they were extremely popular with the general public, they also provided an opportunity for the most powerful organizations and Livery Companies in the City to ingratiate themselves with the new King by providing dramatic presentations, *tableaux vivants*, on street corners and by erecting opulent triumphal arches along the processional route. When James undertook his coronation passage through the City in March 1604, after the plague had died down, seven triumphal arches had been constructed along the route. One of the seven had been sponsored by the Dutch community in London and was erected behind the Royal Exchange in Cornhill.[44]

Austin Friars went to considerable expense on these occasions, as can be seen from the sums spent in 1625 and 1626 when the consistory decided to build a triumphal arch 'in our churchyard and in an isolated

part of the church' in anticipation of Charles I's royal entry. On this
occasion more than £1,000 was spent on the triumphal arch. Unfortunately it was all spent in vain since the entry was cancelled and never
undertaken by Charles. Had it taken place, the triumphal arch would
have been erected in the name of the members of Austin Friars, with
those of the French church who wished to contribute being incorporated under that title.[45] This was a most telling proof of the economic
strength of the Dutch congregation during the early seventeenth
century.

The Star Chamber case of 1619

Besides being the strongest community in economic terms, the Dutch
church also seems to have benefited from better political contacts with
central government during this period. Here it depended primarily on
the membership of the first two ambassadors of the Dutch Republic in
England, Sir Noel de Caron and Sir Albertus Joachimi.[46] These gentlemen played a prominent role in renewing the privileges of the artisan
members of the stranger churches during the difficult years under the
Stuarts. Their services were invaluable during the severe economic
depression which hit England in the decade between 1615 and 1625.[47]
The depression was brought about by several factors. First, Alderman
Cockayne's project for an export trade of dressed and dyed cloth
finally broke down in December 1617 having already generated a
crisis for the cloth industry on which approximately 80 per cent of the
English export trade depended. Second, and of perhaps greater consequence, were a series of currency manipulations on the Continent,
especially in northern and eastern Europe, where the debasement of
silver coins soon priced English cloth out of the market at the same
time as it caused an outflow of bullion from England since no exchange adjustment took place. Third, England suffered two consecu-
tively bad harvests between 1621 and 1622, which caused food prices
to soar. When the economy started to recuperate, the country was
faced with a severe outbreak of plague in 1625.[48] In these conditions
xenophobia was rife, especially in London, and the artisan members
of the alien congregations became its prime targets, as they had been
before during the reign of Elizabeth.

It was in this situation that James I decided to take advantage of the
negative attitude to the strangers in the City while simultaneously making an attempt to solve his own financial difficulties. He initiated the
Star Chamber case against the merchant strangers for illegal export of
bullion in December 1618.

James's action, however, had other antecedents. In 1617 he had contracted two major loans to solve some of his immediate financial problems. One of £100,000 had come from the City, the other of £20,000 had been provided by the merchant strangers. The majority of these merchants belonged to the congregation in Austin Friars, but a fair number were members of the community in Threadneedle Street.[49] The Dutch ambassador, Sir Noel de Caron, who was himself a wealthy man and who had already furnished James with loans on several occasions, had become heavily involved in this business from the beginning. On the King's behalf, he had negotiated the loan from the merchant strangers and it had been arranged that he would forward the £20,000 at 10 per cent interest to James, receiving the King's, as well as the Privy Council's, guarantee of repayment. Caron had subcontracted what he could not provide himself at 9 per cent, not only to the merchant strangers in London but also to Dutch merchants in Amsterdam.[50]

The accusations against 160 alien merchants for illegal export of bullion to the exhorbitant value of £7,000,000 were raised by two courtiers, Sir Henry Britain and Sir Thomas Vavasour. They served two purposes at a time when the Crown's revenues were falling. James could eliminate the insoluble problem of repaying the merchant strangers' loan of 1617 and hopefully also refill some of his empty coffers from the fines imposed on the strangers. Certain optimistic reports mentioned the possibility of a total fine which would cover over half the King's debts.[51] Several contemporaries, including the minister to Austin Friars, Simon Ruytinck, saw the case as primarily directed against Dutch merchants, even if a number of French and Hanseatic merchants were included.[52] Consequently it was not only on behalf of Austin Friars, but of 'the outlandish Church in London' generally that Sir Noel de Caron petitioned James to halt the proceedings during the first months of 1619.[53] De Caron achieved nothing and the case proceeded despite growing doubts about the wisdom of doing so. John Chamberlain informed the English ambassador in the Hague, Sir Dudley Carleton, that the case would be difficult to prove and that it might be 'prejudiciall to our merchants in other parts'.[54]

Apparently the Attorney-General did not find the case an easy one either. In early June his list of accused merchants had shrunk from the original 160 to 33, suspected of illegal export of gold and silver to the value of £700,000, or 10 per cent of the original sum.[55] Less than a week later the number of accused had dwindled to 18 or 19 when, on 18 June James adjourned the case to provide the prosecution with further time to prepare its case.[56]

The merchant strangers put the delay to good use. Again they tried to have the case stopped and de Caron approached several Privy

Councillors to gain their support for the idea.[57] Likewise business contacts were mobilized in the Netherlands, in order to create support for the merchant strangers within the Dutch government. This was a natural consequence since nearly two thirds of the accused belonged to the Dutch community. On 5 November 1619 the States General provided assistance by asking James to withdraw the case, but to no avail.[58] However, when the case was resumed in the autumn even the judges had started to despair. Sir Robert Naunton informed the Duke of Buckingham that it was an extremely difficult and time-consuming business and that 'the rest of the learned council seeme abashed at it, and professe they ar all strangers to the proceedings that have been used'.[59]

Finally in December 1619 18 merchant strangers were fined £140,000 in the Star Chamber. Ten of the convicted were members of Austin Friars whereas only three or four belonged to the congregation in Threadneedle Street.[60] The outcome evidently threatened the economic fabric of the Dutch community to a greater extent than the French, but it should be borne in mind that two members of the French church, Robert de la Barre and Robert de Leau/Lewe, together with Sir William Courten of the Dutch church, were each fined the extraordinarily large sum of £20,000.[61]

The fines were to be paid immediately if the merchants were not to be imprisoned in the Fleet. James showed no mercy at this stage: most of the 18 were imprisoned and their goods and outstanding credits sequestered.[62] In vain the French and Dutch congregations petitioned James for their release, arguing that the imprisonment would lead to their utter ruin.[63] The two consistories' unease about the situation grew during the first months of 1620 since the majority of the merchants remained in the Fleet prison. They decided to establish a committee in conjunction with the Dutch ambassador in order to discover how much money could be raised within the congregations towards the payment of the fines. Each church appointed one minister and two elders.[64] Obviously the economic future of the congregations was at stake, especially in the case of Austin Friars, and it must have been of paramount importance to reach some kind of compromise with the King.[65] It was the Dutch ambassador, Sir Noel de Caron, who finally negotiated a compromise during the summer of 1620 when he managed to have the fine cut to £60,000.[66]

Part of this settlement, however, was to spoil the excellent relations between the stranger churches and de Caron. The Dutch ambassador had happily accepted that the loan from 1617 of £20,000, plus accumulated interest of £6,000, all in all £26,000, for which he had been responsible, would be included in the reduced fine. It was then decided that the ambassador should be reimbursed by the merchant strangers who had been fined.[67] De Caron evidently favoured this arrangement having realized that the likelihood of quick repayment by either James or the Privy Council was slim, whereas he stood a much better chance with the merchant strangers. However, he seriously misjudged the situation. The merchants proved themselves more unwilling to pay than the King. Consequently de Caron spent the next couple of years until his death in December 1624 attempting to obtain the £26,000 by harrassing the consistories of the French and Dutch churches. He had the Privy Council write several letters to the churches on his behalf and he threatened them with litigation.[68] The churches, on the other hand, repeatedly argued that they had never been part of the negotiations which had lowered the fine to £60,000. Neither could they find the amount of money demanded by de Caron among their members and they pointed out that the settlement had been the sole responsibility of the ambassador.[69] Despite the feeling that at this stage it was everyone for themselves, with the unfortunate de Caron left to lick his own financial wounds, the leadership of the two communities managed to collect some money towards the payment of de Caron and subsequently offered him £7,000 which he declined. Eighteen months after de Caron's death the Dutch suggested to the French church that the money which had been collected should be used for the general benefit of the two communities.[70]

The experience of the Star Chamber case had, no doubt, been traumatic for both churches. Gradually they had seen themselves becoming involved in a case which only indirectly concerned the congregations, but which, nevertheless, threatened their existence. The episode provided food for thought within the Dutch church, and the decision of the colloquium of the Dutch churches in 1621 not to allow ministers to involve themselves in political matters in the future, except in absolute emergencies, should be seen in this context.[71]

Archbishop Laud's campaign for uniformity

In effect the Star Chamber case served the foreign communities as a dress rehearsal for the more comprehensive crisis they were to face 15 years later during William Laud's campaign for uniformity within, as well as without the Anglican Church. As Bishop of London, Laud had had his eye on the stranger churches already. In 1632 he had informed his colleagues in the Privy Council that he considered them 'nurseries of ill-minded persons to the Church of England'.[72] It had not escaped his attention that the alien Reformed communities were situated in south-east England, the centre of Puritan opposition. On 7 April 1634, less

than eight months after his promotion to the archbishopric of Canterbury, he summoned representatives from the French and Dutch congregations in Canterbury, Sandwich and Maidstone to Canterbury.[73] It
made sense to initiate the new policy with the smaller, less influential
provincial churches. When the representatives arrived in Canterbury on
17 April they were asked by the Vicar-General, Sir Nathaniel Brent:
(1) Whether they used the Anglican liturgy in Dutch and French, and if
not, what other liturgy they used? (2) How many of their members were
born in England? (3) Whether those born in England would conform to
the Anglican ritual?

The congregations in Kent informed their mother churches in London
that they thought the Archbishop wanted to dissolve all the foreign
congregations in England.[74] After several consultations with the leaders
of the London churches, the three congregations avoided answering the
questions by referring to the Charter of Edward IV.[75] Laud was unim-
pressed and when he finally summoned the delegates from Kent to
appear before him in December 1634, it was only in order to present
them with his Injunctions: all their members who were born in England
should from 1 March 1635 attend their English parish churches and the
remaining members were to use the Anglican liturgy translated into
French and Dutch.[76] Eventually he granted the communities a delay of
the Injunctions' implementation until Easter.[77]

Once Laud had shown his intentions, the need for collective action
was evident. A synod of all the French and Dutch churches in England
was called. When it met on 5 February 1635 the need for immediate
action was recognized and the following day some of the foreign congregations' friends at Court were approached. The former financier to
the English Crown, Philip Burlamachi, was contacted. He was living
under the King's protection after his bankruptcy and was an obvious
candidate, being a member and former elder of the church in
Threadneedle Street.[78] Two elders of the French church in London
visited the Countess of Southampton, a member of their congregation,
and spoke to her husband, who promised to present their case to the
Lord Chamberlain.[79] The Huguenot, Benjamin de Rohan, Duke of
Soubise also promised to assist the synod. He was godfather to Charles I
and since 1626, after having been involved in the Duke of Buckingham's attempt to relieve La Rochelle, he had made his home at the
English Court.[80] A couple of elders of Austin Friars approached the
Dutch ambassador, Sir Albertus Joachimi and the royal physician, Sir
Theodor de Mayerne, who had married one of Joachimi's daughters.[81]
These efforts were rewarded when a large deputation from the synod
was granted an audience with Charles on 12 February. The spokesman,
as always, was one of the French ministers, in this case Ezékiel Marmet.[82]

The churches' main objections against Laud's Injunctions were economic. Among other things they claimed that their congregations not only maintained their own poor, for which they were widely admired by their hosts, but that they also contributed towards the support of the English poor in their respective parishes.[83]

It was probably these economic implications which made Laud soften his attitude towards the stranger churches in March. During an interview with the deputies from Kent, Laud promised that should they wish to petition the King in order to be allowed to keep their members of the first descent, he would *bona fida* forward their petition.[84] The synod rejoiced on hearing the news, but when the Injunctions were published on 1 April 1635, Laud had only granted a minor concession, allowing the born strangers to use their own disciplines.[85] Somehow the churches in Kent managed to engineer a further breathing-space and to have the implementation of the Injunctions postponed until 1 July.[86] Several consultations between the Dutch and French churches took place in London. The petition of the Norwich communities to the Archbishop of 26 June must have evolved out of these meetings. In this document the alien churches acknowledged, for the first time, the real motives behind Laud's actions. Naturally they disclaimed Laud's allegations that they harboured English Puritans within their churches.[87] However, it was during the interview which the Archbishop had granted the deputies from Norwich that Laud returned to his earlier promise of March the same year, allowing the 'natives of the first descent' to remain within the stranger churches. He also promised that those who were to attend their parish churches would still be required to pay their fees to the alien churches as before.[88] The modifications were included when the Injunctions were finally served on 6 September 1635.[89] Thus the Dutch and French churches not only managed to force the Archbishop to modify his Injunctions, but also to delay them for about six months.

The resistance of the stranger churches to the Injunctions did not stop here. Since the churches had been given no clear indication of how to publish them, they took advantage of this loophole and claimed ignorance of their existence.[90] Here they proved as successful as they had been in delaying the Injunctions. As late as in April 1639 it would appear that the Injunctions were widely ignored, not only by the stranger churches but also by the English ministers and church-wardens.[91] According to Peter Heylyn, Laud's apologist, they were only observed after Laud had issued an order to the church-wardens in April that year. The convention of the Long Parliament in November 1640 certified the collapse of Laud's church policy and at best made the Injunctions effective for around a year and a half; not an impressive record for a policy originally introduced in 1634.

Laud's fall, however, did not bring an end to this matter. On 11 March 1641, only ten days after Laud had been transferred to the Tower, information received from the educationalist, Samuel Hartlib, was discussed in the consistory of Austin Friars. Hartlib, who acted as an intermediary for the parliamentary leader, John Pym, had asked the consistory to forward complaints against Laud to the Investigational Committee which was chaired by Pym.[92] It was important for John Pym to have the cases against both Laud and Wentworth concluded during the spring of 1641 and his request to Austin Friars should be seen in this context. Samuel Hartlib was an obvious person to play the part of middleman. He was closely associated, not only with the Dutch community in London but also with Puritan circles in the City.[93] He was strongly involved in the case against Laud and was one of the witnesses against the Archbishop. Pym's urgency in this matter is further illustrated by his renewed request to Austin Friars in May. On 27 May the Dutch consistory decided to appoint the minister, Timotheus van Vleteren, and the elder, Dirick Hoste, to discuss the matter with Pym personally and to invite the French church to participate.[94] Only the deputies of Austin Friars, however, met with John Pym. On the basis of their report, it was decided to provide the parliamentary leader with the necessary information in writing and to present it to the community in Threadneedle Street to receive its assent.[95] This it came about that Laud's treatment of the stranger churches constituted an important part of the accusations directed against him, as reported in William Prynne's pamphlet, *Canterburies Doome*.[96]

In spite of their differences, the French and Dutch churches were firmly based on common ground during the early seventeenth century. Owing to that, they managed to survive two severe crises in less than 22 years. In doing so, they showed a remarkable tenacity and ability, not only to utilize their different assets, but also to co-ordinate their actions within the well-tested framework of coetus. Spiritual leadership was generally provided by the ministers from the congregation in Threadneedle Street who were responsible for the official profile of the churches. Practical, economic leadership came from the elders and merchant members of Austin Friars. Together, both groups secured the continuing existence of the churches during the critical years under the early Stuarts.

Notes

1. See O. P. Grell, 'Continuity and Change; The Dutch Church in London 1550–1650', in *Refugees and Emigrants in the Dutch Republic and England*, Sir Thomas Browne Institute, Leiden 1986, pp. 43–51.

2. A Pettegree, *The Strangers and their Churches in London 1550–1580*, doctoral dissertation, University of Oxford 1983, p. 29. A revised version of this work has been published, *Foreign Protestant Communities in Sixteenth-Century London*, Oxford 1986.

3. Ibid., pp. 29 and 241. The question of ownership of the church of Austin Friars was raised as late as 1605 by the French community, see J. J. van Toorenenbergen (ed.), *Gheschiedenissen ende Handelingen die voornemelick aengaen de Nederduytsche Natie ende Gemeynten wonende in Engeland ende bysonder tot London*, Utrecht 1873, pp. 201–10.

4. The French congregation was represented by Dr Jean Dumas and the Dutch by the elder, Anthony Ashe, see A. Pettegree, op. cit., pp. 145–6.

5. Ibid., p. 281.

6. O. P. Grell, *Austin Friars and the Puritan Revolution, 1603–1642*, doctoral dissertation, The European University Institute, Florence 1983, Chapter II, part 1. See also O. P. Grell, *Dutch Calvinists in Early Stuart London*, Leiden 1989.

7. See ibid., Appendix I and French Church, Soho Square, London, MSS 4 and 5.

8. See I. Scouloudi, 'Alien Immigration into the Alien Communities in London', *Proc Hug Soc Lond* 16, 1938, pp. 27–50, esp. pp. 45–7; Guildhall Library MS 7402/10, f. 9r and *Gheschiedenissen*, p. 337 (the date is 1617 not 1619) – see also O. P. Grell, *Austin Friars*, Chapter II, part 1.

9. M. Prestwich, 'Calvinism in France, 1555–1629', in M. Prestwich, (ed.), *International Calvinism 1541–1715*, Oxford 1985, pp. 71–107, esp. 104. For the arrival in July 1621 of several Reformed ministers with their families from Normandy, see *Gheschiedenissen*, pp. 402–3 and Baron F. de Schickler, *Les Églises du Refuge en Angleterre*, 3 vols, Paris 1892, vol. 1, pp. 390–91.

10. *C.S.P. Dom 14*, CXXI and CXXII. See also French Protestant Church of London, MS 5, ff. 57r–58r. Austin Friars collected £123 on this occasion, see Guildhall L. MS 7397/7, f. 92r.

11. See R.D. Gwynn, *A Calendar of the Letter Books of the French Church of London from the Civil War to the Restoration 1643–1659*, pp. 6–7 (*Hug Soc Lond*, vol. LIV QS) and R. D. Gwynn, *Huguenot Heritage. The History and Contribution of the Huguenots in Britain*, London, 1985, pp. 33–5.

12. See J. Bulteel, *A Relation of the Troubles of the Three Forraign Churches in Kent Caused by the Injunctions of W. Laud*, London 1645; see also R. D. Gwynn, *Huguenot Heritage*, p. 33.

13. For the membership list of Austin Friars from 1635, see Guildhall L. MS 7397/8, f. 34r and J. H. Hessels (ed.), *Ecclesiae Londino-Batavae-Archivum*, vols I–III, Parts 1–2, Cambridge 1887–97, III, no. 2347. For earlier membership lists of Austin Friars, see R. E. G. Kirk and E. F. Kirk, *Returns of Aliens Dwelling in … London*, I, pp. 202–9, and 278–84; II, pp. 378–89 and 462–74, (*Hug Soc Lond*, vol. X QS).

14. See Ecclesiastical Discipline of the French Churches in England, 1641, Des Pasteurs, XVI, reprinted *Hug Soc Lond*, vol. LIV QS, pp. 95–133 and J. J. van Toorenenbergen (ed.), *Acten van de Colloquia der Nederlandsche Gemeenten in Engeland 1575–1609* and *Uittreksels uit de Acten der volgende Colloquia 1627–1706*, Utrecht 1872, Acten, p. 138.

15. Guildhall L. MS 7390/1, p. 63 and French Church MS 4, f. 489v.

16. See French Church MS 4, ff. 423r, 423v, 424r, and 425v. For the number of elders and deacons during the late sixteenth century, see A. Pettegree, op. cit., p. 221.
17. *Acten*, p. 139.
18. See O. P. Grell, *Austin Friars*, Appendix I.
19. See Ecclesiastical Discipline, Des Anciens, XXVIII.
20. French Church MSS 4 and 5; for Gideon Delaune, see MS 4, f. 503v and MS 5, f. 10r, see also *Dictionary of National Biography*; for Jean Payne, see MS 4, ff. 242v and 435r.
21. For Gideon Delaune, see French Church MS 4, f. 503v and MS 5, ff. 10r and 42r; for Robert de la Barr, see MS 4, ff. 429r and 489v; for Jean Fortrie, see MS 4, ff. 424r, 483r and 509r and MS 5, ff. 46r and 74v; for Philip Burlamachi, see MS 4, ff. 483r and 503v and MS 5, ff. 46r, 74v and 77r.
22. For the Dutch consistory minutes, see Guildhall L. MSS 7397/7 and 8; for the French minutes, see French Church MSS 4 and 5.
23. See Baron F. de Schickler, op. cit., vol. I, pp. 403 and 407–8, and vol. II, pp. 14–16; for Primrose see also *DNB*.
24. See A. C. Chamier (ed.), *Les Colloques des Eglises Françaises et des Synodes des Eglises Etrangéres en Angleterre 1581–1654*, (*Hug Soc Lond*, vol. II QS) and *Acten* also *Uittreksels*. For the decision of the Dutch churches to hold triennial colloquia, see *Gheschiedenissen*, p. 256.
25. *Acten*, pp. 100–1 and *Uittreksels*, pp. 304–33.
26. Marten Micron, *De Christlicke Ordinancien der Nederlantscher Gemeinten te London* (1554), ed. W. F. Dankbaar, The Hague 1956, p. 137. Guildhall L. MS 7397/7, ff. 32v, 75r, 143v and 149v; it was suggested in coetus in 1627 that the small Spanish church, which had no proper Reformed structure with elders etc. should join the Italian church – the proposal was rejected see f. 153r.
27. Guildhall L. MS 7410, f. 12.
28. Guildhall L. MS 7397/7, f. 149v.
29. Ibid., ff. 20v and 36r.
30. Marten Micron, op. cit., p. 137 and Guildhall L. MS 7397/8, f. 156v. See also MS 7397/7, ff. 61v, 149v (12 and 19 April 1627), 161v, 162r and 239v.
31. A couple of lists of the 'hommes politiques' have survived from this period, see Guildhall MS 7396/3, ff. 120–29. In 1624 the four members of the French church were Pierre de la Forterie, John Thullier, Jacques Oyels and Marc de Callone. The eight members representing the Dutch were Jacques T'kint, John Hertau, Isaac van Peenen, Joos Croppenburgh, Andries Boeve, Lerois Boeve, Lucas Jacobs and Jacques Jacobs. For the same body in Norwich, see E. R. Briggs, 'Reflexions upon the first Century of the Huguenot Churches in England', *Proc Hug Soc Lond 23*, 1980, p. 105 and W. J. C. Moens, *The Walloons and their Church at Norwich* (*Hug Soc Lond*, vol. 1 QS).
32. Guildhall L. MS 7397/7, ff. 65r, 41v and 147v.
33. Ibid., ff. 201r, 216v and 218v; MS 7397/8, ff. 12v and 24r.
34. Guildhall L. MS 7396/3, ff. 124 and 128; for the standard formula, see Guildhall L. MS 10,055, ff. 72r–v; see also *Gheschiedenissen*, pp. 198–9. For the gift to the Lord Mayor, see Guildhall L. MS 7396/3, ff. 125r, 129r and 135r.

35. Guildhall L. MS 10,055, f. 74r and *Gheschiedenissen*, pp. 196–7 and 244–5; see also Guildhall L. MS 7397/7, ff. 5v, 15v and 174v.
36. Guildhall L. MS 7397/7, f. 179v.
37. *Gheschiedenissen*, pp. 172–3 and 473.
38. See Simon Ruytinck's remarks about Robert le Maçon, *Gheschiedenissen*, pp. 194–5; for Gilbert Primrose, see *DNB*.
39. See Guildhall L. MS 7397/7, ff. 50r and 51v.
40. See my article, 'From Uniformity to Tolerance: The Effects on the Dutch Church in London of Reverse Patterns in English church Policy from 1634 to 1647', *Nederlands Archief voor Kerkgeschiedenis*, LXVI, 1986, pp. 17–40.
41. For the 'banquettes', see Guildhall L. MS 7397/7, f. 51v; for the Exchange, see f. 65v and MS 7397/8, f. 181v.
42. *Gheschiedenissen*, p. 499.
43. Ibid., pp. 460–61 and French Church MS 5, f. 65v.
44. See *Gheschiedenissen*, pp. 189–93 and *Beschryvinghe vande herlycke Arcvs Trivmphal ofte Eere Poort de vande Nederlantshe Natie Opgherecht in London*, Middelburg 1604, f. A2v; see also D. M. Bergeron, 'Charles I's Royal Entries into London', *The Guildhall Miscellany*, III, no. 2, pp. 91–7.
45. Guildhall L. MS 7397/7, f. 124v and MS 7390/1, ff. 227–42; it was to have been erected in Gracechurch Street, see *Gheschiedenissen*, p. 480. See also below, Chapter 8.
46. See *Nieuw Nederlands Biografisch Woordenboek*.
47. *Gheschiedenissen*, pp. 290–302 and Hessels, III, nos 1760 and 1860.
48. See C. Wilson, *England's Apprenticeship 1603–1763*, 2nd edition, London 1984, pp. 52–7.
49. See Hessels, III, nos 1849, 1855, 1904 and 1925.
50. R. Ashton, *The Crown and the Moneymarket, 1603–1640*, Oxford 1968, pp. 22 and 122–7 and *Gheschiedenissen*, p. 390; see also Guildhall L. MS 7411/2, f. 37v and P. C. Hooft, *De Briefwisseling 1608–1687*, (ed.) J. A. Worp, 6 vols, The Hague 1911–17, vol. 1, no. 169.
51. *C.S.P.Dom. 14*, CIV, nos 4 and 112; see also F. C. Dietz, *English Public Finance 1558–1641*, 2 vols, 2nd edition, London 1964, vol. 2, p. 178.
52. *C.S.P.Dom. 14*, CIV no. 4; CV, no. 64; CIX, nos 87, 101, 103 and 112; see also *Gheschiedenissen*, p. 340.
53. *Gheschiedenissen*, pp. 341–2.
54. N. E. McClure, *John Chamberlain's Letters*, 2 vols, Philadelphia 1939, no. 330.
55. British Library, Add. MS 12,497, ff. 53–4.
56. *C.S.P.Dom. 14*, CIX, no. 101 and *Gheschiedenissen*, pp. 350–1.
57. *Gheschiedenissen*, p. 358.
58. Ibid., p. 366.
59. S. R. Gardiner, *The Fortescue Papers*, Camden Society 1871, p. 107.
60. Public Record Office, S.P. 14/111. Simon Ruytinck's list in *Gheschiedenissen* is not correct, see *Gheschiedenissen*, p. 376. Robert de la Barr, Robert de Leau and Philip Burlamachi all served the French church as elders during the early Stuart period, see French Church MS 4, ff. 429r, 483r, 489v and 503v; MS 5, ff. 46r, 74v and 77r; John de Clerck was possibly a member of the community in Threadneedle Street.
61. Public Record Office, S.P. 14/111.

62. Robert de Leau had his shares in the East India Company sequestered and sold with a loss of 20 per cent; the £9,000 which ensued from the sale was confiscated, see N. E. McClure, op. cit., no. 345.
63. *Gheschiedenissen*, p. 382.
64. Ibid., p. 388.
65. See O. P. Grell, *Austin Friars*, Chapter II, Part 1.
66. *Gheschiedenissen*, p. 391.
67. F. C. Dietz, op. cit., p. 178.
68. *Gheschiedenissen*, pp. 398–9 and 466.
69. Ibid., pp. 399–400.
70. Guildhall, L. MS 7397/7, f. 135v.
71. *Gheschiedenissen*, p. 397.
72. *C.S.P.Dom. 16*, CXXXV, no. 81 and P. Heylyn, *Cyprianus Anglicus*, London 1671, p. 218.
73. *Hessels*, III, no. 2288.
74. Ibid.
75. *C.S.P.Dom. 16*, CCXXVI, no. 65.
76. Hessels, III, no. 2316 and *C.S.P.Dom. 16*, CCXXVIII, nos 63 and 64.
77. Hessels, III, no. 2316.
78. *Gheschiedenissen*, p. 388.
79. Guildhall L. MS 7430, f. 55; see also *DNB*.
80. Ibid.
81. Ibid.
82. P. Heylyn, op. cit., p. 263 and Guildhall L. MS 7411/2, pp. 74–5.
83. Hessels, III, no. 2341.
84. Guildhall L. MS 7430, f. 103ff.
85. Hessels, III, no. 2361 and *C.S.P.Dom. 16*, CCLXXXVI, no. 85.
86. Hessels, III, no. 2363.
87. Ibid., nos 2370–73.
88. Ibid., nos 2375 and 2378. See also *C.S.P.Dom. 16*, CCXCVII, no. 4.
89. Ibid., no. 2380.
90. Ibid., no. 2449.
91. P. Heylyn, op. cit., pp. 377–8.
92. Guildhall L. MS 7397/8, f. 98v.
93. See O. P. Grell, *Austin Friars*, Chapter VI.
94. Guildhall L. MS 7397/8, f. 100v.
95. Ibid., f. 101r – see under 9 and 17 June.
96. W. Prynne, *Canterburies Doome*, London 1646, see especially pp. 391 and 401.

CHAPTER THREE

A friendship turned sour: Puritans and Dutch Calvinists in East Anglia, 1603–1660

In March 1659 the consistory of the Dutch church in Colchester informed its mother-community in Austin Friars in London:

> As to our reasons regarding the Parliament, we hope that the Lord will bless this Assembly for the purpose of restoring a good government and discipline in the Church, whereby the unbridled liberty of heretics and sectarians may be restrained and our discipline the more conformed, *as in the time of the Bishops*.[1]

This was a remarkable conversion for a Calvinist congregation which, in conjunction with the other Dutch churches in England, had been widely admired by English Calvinists and Puritans for its doctrine and discipline since the reign of Queen Elizabeth. The statement is even more startling when we bear in mind that the Anglo-Dutch communities, together with godly Englishmen, had been the prime target of Archbishop Laud's anti-Calvinist campaign, and that they had fought a determined rearguard action throughout the 1630s against the Archbishop's Injunctions.[2]

Was the experience of the Dutch congregation in Colchester unique, or was it shared by the other Dutch communities in East Anglia and the rest of England? And why had the 1640s and 1650s, with their *de facto* toleration and religious pluriformity, been so disastrous for the Anglo-Dutch community in Colchester that by 1659 it not only wanted to see the sects restrained, but looked back nostaligically to the period prior to the Civil War, when the bishops had been firmly in control of the Church of England and the Dutch congregations in England forced to fight for their existence? These are the questions which I shall attempt to answer in what follows.

When Charles I succeeded his father on the English throne in 1625 three Dutch congregations had been in existence in East Anglia for more than 50 years. They owed their establishment primarily to the Dutch Revolt against Spain, which had started in the 1560s. The accompanying war and persecution had brought waves of Reformed Dutch and Walloon refugees to England. Here they were welcomed by the government of Elizabeth I, not primarily because of their religion as had been the case of their mother-community in Austin Friars in London under Edward VI, but for their superior skills and enterprise, which Elizabeth and her Privy Councillors considered useful in regenerating the stagnating English economy.

The Dutch church in London, which had received its first charter from Edward VI in 1550, had shared its Marian exile with a number of influential English Protestants. After its re-foundation in 1560 it had been instrumental in creating new Dutch churches in a number of Kentish and East Anglian towns. In this enterprise it had co-operated closely with the Elizabethan government.

In East Anglia, Dutch congregations had existed in Ipswich, King's Lynn, Thetford and Halstead during the 1570s and 1580s. These communities, however, were short lived and had all disappeared before 1590 when only the larger and more vigorous of the Dutch churches, in Norwich, Colchester and Yarmouth, had proved to be of a more permanent nature.[3]

Apart from the church in Yarmouth, which always had a relatively small permanent membership and which primarily survived because of its service to the many visiting Dutch fishermen and traders, Norwich and Colchester constituted the largest Dutch settlements outside London. Most of their members were either weavers or were occupied in trades connected with the new draperies. Both Colchester and Norwich, which had seen a steady decline in trade as well as in population towards the middle of the sixteenth century, benefited tremendously from the arrival of the immigrants. As opposed to London, where strangers never constituted more than 4 per cent of the total population, the Dutch and Walloon communities comprised around a third of the population in Norwich and probably not less than a fifth of the population in Colchester when they peaked towards the end of the 1580s.[4]

Far from all the Dutch immigrants joined the Reformed Dutch churches which Elizabeth had allowed the newcomers to establish. A considerable number of the refugees probably preferred the looser connection of *passanten* with the Dutch churches, thereby sparing themselves a number of economic obligations and simultaneously evading the more rigorous consequences of the discipline exercised by the ministers and elders to the congregations. Likewise, the constant inter-traffic between East Anglia and the Netherlands, and the immigrant communities' involvement in the Dutch Revolt, meant that many refugees only intended to stay in England for a brief period before returning to the Netherlands.[5] Assuming that the situation in London did not differ significantly from that in the provincial towns, the congregations in Norwich, Colchester and Yarmouth never included more than half the towns' Dutch or Anglo-Dutch inhabitants.[6]

At the time of Charles I's accession the Dutch communities in East Anglia were gradually contracting, many of their members having returned to the Netherlands during the last two decades of Elizabeth's reign, with hardly any new immigrants having arrived to take their place since 1590. Further decreases were caused by the migration of members to London following the pattern of the host population during the early seventeenth century. Those who left were often the wealthy and more enterprising, who were greatly missed in their provincial communities, but who, upon joining the Dutch church in Austin Friars, as the merchants Timotheus Cruso from Norwich and John la Motte from Colchester did, were able to serve the congregation in London diligently as elders and deacons.[7]

When the Dutch church in London had been founded in 1550 as a separate *corpus corporatum et politicum* under its own superintendent, Johannes a Lasco, its establishment had been furthered by leading Protestants within the government of Edward VI who wanted to help create a Reformed congregation which could serve as a model for the Church of England. After the church's re-establishment in 1560, and the creation of additional congregations in Kent and East Anglia in the 1560s and 1570s, that role was not to be resurrected, and limitations were applied to the original Charter. The Dutch churches were still allowed their own church order and discipline, but they were placed under the supervision of their respective bishops. Moreover, these Calvinist congregations found new admirers among the Puritan opposition to the Elizabethan church settlement and were suspected on occasion of harbouring English dissenters. In 1573, at the climax of the presbyterian agitation against the government and liturgy of the Elizabethan church, the Privy Council warned the Dutch church in London not to accept any English dissenters in their congregation.[8] That the religious example of the Dutch communities was also appreciated among the godly at Colchester during the reign of Elizabeth is evident from letters of support for the strangers, written by three English ministers in Colchester to Secretary Walsingham, in which they claimed that the good example 'both for liefe and religion generallie geeuen bie the straungers durynge their abode in Colchester haue ben comfortable to all those that be godlie minded'.[9]

Thus the Dutch Reformed communities in England were already associated with the godly or 'puritan' opposition within the Church of England well before the reign of Charles I and Archbishop William Laud's campaign for religious uniformity in the 1630s. The separatist minister, Henry Jacob, saw the status of the Dutch and French congregations in England as separate congregations outside the Anglican Church, but in 'brotherly communion with the rest of our English

churches', as a model for the separatist congregations which he, in
1605, together with other godly clergymen, wanted James I to permit.
This admiration for the stranger churches was, however, not shared by
the 'Anglican' clergy within the Church of England. In 1610, for instance, the 'Anglican' controversialist, David Owen, chaplain to Sir
John Ramsay, Viscount Haddington, published a pamphlet in which he
implicated the Dutch church in London with the 'Modern Puritans',
indicating that both were dangerous to Crown and Church. The Dutch
church, of course, denied the accusation and complained to the Bishop
of London, George Abbot; but such contemporary correlations, whether
constructed or real, were numerous and only waited for an ardent, anti-
Calvinist disciplinarian like William Laud to seize upon them and bring
them into play.[10] Furthermore, the fact that the Dutch communities
were all situated in the southeast of England, the heartland of English
dissent, retaining close contacts with leading Counter-Remonstrants
such as Festus Hommius and Franciscus Gomarus in the Dutch Republic, and enjoying particularly good relations with the Reformed churches
in the province of Zeeland, the home of hardline Dutch Calvinism
within the United Provinces, can hardly have escaped the Archbishop's
notice. Moreover, the Dutch Republic simultaneously provided an asy-
lum for refugee English Puritans. Small wonder that Laud included the
English congregations in the Netherlands and the Anglo-Dutch churches
in England in his campaign for religious uniformity when he succeeded
George Abbot as Archbishop of Canterbury in 1633.[11]

Until the late 1620s and the ascendancy of Laud and the 'Arminian'
faction within the Church of England, the Anglo-Dutch communities
had been extremely fortunate in most of the bishops and archbishops
under whose authority they had rested. Many of these bishops, like
Edmund Grindal, Edwin Sandys, George Abbot and John King, were
solidly Calvinist in doctrine and were accordingly sympathetic to the
foreign Reformed churches. Those, like most of the bishops of Norwich
under whose authority the Dutch congregations in Yarmouth and Norwich rested, and who, like John Jegon, Samuel Harsnett, Richard Corbett
and Matthew Wren, were not attracted to continental Calvinism, were
either too busy dealing with local English Puritans, such as the outspo-
ken Ipswich minister, Samuel Ward, or else had no ambition to tinker
with the well-ordered Dutch and Walloon churches, which generally
kept a low profile. Likewise, until the mid 1620s, the Dutch congregations were prepared, on occasion, to appeal to the English bishops for
assistance when the consistories found it impossible to control recalci-
trant members. Thus in 1624, when the Colloquium of the Dutch
churches debated whether a blasphemer could be brought before the
bishop, it was decided that, since experience showed that the English

bishops did not attempt to infringe their Discipline, it was permissible for the congregations to seek the bishops' assistance when the normal disciplinary measures had been exhausted.[12]

The Dutch communities did their best to steer clear of issues which might involve the churches in religious controversy. Hence, in 1606, when the Dutch Reformed churches of Amsterdam wrote to the consistory in Austin Friars asking it to recommend a suitable English minister for the newly established English Reformed congregation there, preferably one of those who had been discharged in the wake of the Hampton Court Conference, the members of the consistory in London refused to co-operate. They pointed out to the church leaders in Amsterdam that they dared not approach such candidates, since their whole existence depended on good relations with the English authorities. They did, however, offer to check the reputation of any particular candidate whom the churches in Amsterdam might have in mind. Evidently the Dutch church in London had the necessary contacts with English Puritan circles to be able to procure information about specific ministers, even if it found itself forced to decline the more active and potentially dangerous role of finding candidates.[13]

Under the early Stuarts the attitude of the Dutch churches to the Church of England was at best ambivalent. For obvious reasons the congregations refrained, if at all possible, from advertising their opinions. However when, in 1621, the Colloquium of the Anglo-Dutch churches was asked if it were possible for someone who had signed the *Ceremonien ende Ordinantien van de Engelsche kerche* to become a minister to one of the Dutch congregations, the answer was revealing, namely: that it was possible to elect such a person as a minister, since no National or Provincial Synod of the Reformed churches had found the discipline or ceremonies of the Church of England to be contrary to the word of God. Likewise, the deputies found 'that Christian charity would prohibit them from expressing any antipathy against the Church of England under whose wings they were sheltering and whose ceremonies they occasionally used in the English churches'. Still, the Colloquium emphasized that such a candidate was only bound to use these ceremonies in English churches and not in the Dutch, which had 'their own privileges granted by the King and Council' and confirmed by *de Approbatie vande Bisschoppen ende Langheduerighe prescriptie* (the approval of the bishops and established custom), provided that he promised to submit himself to the discipline and doctrine of the Dutch churches. Evidently this halfhearted acceptance of the Anglican church was determined by political reasoning rather than any feeling of religious affinity.[14]

A similarly cautious approach can be seen in 1639 when Austin Friars decided to appoint the former minister to the Reformed Italian

church in London, Cesar Calandrini, who since 1620 had occupied the
rectory of Stapleford Abbots in Essex. In spite of Calandrini having
received his ordination by the Coetus of the foreign Reformed churches
in London in 1618 and not having been forced to take any episcopal
ordination on his entry into the Church of England, thanks to the
support of Thomas Morton the Calvinist Bishop of Lichfield, the
consistory in Austin Friars appears to have been nervous about this,
their first appointment from within the ranks of the Church of England.
Calandrini produced a certificate proving his Calvinist orthodoxy signed
by English Calvinist and Puritan divines such as the London minister
William Gouge, Thomas Winniff, Dean of St Paul's, and two Essex
ministers, Theodore Herring and Samuel Hoard. In 1629 Herring and
Hoard had supported Thomas Hooker, the lecturer at Chelmsford in
Essex, who later left for the United Provinces, in connection with his
prosecution for nonconformity. Austin Friars obliged Calandrini to sign
three clauses in the consistory book, promising to end his ministry in
Stapleford Abbots and to observe the discipline and order of the Dutch
churches in England 'exactly as the ministers in this and other Reformed churches are sworn to observe and not to become an instrument
for any changes, or cause for anxiety, to the traditional discipline, order
and propriety of this congregation'. Having tasted Archbishop Laud's
anti-Calvinist medicine the leaders of the London community were not
prepared to take any chances in 1639.[15]

Caution had also guided the Anglo-Dutch communities when, in
1575, they decided to hold triennial Colloquia rather than to organize
themselves into the formal structure of a Classis, as they had been
admonished to do by the first General Synod of the Reformed churches
in the Netherlands, which had met in Emden in 1571. The fact that this
suggestion had displeased the Elizabethan government had not been
wasted on the leaders of the Dutch churches in England. Attendance at,
as well as adherence to the decrees issued by, the National Synods of the
Dutch Reformed churches posed the problem of conflicting authority
for the Dutch congregations in England. The exiled communities owed
their existence to the English government; they acknowledged that if
conflict arose self-preservation would force them to obey the English
government and to disregard the Synods. Accordingly, the Anglo-Dutch
communities were only represented at two out of the four Synods of the
late sixteenth century.

It must have been similar worries about conflicting authority which
caused the Norwich community to ask the Colloquium in 1615 whether
or not someone who had taken the Oath of Allegiance, which had been
introduced in the wake of the Gunpowder Plot in order to secure the
civil obedience of English Catholics, was eligible as an elder or a deacon.

The Colloquium told the representatives from Norwich that the Oath constituted no problem for potential elders and deacons since it had only been introduced to exclude 'foreign interference and jurisdiction'. The offices of elders and deacons were not *contra leges* but *praeter leges* and served 'to reinforce peaceful order through the strengthening of virtue and bridling of licentiousness among the King's subjects and through Christian care for the poor'.[16]

The National Synod of Dort (1618–19), the only General Synod to be held in the early seventeenth century, which became a highly politicized event with its confrontation between the staunch Calvinist, Counter-Remonstrant, wing of the Reformed churches in the Netherlands and the Arminians, who were subsequently expelled, was only attended by an observer from the Dutch churches in England. In spite of the close connection between the Dutch community in London and leading Counter-Remonstrants in the Netherlands, and the fact that the Colloquium which met in June 1618 had already appointed an official delegation (consisting of Simon Ruytinck, minister to the London church, Jonas Proost, minister to the Colchester community, and Carolus Liebaert, a fully trained minister who served Austin Friars as an elder from 1617 until 1624 when he became a minister to the Dutch church in Norwich), the interest of the English authorities in the Synod meant that the official presence of the Anglo-Dutch churches was considered politically undesirable by the States General. Consequently only Carolus Liebaert was dispatched as an observer.

The Colloquium of 1618 considered Arminianism a problem which was geographically limited to the United Provinces, even if the deputies realised that those students who were trained at the universities in the United Provinces and whom the Anglo-Dutch congregations might employ, might turn out to be crypto-Arminians. It was discussed whether or not representatives from the Colloquium should examine future candidates for the ministry in order to guarantee that Arminian tendencies did not sneak in to the churches by the back door. Likewise, the community in Norwich was worried about new members recently arrived from areas in the United Provinces which were known to be served by Arminian ministers. It was decided that these newcomers should not be accepted into the congregations immediately, but that they should be examined by one minister and two elders. Those who were willing to be taught and to accept the Counter-Remonstrant position should be welcomed as members after a trial period, whereas those who persisted in their beliefs were to be excluded until they had been made to see their errors.[17]

The fact that the English delegates, in spite of having supported the Counter-Remonstrants throughout the Synod, did not sign the canons of Dort must have been the reason why the Dutch churches in England refrained from subscribing to the 93 canons of the Synod of Dort. Calvinists within the Church of England later attempted on several occasions to make the articles binding on England, but the Anglo-Dutch communities, realizing the risks involved, only dared to subscribe to them after the fall of Archbishop Laud and the call of the Long Parliament.[18]

Despite the guarded attitude of the stranger churches to all issues which might be considered controversial by the English authorities, there is no doubt where their sympathies lay. They identified with what they described as the 'godly and well-disposed English' for whom they saw their churches serving as 'examples of godliness'.[19] This was a clear reference to those Calvinists or Puritans within the Church of England who wanted to carry the reformation further. It did not, however, include early Separatists, or 'Brownists' as the Anglo-Dutch churches generally labelled them.[20]

On its own, carefully expressed sympathy for the English Calvinists and Puritans can hardly have justified Archbishop Laud's view of the stranger churches as providing examples of 'ill consequence' to English subjects, confirming many 'in their stubborn ways of disobedience to the church-government' and attracting Englishmen 'who will not conform to our Church government', thereby breeding 'a nursery of ill-minded persons to the Church.'[21]

Obviously it must have been tempting for those disaffected Englishmen who understood Dutch and who would have been relatively numerous in places such as Colchester, Norwich and Yarmouth, which had close trading links with the United Provinces, to hear the 'pure' Word of God preached in the Dutch churches. In most cases they would have been able to attend discreetly as *passanten*, which meant that they did not have to provide attestation or to take out membership, while the stranger churches, at the same time, could pretend to have no knowledge of their presence. It was the same cautious approach which the Colloquium had advised the congregation in Colchester to follow in 1612. The Colchester community had wanted to know if it could accept English men and women who had married into the community as members, and if membership could also be extended to young Englishmen apprenticed to Dutch masters. Permission was given to allow these people in as *passanten*, with the proviso that it could only be done so long as this did not cause offence to the local English clergy.[22]

It is, however, just as likely that William Laud was equally worried about the close contacts which existed between individual ministers and elders of the Dutch churches and English Puritans. These contacts had been expanded in the late 1620s and early 1630s in the collections for those refugee Reformed ministers and schoolmasters from the two German Palatinates who had fallen victim to the Thirty Years' War. The first two royal collections for the refugees were administered by the consistory of the Dutch church in London, and saw elders like the Colchester-born John la Motte, who was later included in Samuel Clarke's hagiography of Puritans, co-operating closely with leading Puritan ministers such as John Stoughton, William Gouge, John Goodwin and John White, the Patriarch of Dorchester, and laymen such as the future Lord Mayor of London, John Kendrick, and the educationalist, Samuel Hartlib. In East Anglia the same collections saw the involvement of Samuel Ward of Ipswich, Samuel Collins of Braintree in Essex, and Cesar Calandrini, then Rector of Stapleford Abbots.[23]

Small wonder that William Laud decided to remove the responsibility for the third royal collection, which began in April 1635, from the hands of the Dutch consistory in London. Being a great believer in conspiracy theories, and seeing dissenters everywhere, the Archbishop must have felt considerable unease about the first two collections, which had brought leading members of the Feoffees of Impropriations, the great Puritan scheme for the infiltration of the Church of England with godly ministers, into close co-operation with Dutch Calvinists in England and the Netherlands.[24] Furthermore, Laud might well have known that several of the ministers of the Dutch churches had close personal contacts with leading Puritans such as John Cotton, Arthur Hildersam and Thomas Gataker. Some of the Dutch ministers even attended the household academies of Thomas Gataker and Richard Blakerby, the latter having opened his academy in Essex after he had lost his living in Norfolk on account of his nonconformity.[25]

Jonas Proost, who became a minister to the Dutch church in Colchester some time before March 1600 and served the community until he was transferred to the Dutch community in London in 1644, attended Blakerby's household seminar:

> Divers young Students (after they came from University) betook themselves to him to prepare them for the Ministry, whom he taught the Hebrew Tongue, to whom he opened the Scriptures, and read Divinity, and gave them excellent advice for Learning, Doctrine and Life; and many eminent persons proceeded from this Gamaliel.

Jonas Proost, son of Willem Proost, an elder to Austin Friars, had been born in London in 1572. He might well have been an alumnus of Austin Friars, since we find him matriculated in Heidelberg in 1588 together with a group of alumni from the London church.[26] Four years later Proost matriculated as a student of theology at the University of Leiden[27] and upon finishing his studies there he must have joined Blakerby's seminar. Proost was succeeded in 1645 by Johannes Ruytinck, son of the former minister to Austin Friars, Simon Ruytinck. Like Proost, he had been an alumnus of the London community and had studied in Cambridge as well as in Leiden before being appointed minister to the Yarmouth congregation in 1641.[28] A young student of theology, Johannes Meulenaer, who had matriculated at Leiden University in April 1616, had by June 1618 served the Colchester community for a considerable period as a 'proponent' or trainee minister. The Colloquium of that year, on the request of the church in Colchester, accepted Meulenaer as a fully trained minister. The regular absence from Colchester of the minister, Jonas Proost, in *publicke affaijren* had meant that many children had gone without baptism for several months. It was hoped that the appointment of Meulenaer would remedy this unsatisfactory situation. Meulenaer was not, however, to serve the congregation in Colchester for long. Two years later, in July 1620, he was suspended from Communion and was never again to serve the congregation in Colchester. In 1624 he found new employment when he was elected minister to the Dutch congregation in Maidstone, a post he retained until he eventually moved to London in 1639 to make a living as a brewer's clerk. Meulenaer might well be the only Dutch minister whom Archbishop Laud managed to have silenced during his anti-Calvinist campaign in the 1630s, yet his reasons for leaving the small Dutch community in Maidstone are far from clear.[29]

By August 1621 the congregation in Colchester had found a replacement for Meulenaer. That year the Colloquium allowed the church in Colchester to accept Thomas Cool as *proponent*. Cool, who was born in Colchester, differed from his predecessor and most of his future colleagues in having had no university training. The church in Colchester referred to him as a devout man 'experienced in the Word of God'. He had spent the years between 1619 and 1621 being trained, while preaching to the community in Colchester.[30]

He was most likely a product of the prophesying sessions which had originally been introduced by Johannes a Lasco and Maarten Micron in 1550 when the Dutch church in London, Austin Friars, had been founded. The Zurich-inspired prophesying sessions, which took place on Sundays after the services, were used by the Dutch ministers to explain their sermons and by the membership to question the clergy. They were far more democratic and open than the equivalent sessions among the English Calvinist clergy, who might allow laymen to listen in on their discussions but never to participate. By contrast, English Puritan ministers organized their meetings on a weekly or monthly basis for mutual edification and for the improvement of their ignorant brethren. In Scotland, however, prophesying sessions seem to have followed the same pattern as among the Anglo-Dutch congregations. Patrick Collinson is no doubt right when he claims that, had English Calvinists or

Puritans been left to themselves, undisturbed by the authorities, they would have allowed laymen to take an active part in their prophesying sessions.

By the 1620s prophesying was in use in the Dutch congregations in London, Sandwich, Canterbury, Norwich and Colchester, and the Colloquium of 1621 considered these meetings to be of the greatest importance to the Anglo-Dutch congregations. The Colloquium emphasized that not only did the prophesying sessions promote godliness among the membership at large, but they had also served to call several members to the ministry of the church, a number of whom now served the Dutch communities in England.[31]

Nearly all the ministers who served the Dutch communities in East Anglia during the first half of the seventeenth century were educated either in Leiden, under the guidance of Counter-Remonstrants, or supervised by Calvinists in Cambridge. This, at least, was the case until 1629, when Calvinism appears finally to have been muzzled within the University of Cambridge.[32] Theophilus Elisonius, son of the Norwich minister, Johannes Elisonius, who in 1639 succeeded his father as minister to the Dutch church in Norwich, received his BA from Cambridge in 1629 and matriculated in theology in Leiden the following year, together with the Austin Friars' alumnus, Johannes Ruytinck, mentioned above. He was thus following in the footsteps not only of his father, who had commenced his studies in Leiden in 1596, but also of his and his father's colleague, Carolus Liebaert, who had matriculated in theology in 1607.[33] Liebaert, who originated in the Dutch community in Sandwich, had moved to London only the year before he commenced his studies at Leiden University. After having graduated there he became a *proponent* or trainee minister in Norwich under the guidance of Johannes Elisonius. In 1615 the Colloquium of the Dutch churches in England recognized Carolus Liebaert as a fully trained minister, he did not, however, find full-time employment until nine years later when the Norwich community elected him as a second minister. During the intervening years he appears to have lived at the house of his brother, the merchant John Liebaert, in Bishopsgate Ward in London. On occasion he ministered to the congregation in London while at the same time serving that community as an elder from November 1617 until he was elected a minister in Norwich in 1624.[34]

The ministers to the three Dutch communities in East Anglia were theologically indistinguishable from most of the ministers whom Bishop Wren of Norwich and Archbishop Laud had deprived during the late 1630s. William Bridge, Samuel Ward and Jeremiah Burroughes were all former ministers in Norwich who sought sanctuary in Rotterdam where they became active within the English Reformed church, thus underlining the Dutch aspect of English nonconformism. Matthew Wren's energetic campaign against nonconforming Calvinists within the Church of England eventually led to an exodus of several hundred godly people from Norfolk to the Netherlands and New England.[35]

Bearing in mind the growing integration and anglicization of the Dutch communities in Yarmouth, Colchester and Norwich – by the 1630s most of their members would have been at least the first, if not the second, generation born in England – one should expect that these weakened communities would have suffered from William Laud's and Matthew Wren's campaign for uniformity even more than their English counterparts. Instead, it would retrospectively appear that Laud's Injunctions issued against the stranger churches in 1634/35 – ordering their members of the second descent to join their parish churches – benefited the Dutch congregations rather than harmed them. No evidence can be found in either London or East Anglia to support John Rushworth's and Clarendon's claims that many members and ministers of the foreign churches returned to the Continent. The Injunctions rather served to sharpen the Dutch churches' consciousness of their Reformed religion and Dutch culture, thus giving them an extra lease of life and reinforcing their position as 'model communities' for the Puritan opposition. Besides, the Anglo-Dutch churches in Colchester and Norwich demonstrated considerable skill in dodging the Injunctions. Jonas Proost in Colchester was of the opinion that, since the stranger churches had received no instructions on how to publish the Injunctions, the best thing they could do was to keep quiet about them, making it possible for members of the second descent to plead ignorance of their existence. In Norwich, where they were published, the consistory appears to have allowed those excluded to return through the back door as *passanten*.[36]

It was, however, not only the religious aspects of the activities of the Anglo-Dutch communities which caused serious concern within the government of Charles I in the decade leading up to the Civil Wars. In the autumn of 1640 it was reported that resident Dutchmen had armed themselves 'both here in London and other places especially Ipswich, Yarmouth, and Norwich, where the French, Walloons and Dutch are as many if not more than the natives, and exercise military discipline once a fortnight'. This was obviously a reference to the trained bands in those places where the Dutch appear to have played a prominent part.[37] This provided a natural domain for the exiles to become involved in, bearing in mind the strong Dutch civic traditions in this field, as portrayed in the famous paintings of Frans Hals and Rembrandt of the city companies in Haarlem and Amsterdam.

In Norwich a Dutch/Walloon company had been in existence since at least 1621. It was commanded during most of the 1630s and 1640s by a

Dutch/Walloon captain, John Cruso, who was an elder of the Dutch church, and also a close friend of the minister to the Dutch community in Norwich, Johannes Elisonius (who left him a folio volume in his will), and the Colchester minister, Jonas Proost (to whom he gave a copy of his first military work, *Militarie Instructions for the Cavallerie*, a folio edition published in Cambridge in 1632) was a prolific author and translator of military works.[38] His authorship, however, was not restricted to military matters: he also wrote an *Elegy on the premature decease of the most learned and God-fearing Dominus Johannes Elisonius, faithful minister of the Dutch congregation in Norwich*, and a commentary on Psalm VIII, which was published in Amsterdam in 1642.[39] In the same year he also published a work on castrametation, which he dedicated to 'the right worshipfull My ever honored Friend Philip Skippon' and added, 'I could not present it to any other but your Worthy Selfe, since you have been pleased, in the perusall of it, to give it such perfection'. Skippon, who since 1639 had been in charge of the Honourable Artillery Company in London, was an experienced soldier who had served both in the Palatinate and the Netherlands before becoming one of the Parliament's generals in the Civil War. He belonged to a Norfolk family of minor gentry[40] and had returned to England in 1638, when, together with his Dutch wife from Frankenthal, Maria Comes, he had settled at Foulsham. He appears to have formed a close friendship with several members of the Cruso family, especially Timotheus Cruso, John's brother, a London merchant and deacon to the Dutch church in Austin Friars, who was a lieutenant in the Honourable Artillery Company.[41]

The Dutch in Colchester also appear to have been active in the trained bands. The Alderman and later Mayor of Colchester, John Langley, who was captain of the trained bands there and led his company to the defence of London against the Royalist forces in November 1642, is most likely the same John/Jan Langele who served the Dutch church in Colchester as a deacon and elder between 1621 and 1627.[42]

Most members of the Anglo-Dutch communities sided with Parliament when the Civil War broke out in 1642;[43] several, like John Langley/Langele in Colchester, Samuel Voute and John Cruso in Norwich, and the master of the Brewers' Company in London and deacon to Austin Friars, John de Groote/Great, were heavily involved. Moreover, the Dutch congregation in London was no doubt correct when it claimed in 1649 that 'many of them haue not only emtyed their purses, but hazarded their persons in the Parliaments seruice'. Yet by the time the second Civil War started, their enthusiasm had waned, and many had changed sides or become moderates. Thus, in February 1649, John de Groote/Great was fined for having 'sent an armed foot soldier to serve under

Lord Goring in the Essex insurrection'; an incident which was to cause devastation to the Dutch community and to the town of Colchester.[44]

The bewildering and chaotic years of the Civil Wars and the Interregnum were to prove detrimental to the Dutch congregations in East Anglia and extremely difficult for the mother-community in London. That most of their problems were generated by former sympathizers and admirers among the ousted English divines, who had radicalized their religious positions during their exile in the Netherlands, can only have served to disappoint the leaders of the Dutch communities.[45]

The smallest of the Dutch communities in East Anglia, Yarmouth, had a tiny membership of 28 householders in 1605. Since the beginning of James I's reign the congregation had only survived because of financial support from Austin Friars. Its minister, Engel Hallinck, who served the community from 1601 to his death in 1640, was struggling to maintain his family on a modest stipend. Consequently the Colloquium of 1609 took the unusual decision to allow him to continue to sell socks to Dutch skippers and fishermen, even if he had to conduct his trade in inns and taverns.[46] This practice would only have served to make the Dutch churches yet more unpopular with Matthew Wren's successor in Norwich, Bishop Richard Montagu, who in 1639 reported to Laud that it had come to his knowledge that many clergymen frequented 'alehouses, taphouses and tobacco houses, especially in parts towards the seaside, to the foul scandal of their calling'.[47]

Austin Friars' annual contribution to the congregation in Yarmouth – between £12 and £20 – was justified by the church's importance to visiting sailors and fishermen from the Netherlands arriving twice a year for the herring fisheries. They used Yarmouth as their base to dry and repair nets and to take in supplies, and on Sundays a number of them attended service in the Dutch church. In the 1630s the Yarmouth community had argued for continuous financial support on the basis · that, without a Dutch church in the town, these sailors and fishermen were likely to spend their Sundays drinking in the local inns. Such a practice might, in the church's opinion, reflect badly on all the Dutch communities in England.

After the call of the Long Parliament the Yarmouth community was faced with accelerating decay, with several members joining the English churches where the preaching of ministers such as William Bridge, returning from exile in the Netherlands, might have proved particularly attractive.[48] The leaders of the community only managed to stop the independents from taking over their church because their objections were shared by the local authorities. They wished to preserve the Dutch church, 'which is necessary, not only for the maintenance of the poor, but for all other Dutch strangers who arrive here and require our assistance'.[49] Johannes Ruytinck, who left for Colchester in 1645, was to be the last permanent minister to the community. From then on the church had to make do with young trainee ministers – *proponenten* – who generally came over from Zeeland to serve the community for two-year stints, in order to learn English before returning to the Netherlands to take up permanent positions.[50]

The growing number of independent churches in Colchester and Norwich created similar problems for the Dutch communities there. Both were considerably larger than the Yarmouth community – Colchester had around 700 heads of households as members in 1635 and Norwich around 360 – and both could afford to employ two ministers, but the 'Separatists' nevertheless made severe inroads into their membership. Members left, claiming that they felt better edified among the 'Separatists' who did not, as the Dutch congregations did, allow 'scandalous people' as members. The Dutch churches decided to tackle the situation in two ways until 'the chiefest remedie against this grivance is to be expected from the Parliament'.

First, the discipline of the churches was to be tightened to satisfy 'tender consciences', and in order to encourage upright and godly behaviour among old and new members. Members were to be regularly catechized and examined in the main tenets of the Faith. New members should not be allowed to come to communion before they had been properly examined by a minister. They were required not only to be able to repeat the 'Kort Ondersoeck ofte Begrip' (an abridged version of the Heidelberg catechism written by the Middelburg minister, Herman Faukelius)[51] but to prove that they had reached a clear understanding of it, and not merely learned it by rote.

Secondly, the ministers were admonished 'to reduce such as begin to stray, both in private and in publick' and the consistories were to refuse to grant such members an attestation, 'lest we should seeme therby to countenance their separation'.[52]

The community in Colchester felt that the Dutch churches ought to oblige the separatists further by abolishing religious festivals and holidays in accordance with the *Directory*, which had replaced the Book of Common Prayer in 1645. The Colloquium of 1646 rejected this suggestion in spite of the Walloon/French churches' having already abolished festivals in 1644. It pointed out to the Colchester community that the Dutch churches were not bound by the *Directory*, and should stick to their own Order and Discipline, which was only to be abandoned by special order of Parliament.[53]

The Dutch congregations continued to lose members to the gathered churches, especially the Baptists and the Antinomians, throughout the 1640s and 1650s. Whether the decision of the Colloquium of 1644 to stay in close contact and regular correspondence with the Classis of Walcheren in Zeeland made it any easier for the churches to uphold their traditional Order and Discipline is questionable: members defecting to the sects continued to be a problem. Only the issues changed – from the question of having the membership restricted to the godly in the 1640s, to the question, in the 1650s, of whether the form of baptism used by the Dutch churches was sound and in accordance with the Word of God. This came at a time when the Dutch communities also began to feel the first effects of Quakerism.[54]

The call of the Westminster Assembly in 1643 and the prospects of a Presbyterian settlement for the English church were seen as positive developments by the Dutch churches. In 1645 they decided to try to promote the Presbyterian cause by having their Discipline translated into English and printed. Likewise, the London community paid for the translation and printing of the Middelburg minister Wilhelm Appolonius's caution against religious radicalism, which the Classis of Walcheren had forwarded to the Westminster Assembly in 1644. By the end of August 1647, however, Presbyterianism had been defeated by the army after its march on London, and hopes of some order and equilibrium being restored in religion had evaporated. Consequently, the Dutch communities finally shelved their plans for petitioning Parliament to have their Charter confirmed, something which had been at the top of the churches' agenda since 1644.

Instead, the Dutch churches in East Anglia were left to fight a losing battle, trying to retain their members while attempting not to anger the gathered or independent churches.

Norwich, seeking advice and help from the Colloquium on how to force unwilling members to continue their contributions to the congregation, suggested that those members who spent their Sundays in 'sectarian gatherings' or in 'profanity' should be fined one shilling for the church's poor-box; but it was allowed only to let its 'political men ... visit the public houses where the desecrators of the sabbath normally hide, so that they can be properly punished'.[55]

The Colchester community also found itself under great pressure and in 1652 its leaders suggested that the next Colloquium of the Dutch churches should not take place in Colchester. They pointed out that such an unusual gathering might prove counter-productive 'in a town where the Magistracy and its Minister and most of the inhabitants are great Independents, who hate and despise even the name of Presbyterian Government'. They had also heard about the recent attack on Presbyterianism by Peter Sterry, preacher to the Council of State, in a sermon entitled, 'England's deliverance from the Northern Presbytery, compared with its deliverance from the Roman Papacy'. They were therefore forced to conclude that, since 'our Church government is in bad odour in this country, and in this town consisting mostly of Independents, Anabaptists and Separatists, such an assembly would not be welcome'.[56] It is hardly surprising, when a split between radicals, pro-Cromwellian supporters and moderate anti-Cromwellians occurred in Colchester in the mid-1650s, that we find several members of the Dutch church among the moderates. By then the Dutch churches in England found themselves in the unenviable position of having been totally overtaken by religious developments. Long gone were the days of their much admired resistance to Laud's Injunctions, when their Puritan friends had told them that 'the Liberty of the Gospel, and the most desirable freedom of the Church from Episcopal Tyranny, depended chiefly on their Courage and Resolution'. Instead they found that their former friends, who had often sought refuge in their country of origin, were now among their leading antagonists.[57]

Notes

1. J. H. Hessels (ed.) *Ecclesiae Londino-Batavae Archivum* (Cambridge 1887–97), 3 vols in 4 parts (hereafter Hessels), no. 3475 (my italics).
2. O. P. Grell, *Dutch Calvinists in Early Stuart London* (Leiden 1989) (hereafter *D.C.*), 224–48.
3. I have not included the small Dutch congregation which came into existence in Canvey Island in the early seventeenth century as a consequence of the draining project launched by the merchant-member of Austin Friars, Joos Croppenburgh. For the establishment of a Dutch church in Canvey Island in 1627, see J. J. Van Toorenenbergen (ed.) *Acten van de Colloquia der Nederlandsche Gemeenten in England 1575–1609 & Uitreksels uit de Acten der volgende Colloquia 1627–1706* (Utrecht 1872) (hereafter *Acten*), 298, and J. J. Van Toorenenbergen (ed.) *Gheschiedenissen ende Handelingen die voornemelick aengaen de Nederduytsche Natie ende Gemynten wonende in Engeland ende bysonder tot London* (Utrecht 1873) (hereafter *Gheschiedenissen*), 502–3. The Dutch church in Ipswich existed from 1568 to 1576, see V. B. Redstone, 'The Dutch and Huguenot Settlements of Ipswich', *PHS* 12 (1919–24), 183–204, especially 185–6. The Thetford community consisted of a colony of weavers from 1573 to 1578, who were recruited from the Dutch congregation in Norwich, see W. J. C. Moens, *The Walloons and their Church at Norwich*, Lymington 1888, 1. The Halstead community, consisting of forty weaving families coming from Colchester, existed from 1576 to 1589; see W. J. C. Moens, *Register of Baptisms in the Dutch Church at Colchester*, London 1905, (hereafter Colchester), ii. See also Grell, *D.C.*, 12.
4. Grell, *D.C.*, 16; the Dutch and Walloon population of Norwich numbered around five thousand during the 1580s, see P. Slack, *The Impact of Plague in Tudor and Stuart England* (London 1985), 140. The estimate for Colchester is based on information found in *The Victoria History of*

the County of Essex, vol. ii (London 1907), 331–2, 339; and W. J. Hardy, *Foreign Settlers at Colchester and Halstead*, Pub. H.S. 2 (1887/8), 182–96, especially 189. In 1622 the Anglo-Dutch population in Colchester totalled 1535.

5. See A. Pettegree, *Foreign Protestant Communities in Sixteenth-Century London* (Oxford 1986), 252.
6. Grell, *D.C.*, 3.
7. Ibid., 82 and 269.
8. Ibid., 12–14.
9. Moens, *Colchester*, vi.
10. For Henry Jacob's interest in the Dutch and French communities in England, see M. Tolmie, *The Triumph of the Saints: the Separate Churches of London, 1616–1649* (Cambridge 1977), 8; Grell, *D.C.*, 5.
11. For contacts between Calvinists in the Netherlands, English Puritans and Anglo-Dutch Calvinists, see K. L. Sprunger, *Dutch Puritanism: a History of English and Scottish Churches of the Netherlands in the Sixteenth and Seventeenth Centuries* (Leiden 1982), and Grell, *D.C.*, *passim*.
12. R. W. Ketton-Cremer, *Norfolk in the Civil War* (Norwich 1985), 51–62. An exception to this general tendency of non-interference was Bishop Samuel Harsnett's attempt in 1619 to force the Dutch and Walloon churches in Norwich to take communion kneeling. It was probably inspired by James I's success in imposing the Anglican liturgy on the Scottish church at the Assembly of Perth in August 1618, but was firmly resisted by the two Norwich communities, see Van Toorenenbergen, *Gheschiedenissen*, 328, and P. Milward, *Religious Controversies of the Jacobean Age* (London 1978), 24. For the example from the Colloquium of the Dutch churches in England in 1624, see Guildhall Library, London (hereafter GL) MS 7411/2, 50r–v.
13. Grell, *D.C.*, 15. The Anglo-Dutch churches sympathized with those among the English clergy who refused subscription after the Hampton Court Conference and who were consequently ejected from their livings. In the words of the minister to the Dutch church in London, Simon Ruytinck, these ministers 'were dismissed to the sorrow of many good Christians', see Van Toorenenbergen, *Gheschiedenissen*, 187.
14. GL MS 7411/2, 37r.
15. Grell, *D.C.*, 65–7, and N. Tyacke, *Anti-Calvinists: the Rise of English Arminianism c. 1590–1640* (Oxford 1987), 189.
16. Grell, *D.C.*, 31–2. For the Oath of Allegiance, see Milward, *Religious Controversies of the Jacobean Age*, 114–19, and W. K. Jordan, *The Development of Religious Toleration in England from the Accession of James I to the Convention of the Long Parliament* (London 1936), 76–83. For the concern of the Dutch church in Norwich about the oath, see GL MS 7411/2, 19v.
17. See Grell, *D.C.*, 32–3 and 264. For the Colloquium's concern about candidates for the ministry who might have Arminian leanings, see GL MS 7411/2, 26r–v; and for the special concern of the Norwich community, ibid., 28r.
18. Tyacke, *Anti-Calvinists*, 87–106 and 176–7 and *Acten*, 315 and 333.
19. See below, Chapter 9 'Calvinist *Agape* or Godly Dining Club?'.
20. Grell, *D.C.*, 37 and 144. For Brownists, see M. Tolmie, *The Triumph of the Saints: the Separate Churches of London, 1616–1649*, 14–27.

21. Cited in Grell, *D.C.*, 225 and 227.
22. GL MS 7411/2, 7v.
23. Grell, *D.C.*, 176–223; for Samuel Collins, see also Tyacke, *Anti-Calvinists*, 189; for Samuel Collins' and Samuel Ward's involvement in the collections for the Palatinate, see documents preserved in *Reformierten Pfarrants St Martha, Nuremberg*, West Germany, nos 73, 74. See also W. Hunt, *The Puritan Moment*, London 1983, 253–8.
24. Grell, *D.C.*, 176–223.
25. For the Puritan academies, see Grell, *D.C.*, 58–9, 266 and 276; see also J. Morgan, *Godly Learning* (Cambridge 1986), 296–7. For Richard Blakerby, see also *Dictionary of National Biography* (hereafter *DNB*).
26. For Jonas Proost, see G. Toepke, *Die Matrikel der Universitat Heidelberg*, II Teil (Heidelberg 1886), 139, and Hessels, nos 1156 and 1467.
27. *Album Studiosorum Academiae Lugduno Batavae MDLXXV–MDCCLXXV* (The Hague 1875), 33.
28. See Grell, *D.C.*, 145–6 and 282.
29. For Johannes Meulenaer/Miller, see GL MS 7411/2, 25v, Moens, *Colchester*, 89–90, Hessels, nos 1786, 1787, 1827 and 2519, and *C.S.P. Dom. Charles I*, CCCCXCIX, 520–21 (1643).
30. For Thomas Cool, see GL MS 7411/2, 36r and 42r; see also Moens, *Colchester*, 89–90; Cool was ordained by the London minister Wilhelm Thilenius in February 1628; see GL MS 7397/7, 146r.
31. For prophesying within the Dutch churches in England, see Grell, *D.C.*, 34–5 and 37; for prophesying among English Puritan ministers, see P. Collinson, *The English Puritan Movement* (London 1971), 168–75.
32. Tyacke, *Anti-Calvinists*, 45–57; see also below Chapter 11, 'The Attraction of Leiden University for English Students of Medicine and Theology'.
33. For Theophilus Elisonius, see J. Venn (ed.) *Alumni Cantabrigienses*, part I, 4 vols (Cambridge 1922–24) and *Album Studiosorum Academiae Lugduno Batavae*, 228. He was born in Norwich in 1609 and served the Dutch community in the city from 1639 to 1676. His father, Johannes, was born in 1581, presumably also in Norwich – he registered as 'Anglus' when he matriculated at Leiden University in 1598 (*Album Studiosorum Lugduno Batavae*, 53). Johannes Elisonius was highly esteemed within the Dutch communities in England. Austin Friars attempted to hire him twice, in 1621 and again in 1638 (Grell, *D.C.*, 57 and 62). Johannes married Mary Bucknoll, and served the Norwich community from 1603 to 1639. Their eldest son, also Johannes, became a successful merchant in Amsterdam and, during a visit from his parents, had their portraits painted by Rembrandt, who had by then become the most fashionable and expensive portrait-painter in Europe (A. V. Moore, *Dutch and Flemish Painting in Norfolk* (London 1988), 3–6). In his will, dated 17 October 1639, Johannes Elisonius left forty shillings to the poor of the Dutch congregation, and twenty shillings to the poor in the ward where he lived. He left his eldest son, Johannes, a silver wine cup; all his books and papers to Theophilus; two folio volumes to his colleague, Carolus Liebaert; and one folio volume to the elder and captain of the Dutch/Walloon company of the trained bands, John Cruso (E. A. Kent, 'Notes on the Blackfriars' Hall or Dutch Church, Norwich', *Norfolk Archaeology*, 22 (1924–26), 86–108, especially 98–100).
34. For Carolus Liebaert, see Grell, *D.C.*, 33, 70–71, 90n., 264. He became a

member of Austin Friars in August 1606, having arrived from the Dutch community in Sandwich (W. J. C. Moens, *The Walloons and their Church at Norwich* (Lymington 1887/8), Publications of the Huguenot Society of London, 1 (hereafter *Norwich*), 315) and is listed as living at his brother's house in London in the returns of 1618 (R. E. G. and E. F. Kirk (eds) *Returns of Aliens Dwelling in the City and Suburbs of London under James I*, 4 vols, Pub. H.S. 10, vol. 3 (London 1908), 194). For his acceptance as a fully trained minister, see GL MS 7411/2, 23v.

35.   See K. L. Sprunger, *Dutch Puritanism*, 168–72, and Ketton-Cremer, *Norfolk in the Civil War*, 68–9 and 76–88.

36.   Hessels, no. 2449.

37.   Grell, *D.C.*, 243–4 and Moens, *Norwich*, 82–3. John Cruso was the eldest son of the refugee merchant of the same name from Flanders who settled in Norwich some time during the 1570s or 1580s. Like his brothers, Timotheus and Aquila, the former a successful London merchant and deacon to Austin Friars, the latter accepted as an alumnus of the Dutch community in London, John was born in Norwich (Grell, *D.C.*, 68, 78, 82, 132, 137–8, 238–9, 269, 281; Moens, *Norwich*, 190). The *DNB* identifies him mistakenly with his son John, who matriculated at Caius College at the age of fourteen in 1632. By then John Cruso senior had been an elder to the Dutch church in Norwich for several years, and had advanced from musketeer to Captain of the Dutch company of the trained bands in Norwich (J. Venn, *Biographical History of Gonville and Caius College 1349–1897*, 2 vols (Cambridge 1897), i. 304; Moens, *Norwich*, 82–3, 226; *Acten*, 295).

38.   Cruso appears to have become captain of the Dutch/Walloon company in Norwich by 1632. There is a copy of his *Militarie Instructions* (Cambridge 1632), with a handwritten dedication from Cruso to the minister of the Dutch church in Colchester, Jonas Proost, in Cambridge University Library. He also published a number of other military works, among them, *The Art of Warre* (Cambridge 1639); *The Complete Captain, or An Abridgement of Cesars Warres (Written by the Late Great Generall the Duke of Rohan)* (Cambridge 1640). When Cruso published a second edition of the *Militarie Instructions* (Cambridge 1644), it included a poem to him from the radical London mercer, Colonel Edmond Harvey, for whom see below, Chapter 6, 'From Persecution to Integration: the Decline of the Anglo-Dutch Communities in England, 1642–88'.

39.   *Uytbreydinge over den Achsten Psalm Davids* (Amsterdam 1642); see also W. Woods, 'Poetry of Dutch Refugees in Norwich', *Dutch Crossing*, 8 (1979) 71–3.

40.   Ketton-Cremer, *Norfolk in the Civil War*, 164–5.

41.   Grell *D.C.*, 243–4.

42.   J. H. Round, 'Colchester and the Commonwealth', *English Historical Review*, 15 (1900), 641–64, especially 642; for the deacon and elder John/Jan Langele, whom I identify with him, see Moens, *Colchester*, 92.

43.   Grell, *D.C.*, 50; Moens, *Norwich*, 83, and Hessels, no. 3067.

44.   M. A. Everett Green (ed.), *Calendar of the Proceedings of the Committee for Advance of Money 1642–56*, 3 vols (London 1888), ii. 1015.

45.   See below, Chapter 4, 'From Uniformity to Tolerance: the Effects on the Dutch Church in London of Reverse Patterns in English Church Polity,

1634–1647', Ketton-Cremer, *Norfolk in the Civil War*, 73–5 and 257;
Sprunger, *Dutch Puritanism*, 168–72.
46. Grell, *D.C.*, 84.
47. Ketton-Cremer, *Norfolk in the Civil War*, 125. Hallinck was already an
elderly man by 1628: 'his age and increasing weakness made it difficult
for him to preach four or five times in succession on special occasions',
see Hessels, no. 1941.
48. Ketton-Cremer, *Norfolk in the Civil War*, 257.
49. *Acten*, 322–3.
50. Hessels, nos 2807, 2827, 3274 and 3544.
51. See *Biografisch Lexicon voor de Geschiedenis van het Nederlandes
Protestantisme* (Kampen 1988), vol. 3.
52. Hessels, no. 2347; *Acten*, 321–2, 328–9, 333–4, 342–4.
53. *Acten*, 336–7. For the *Directory* see C. H. Firth and R. S. Rait (eds),
Actes and Ordinances 1642–66 (London 1911), i. 582–607, especially
607; also see above, Chapter 2, 'The French and Dutch Congregations in
London in the Early 17th century'.
54. *Acten*, 324–6, 328–34, 353–6, 362–7; L. F. Roker, 'The Flemish and
Dutch Community in Colchester in the Sixteenth and Seventeenth Centuries', *PHS*, 21 (1966) 29; GL MS 7397/8, 241r–v and 242r; Hessels, no.
3388.
55. *Acten*, 337–8 and Hessels, no. 2908.
56. Hessels, no. 3130.
57. J. H. Round, 'Colchester and the Commonwealth', 651; P. Heylin,
Cyprianus Anglicus (London 1671), 265.

Abbreviations

PHS: Proceedings of the Huguenot Society of London
Pub. H.S.: Publications of the Huguenot Society of London

From uniformity to tolerance: the effects on the Dutch church in London of reverse patterns in English church policy, 1634–1647

During the years between 1634 and 1647 the Dutch church in Austin Friars saw a shift in English church policy from one extreme to the other, moving first towards a uniform Anglican discipline and then towards a general tolerance. From 1634 until the convention of the Long Parliament in 1640 the Dutch Reformed communities in England, like many of their Puritan friends and sympathizers, became targets for the new Archbishop, William Laud's drive for total uniformity within, as well as without the Anglican Church. From 1640 until around 1647 the equilibrium which came into existence after the fall of Laud and the collapse of his church policy in effect produced a state of religious tolerance. A substantial number of Independent congregations established themselves in and around London during the early 1640s often under the guidance of ministers returned from exile in the Netherlands. The call of the Westminster Assembly in 1643 and the general ambition to create a Presbyterian church discipline only served to widen the gap between former Puritan allies. Some recognized the need for a unified church policy and supported Presbyterianism whereas others, the Independents, who had often spent some years in exile under Laud, were against any kind of coercion and wanted nothing less than religious tolerance. The struggle was finally won by the Independents during the summer of 1647. The support of their cause by Oliver Cromwell and the army ensured the defeat of Presbyterianism.

For an alien and Calvinist minority, like the Dutch congregation in Austin Friars, it was obviously difficult to absorb the effects of two such thorough changes in religious policy, having experienced the relative tranquility of the reigns of Elizabeth I and James I. Moreover the Dutch congregation in London had seen a slow decline in membership during the first two decades of the early seventeenth century while the English population of the City had grown rapidly. It was, however, of greater significance that over a third of the congregation's members were by then born in England.[1] This meant that the Reformed discipline and service of Austin Friars which based itself wholly on Dutch language and culture was already threatened from within before Laud became Archbishop of Canterbury. The consistory had recognized this problem from at least the late 1630s and as a consequence had tried to engage a schoolmaster under the auspices of the congregation in order to guarantee that the younger generations could be taught in their mother-tongue.[2]

During the late sixteenth and early seventeenth centuries it was the official policy of the consistory, the governing body of Austin Friars, to co-operate with the English authorities on whose good-will the community depended. In spite of its outward co-operation the congregation was already suspected of harbouring English religious dissenters during the reign of Elizabeth. In 1573 the Privy Council in its attempt to stamp out English Presbyterianism warned the Dutch church not to accept any Puritans in their congregation. The consistory of Austin Friars was, as always in these sensitive matters, very careful in delivering its answer to the Councillors.

> They prayed, that it would please them not to believe or regard malicious reports to their prejudice: for that they countenanced no such tumultuous people, nor approved either of their words or actions. They that were none of those that despised the ceremonies of other churches; and that submission was due to what a pious magistracy had established, and what they judged was most fit for the people, and that ended the promoting of godliness.

and added:

> And that no English should be admitted among them, who on such principles sought to separate themselves from the religious customs of their own country. That they had but four of the English nation in their church: and of each they gave account: two whereof had been exiled; and ever since their return had remained with them.[3]

The Dutch congregation apparently managed to convince the Privy Council in this situation, but in 1634, over 60 years later, the newly created Archbishop of Canterbury, William Laud, had identical suspicions when he endorsed a report entitled *The state of the French and Dutch Churches in England*. This document stated that,

> Contrary to their charter, and to the disturbance of our Church government, they admit of our own nation, and his Majesty's subjects, who will not conform to our Church government, to be members of them, and thereby breed a nursery of ill-minded persons to the Church.[4]

Laud's views were not unfounded even if they were difficult to prove. Most of the English attending the services in Austin Friars would not have partaken in the Communion and if they did, then only as *passanten*. Accordingly they would not have figured in any of the registers of the church. Surprisingly enough though, a couple of Englishmen with Puritan sympathies had themselves registered as members of Austin Friars. For instance the Alderman and later Lord Mayor, Sir Thomas Middleton, became a member of the Dutch church as early as 1582, after having lived in Antwerp for several years.[5] He was a typical Puritan, London merchant connected through marriage with Puritan colleagues, as for instance Richard Saltonstall. When he was elected Lord Mayor in 1613 he requested the consistory to be remembered in the congregation's public prayers in order that God would show him mercy and help him perform his duty well.[6]

Another example was Sir Henry Marten, Dean of the Arches, who was listed as a member of Austin Friars in November 1636, even if he was only included under the unusual heading of 'other members'. This was obviously a practical and personal consequence of his attitude in 1628 when he had promoted a bill in Parliament which was intended to ensure that no one could be persecuted for absence from his parish church if he were listening to the Word of God in another church or chapel.[7]

Of perhaps greater consequence were the friendships and contacts which existed between elders and ministers of Austin Friars on one hand and Puritan ministers and laymen on the other. One of the richer merchant members of Austin Friars, the elder John la Motte, who was a Freeman of the Company of Weavers and who served the Company as Upper Bailiff in 1629, provides an excellent example of the close friendships between English Puritans and individual governors of the Dutch church.[8] Through his daughter's marriage to Morris Abbot, son of Sir Morris Abbot, he was automatically connected with one of the mightiest Puritan merchant families in London. The collections in England for the refugee ministers from the Palatinate which officially commenced in June 1628 furthered la Motte's involvement with Puritans in and around London.[9] John Goodwin, John Davenport's successor in St Stephen's, Coleman Street, dedicated one of his early works to la Motte, and Samuel Clarke included him in his biographies of eminent Puritans.[10]

Originally Charles I had made the consistory of the Dutch church responsible for the transfer and distribution of the sums collected in the first two Royal collections for the exiled ministers from the Palatinate, in 1628 and again in 1630. This responsibility was not given to Austin Friars for the third Royal collection which started on 9 April 1635. The hand of Archbishop William Laud was clearly visible here. Laud's general drive for uniformity also included organizational matters like the collections and accordingly he had both the wording of the Letters Patent changed and the original distributors, the consistory of Austin Friars, removed.[11] Thus he was able to exclude Austin Friars from any further involvement in this work, but not individual, highly committed elders, like John la Motte, who remained a central figure in this enterprise. It is evident from a letter written in 1636 by John Stoughton, the rector of St Mary Aldermanbury in London, to Samuel Hartlib that la Motte was still closely associated with both these gentlemen and others, like for instance, the refugee ministers from the Palatinate, Theodor Haak and John Rulice, and the rector of Holy Trinity and St Peter's in Dorchester, John White, in raising money for the refugee ministers.[12]

It was, however, not only the elders of Austin Friars but also the ministers who were affiliated with Puritan Circles. The relations between some of the most influential pastors of the Dutch church and leading Puritan divines appear to have been close. Jonas Proost, who did not become a minister to the Dutch church in London until after 1642, and Wilhelm Thilenius, who served Austin Friars from 1624 until he retired because of illness in 1630, attended the academies of Thomas Gataker and Richard Blakerby. Timotheus van Vleteren, who commenced his ministry to Austin Friars in 1628, corresponded with John Cotten and forwarded Arthur Hildersam's tracts to his friends in the Netherlands. Cesar Calandrini, who was called to the ministry of Austin Friars in April 1639, was a former minister to the Italian church in London and had close links with both the community in Austin Friars and the French congregation in London. He held an English living until 1639 as rector of Stapleford-Abbots in Essex.[13] Anthony Wood described him as 'by birth a German, by profession a puritanical theologist'. This statement is confirmed by Calandrini's extensive list of correspondents, which includes the names of prominent Puritan ministers such as Dr Cornelius Burges, Hebert Palmer, Stephen Marshall, Thomas Edwards, Thomas Gataker, Dr Thomas Horton and John Davenport.[14]

The connections were many and certainly sufficient to fuel Laud's suspicions that the aliens with their half-independent Presbyterian congregations were part of what he considered a general Puritan threat to the Anglican Church. Furthermore the fact that all the foreign Presbyterian communities were situated in southeast England, the centre of the Puritan opposition, cannot have escaped the Archbishop. William Laud had had his eyes on the foreign congregations for some time before his elevation in 1633 to the archbishopric of Canterbury placed him in a position from which to act. While Bishop of London, in 1632, he had, according to his apologist, Peter Heylyn, brought these matters to the attention of the Privy Council:

> He had long teemed with this Design, but was not willing to be his own Midwife when it came to the Birth; and therefore it was so contrived, that Windebank should make the Proposition at the Council-Table, and put the business on so far, that the Bishop

> might be moved by the whole Board to consider of the several
> Points in that weighty Business: who being thus warranted to the
> execution of his own desires, presented two Memorials to their
> Lordships, at the end of this year, March 22.[15]

The new Archbishop did not waste any time. On 31 March 1634, only
seven months after his promotion to the see of Canterbury, he obtained
a Commission from Charles I to make a visitation of all churches,
hospitals, almshouses and schools within the province of Canterbury.[16]
With this in hand, on 7 April, Laud summoned representatives from the
French and Dutch communities in Canterbury, Sandwich and Maidstone to appear in the consistory of the Cathedral in Canterbury a week
later.[17] It obviously made sense to initiate his new policy with the
smaller, less influential provincial churches. On 17 April the representatives of these congregations met with the Vicar-General, Sir Nathaniel
Brent, who asked them three questions: (1) Whether or not they used
the Anglican liturgy translated into Dutch and French, and if not, what
other liturgy they used? (2) How many of their members were born in
England? (3) Whether or not those who were born in England would
conform to the ritual of the Church of England?[18]

In spite of an amicable interview with the Vicar-General, the congregations in Kent informed their respective mother-communities in London that they were afraid that the Archbishop sought nothing less than
the destruction of all the foreign congregations in England.[19] That
Laud's attitude to the aliens had not softened can be seen from the
report he endorsed only three days after the Kentish representatives had
met with Brent. Here he accused the foreign churches of being nurseries
of dissent to the Church of England.[20] When the congregations in Kent
finally, around the beginning of May, after many consultations with the
leaders of the London communities, responded to the three questions
posed to them by the Vicar-General, they, in fact, avoided answering by
referring to the Charter they had received from Edward VI in 1550.[21]

Their claim that they were exempted from the jurisdiction of the
Archbishop and Bishops certainly did not hold true. Elizabeth I had
altered Edward VI's Charter on exactly this point when she allowed the
Dutch church in Austin Friars to be refounded in 1560 from whence the
congregation had been under the supervision of the Bishop of London.
Accordingly this answer cannot have impressed Laud. The Archbishop
did not bother with the communities in Kent until he finally summoned
their representatives to appear before a Committee of Enquiry on 19
December 1634 where he presented them with a *fait accompli*, in the
form of the Injunctions.

> 1. That all the Natives of their Wallon Congregations must resort
> to the severall parish Churches of those parishes where they in-

habit, to hear divine service and sermons, and performe all duties
of parishioners required in that behalfe.
2. And that the Ministers and all others of the same Wallon or
French Congregations which are aliens borne shall have and vse
the Lyturgy vsed in the English Churches, as the same is, or may be
faythfullie translated into French (and Dutch). Et monuerunt eos,
to informe their Congreations hereof, and conforme them and
themselves hervnto by first of March next.[22]

The deputies of the foreign congregations only managed to obtain a
concession with regard to the date of the introduction of the Injunctions
which was delayed until Easter.[23] Now that Laud had shown his real
intentions the need for collective action was paramount to all the alien
communities in England. It was decided to employ the unusual measure
of calling a Synod of all the Dutch and French churches in England.
When it met on 5 February 1635 the need for urgent action was
generally recognized and the following day some of the foreign communities' friends at Court were approached. The merchant and former
financier to the English Crown, Philip Burlamachi, was contacted. He
was now living under the King's protection after his bankruptcy and
was an obvious candidate being a member and former elder of the
French congregation in London.[24] Two elders of the French congregation in London visited the Countess of Southampton, a member of their
congregation, and spoke to her husband, who promised to present their
case to the Lord Chamberlain, Philip Herbert, Earl of Pembroke, and to
Lord Holland.[25] The Huguenot, Benjamin de Rohan, Duke of Soubise
also promised to assist the Synod. He was godfather to Charles I and
since 1626, after having been involved in the Duke of Buckingham's
attempt to relieve La Rochelle, had made his home at the English
Court.[26] A couple of the elders of Austin Friars approached the Dutch
Ambassador, Sir Albertus Joachimi and the royal physician, Sir Theodor
de Mayerne who, like Philip Burlamachi, was a French Protestant of
Italian origin.[27]

These efforts by the Synod were rewarded when a large deputation
was granted an audience with Charles I on 12 February. The deputation
asked the King to grant them a hearing in the Privy Council and
presented him with a petition. Charles immediately passed it on to
Philip Herbert, his Chamberlain, who was asked to forward it to one of
the King's secretaries. Apparently the Earl of Southampton kept his
promise of a week earlier and managed to convince the Earl of Pembroke
to support the cause of the foreign churches.

> And though Pembroke, either out of love to the Cause, or hate to
> the Archbishops Person, chose rather to deliver it to Cooke than
> Windebank; yet neither Cooke himself, nor Weckerly his chief

Clerk (a Walloon by birth) who had very much espoused the Quarrel, could do anything in it.[28]

The foreign churches' main objections against Laud's Injunctions were economic. The members of the Dutch and French churches contributed not only towards the maintenance of their own poor for which they were widely admired by their hosts, but also towards the support of the English poor in their respective parishes. The Dutch and French, in their petition to the King, pointed out that if all their members who were born in England were forced to leave their congregations the churches would not be able to maintain their poor. These poor people would then be a burden to be relieved by the parishes where they lived.[29] In addition most of their members born in England belonged to the wealthier layer of merchants and entrepreneurs and might leave England if they were forced to join the parish churches.

> by reason of that many good workmen will retire themselves else where who do dayly furnish excellent manufactures to this Kingdome, and of all kinds, and by their retiring many thousands of your subjects who are employed by them will find themselves destitute of worke, yea from thence your Custome is like to receive a great prejudice.[30]

These were probably the most useful arguments the alien congregations could have employed, bearing in mind that the main incentive for Elizabeth's government to encourage the Dutch and French to settle in England after 1560 had been the economic benefit the country might harvest from their immigration.

Laud also realized the value of these arguments, and later the same year he pointed out to the town Council in Canterbury that those members of the foreign churches who were born in England and according to the Injunctions should now join their parish churches would have to continue their contributions to the poor of the Dutch and French communities until some other solution to this problem could be found.[31]

It was probably these economic implications which in March made Laud soften his attitude towards the stranger churches. During an interview with the deputies from the communities in Kent, Laud promised that should they wish to petition the King in order to be allowed to keep their members of the first descent, he would *bona fide* forward their petition.[32] The news of the Archbishop's change of heart caused the Synod to rejoice, but its hopes were quickly dashed. When the Injunctions were published on 1 April 1635 only a minor concession had been granted. The strangers born abroad who were allowed to remain members of the Dutch and Walloon churches were permitted to have and use their owne discipline, as formerly they have donne. Yet it is thought fit that the English Lyturgie should be translated in French and Dutch, for the better fitting of their children to the English government.[33]

Somehow the communities in Kent managed to engineer some further breathing space; the implementation of the Injunctions was postponed until 1 July.[34] In the meantime the foreign churches held several consultations with each other in London. The petition of the Dutch and French churches in Norwich to the Archbishop on 26 June 1635 must have evolved out of the decisions taken during these meetings. As in the earlier petitions from the Synod it emphasized the economic damage the Injunctions would cause. They would eventually be responsible for the dissolution of the foreign churches in England and the poor now maintained by the foreign congregations would in the future be a burden on the English parishes. Furthermore a substantial number of English workmen dependent on Dutch and French employment would be reduced to poverty. A new aspect was, however, included in the petition from Norwich. For the first time the aliens officially acknowledged the real motive behind the Archbishop's actions. At the same time they disclaimed that there was any truth in Laud's allegations. They stated that all their members

> both Aliens and Natiues do demeane themselues respectively towardes the English discipline, neither doe they harbor any factious English persons, as members of their Congregations.[35]

It was during this interview which the deputies from Norwich were granted by the Archbishop that Laud returned to his suggestion of March the same year. He promised that the 'natives of the first descent' would be allowed to stay as members of the foreign churches. Those after the first descent would have to move to their English parish churches, but would still be required to pay their fees, as before, to the foreign communities. Likewise it was emphasized that any interference or obstruction of the aliens' civil occupations would not be tolerated by the English authorities.[36] These modifications were included when the Injunctions were finally served on Sunday 6 September 1635.[37] Thus the Dutch and French churches had not only managed to force the Archbishop to modify his original Injunctions but also to delay them for about six months. The fact that the Injunctions had now been served did not make the Dutch churches give in. Since the foreign churches had not been given any clear indication of how to publish the Injunctions they immediately took advantage of this loophole. The Dutch minister in Sandwich informed his colleagues in London:

> I understand from the letter of Mr Proost that Sir Nathaniel Brent
> has not mentioned anything about the reading to the congregation,
> and possibly not to you either; if that is so, then our members of
> the second descent have the advantage of being able to pretend
> ignorance.

This pretence of ignorance was apparently successful in making the
Injunctions less than effective, as pointed out by the Dutch minister in
Sandwich:

> In the meantime we continue in our customary ways except that
> we have to show deference towards the English ministers with
> whom we try to keep on friendly terms.[38]

Ironically, Laud's attempts to discipline the foreign communities and
include them in his drive for uniformity probably served to make them
even more of an example to Puritan Englishmen than they had been.
His chaplain, Peter Heylyn, regretfully had to admit that later,

> If any Minister began to look strictly to them they would find some
> means to take him off by Gifts and presents, or by some powerful
> Letter from some of the Grandees residing in London, and some-
> times from a neighbouring Justice, whose displeasure must not be
> incurred. And that they may not want encouragement to stand it
> out as long as they could, the leading men of the Geneva Faction in
> most parts of the Realm, did secretly sollicite them not to be too
> forward in conforming to the said Injunctions, assuring them of
> such Assistances as might save them harmless, and flattering them
> with this Opinion of themselves, That the Liberty of the Gospel,
> and the most desirable freedom of the Church from Episcopal
> Tyranny, depended chiefly on their Courage and Resolution.[39]

As late as 1639 the Injunctions were still not properly adhered to by the
affected members of the foreign congregations. Laud found it necessary
to issue an order to the church wardens in April 1639, commanding
them to perform their duties carefully in their several parishes according
to the specifications of the Injunctions.

> Such care being taken to prevent all inconveniences which might
> come from Scotland, he casts his eye toward the Execution of his
> former Orders for Regulating the French and Dutch Churches here
> in England. It had been to no purpose in him to endeavour a
> Conformity amongst the Scots, as long as such examples of separa-
> tion did continue amongst the English. If the postnati in the
> Churches, born and bred in England, should not be bound to
> repair with other of their Neighbours to their Parish Churches, it
> might create a further mischief than the present Scandal, and come
> up close at last to formal Schism. His Orders had been published in
> all the Congregations of strangers within his Province, as before is
> said; but Executed more or less, as the Ministers and Church-
> Wardens stood affected to those Congregations. And therefore that

the Church-Wardens might more punctually proceed in doing their duty, It was thought fit that certain articles should be framed and commended to them for their future direction. The Reformation being pursued in his own Diocess, and the Metropolitical City first, it was to be presumed, that those in other places would gladly follow the example. Of laying Taxes on those strangers in their several Parishes for repairing of, and adorning their several Parish-Churches, and providing Ornaments for the same they were in all places careful enough; because their own profit was concerned in it. And for their proceedings in the rest they were directed by these Orders to inquire of all such strangers as lived amongst them, the names of all married persons in their Congregations as of the second descent in their several Parishes, to the end that order might be taken for decent seats for them, according to their Estates and qualities: that they should return the names and ages of those unmarried of the second descent, and whose children and servants they were; to the end that the like case might be taken of their due resort to the Church, there to be Catechised, and Communicate according to their ages: that those at sixteen years and upwards, that had not already Communicated should prepare themselves to receive the Blessed Sacrament in their Parish-Church at the next Communion; and from thence forward thrice in the year afterwards as the Canons of the Church require, as they would avoid presentment to their Ordinary for their neglect therein: that such as were Parents and Masters of Families of the first and second descent, did thenceforth every Lords day, half an hour after Evening Prayer, send all such, their Children and Servants as were under sixteen to their Parish-Church, there to be Catechised according to the Orders of the Church, as they themselves upon presentment would answer the Contrary. These Articles being given in the middle of April, were Executed for the rest of the year more punctually then in any of those before. But it held not much longer then the rest of that year.[40]

Heylyn was probably right when he claimed that the Injunctions were only obeyed punctually for the remaining part of 1639. The convention of the Long Parliament in November 1640 certified the collapse of Laud's church policy. Thus the Injunctions were at best effective for a little under a year; not an impressive record for a policy originally introduced in 1634. However, this does not imply that Laud's policies left all the foreign communities totally undisturbed. John Rushworth had no doubt that the Archbishop caused trouble for some of them:

By these Injunctions the Foreign Churches were molested and disquieted several years together, for refusing Conformity and some of their Ministers and others of their congregations deserted the Kingdom and went beyond seas.[41]

None of the ministers to the Dutch church in London left the community in the 1630s though, nor did any of the principal members of the congregations. The most serious part of Rushworth's allegation can only have been true for one or two of the smaller provincial churches. Neither were there any extraordinary changes in the recruitment of new elders for the consistory. Such changes as did take place during the 1630s were in fact less drastic than those of the previous decade. Between 1632 and 1638 only four elders left office and from then until 1641 only one retired, while, for instance, six elders had left office between 1624 and 1626.[42]

It was the weaker members of Austin Friars who were affected. They took the opportunity to leave the church if and when they ran into trouble with the consistory over moral and disciplinary matters in the 1630s. The congregations lost members during this period and the situation was serious enough to command the attention of at least one consistory meeting, on 30 August 1638.[43] Still it is revealing that the problem was not of greater concern to the leaders of the Dutch church. It can be concluded that the Injunctions failed to achieve what Laud had intended. If anything, the Dutch church in London gained cohesion through the Injunctions, an experience identical to that of their Puritan friends.

The convention of the Long Parliament signalled the end of the Laudian era. Six weeks later, on 19 December 1640, the Archbishop was impeached for high treason. John Pym, who chaired the parliamentary Investigational Committee which was in charge of the case against Laud, contacted the consistory in Austin Friars in March 1641 in order to ask the ministers and elders to provide evidence for the forthcoming trial. Their evidence was later to form part of the accusations against the Archbishop.[44] During 1641 a sense of relief and optimism emerged among the foreign congregations and in September a Synod of the foreign churches in England met in London. The Synod, the third of its kind, agreed that the French and Dutch churches in England should stay in closer contact in the future.

> It being resolved to keep our triennial Colloquies of both the Nations, It is agreed that they shall be appointed at the same time; that so in matters of moment we may take advice one of another; viz. The next Colloquie to be within three years from Easter last, upon the first Thursday after Easter week, if no extraordinary occasion require it sooner.

As a consequence of this attitude the Synod decided,

> that both the Disciplines of our Churches be revised to which they intend to keep themselves, each Nation revising her own; and out of both one generall Discipline to be made, for a bond of neerer union between the two Nations, and be translated into English, that it may be in readiness to be shewed, in case the King or Parliament should call for it.[45]

The expectations of the Synod were not unrealistic bearing in mind the co-operation of the consistory of Austin Friars with John Pym in the case against Laud and the close liaison between leaders of the Dutch congregation and leading Puritan figures during the 1620s and 1630s. The disciplines of the foreign churches might well have provided the basis for a religious reconstruction of the English church had it taken place during the following months. This was also the impression of the author of the royalist pamphlet of 1648, *Persecutio Undecima*, who described how leading Puritans had consulted Austin Friars on future church government:

> Members also of the Faction, came to the Elders of the Dutch Church in London, to know of the state and government of their church, telling them that they would follow their patterne, though some of those Elders counselled them not to pull downe their House, till they knew where else to lie dry, adding also, that the English people were not like the Dutch, nor would ever endure their government.[46]

The attempt to unite the discipline of the Dutch and French churches came to nothing. By the time the Dutch church decided to go ahead with a translation of its discipline in March 1642 the French congregation's discipline had already been translated into English.[47] The question was raised again, whether or not 'both the Disciplines of our Churches be revised and one generale Discipline be made out of them both for a bond of neerer union between the two nations', when the fourth Synod of the foreign churches met in May 1644. It was decided not to abolish this attempt but to postpone it until the next Synod, 'in regard of the sad distractions of this Kingdome, and that Parliament itself is now about a Reformation'.[48] As developments were to show the Synod was to be sadly disappointed in its expectations.

Yet, the main point on the agenda of the third Synod in 1641 was the confirmation of the privileges of the foreign churches:

> The Synod considering the great disturbances brought upon some of our Churches where the late Injunctions of the Archbishop have been pressed; and the danger of the overthrow of all our churches if not prevented; thought this to be a fit season to petition to the Parliament for a setlinge by an Act of the said Parliament of the libertie of exercise of our Religion and Discipline, as they are respectively used beyond the Seas in the reformed Churches of our severall nations, and we have hitherto enjoyed them in this Kingdom.

In accordance with this decision an act was drawn up 'by learned Councell at law' for presentation to Parliament in due course.[49] It was, however, never presented to the Long Parliament. It had been an easy

task for Parliament during the spring of 1641 to agree to abolish the
Court of High Commission and Laud's hated innovations in the ritual
of the Anglican Church.[50] In the fight against Laud the Puritans had
remained united, but in the constructive policy of establishing a new
ritual and discipline they immediately started to disagree among themselves. The alternatives were Presbyterianism or some looser Calvinist
church structure with a wide measure of religious tolerance, and it
turned out to be impossible to find a compromise between the two.
Repression had fostered cohesion among the Puritans whereas liberty
was to create division.

Since Parliament could not agree on the discipline to be introduced in
the Church of England the foreign churches were obliged to keep post-
poning their planned petition to Parliament for the renewing of their
privileges.[51]

In connection with the internal divisions of the French congregations
in London and Canterbury during the early 1640s all the foreign churches
received what amounted to a partial confirmation of their privileges
from the House of Lords. This order, of January 1643, emphasized two
important points:

> 2. That no member of their Congregations, being under the Cen-
> sure of their Discipline by reason of some scandalous offence com-
> mitted, be received as a member of any other Church.
> 3. That no Church or congregation of Foreigners be authorized in
> this realme who are not subject respectively to the Synods of theire
> severall nations.[52]

In spite of having been born of the internal strife of the French churches
this order was to be a very useful point of reference for the Dutch
consistory during the mid-1640s. The Dutch congregation saw no split
in its leadership of ministers and elders during the 1640s, but the loss of
important members, which the community had managed to evade under Laud in the 1630s, began in the 1640s. Several members left for
either their own parish church or for one of the many Independent,
often Baptist, congregations which had come into existence in London
after 1640.[53] Those who drifted towards their local parish churches
were often already in trouble with the consistory of Austin Friars. One
of the major instances of this type was Salomon vanden Broecke, a
deacon to the congregation between 1630 and 1636, who stopped
attending services and partaking in the Communion during the autumn
of 1642.[54]

A disagreement had emerged between the consistory and him over
some money left in the hands of the ministers and elders by his uncle,
Franchoys vanden Broecke.[55] When the minister, Cesar Calandrini, and
the elder, Joos Godschalck, informed the rest of the consistory of their

conversation with Salomon vanden Broecke, they pointed out that Salomon had not stayed away from both service and Communion in order to separate himself from the church. He had informed them that he had been elected church-warden in the parish where he lived and that he accordingly had received the Communion there. He admitted, however, that the consistory's handling of the money originally left in its hands by his uncle had upset him. The consistory of Austin Friars repeatedly tried to reason with Salomon during 1643, but to no avail.[56] Early in 1644 the consistory decided to appeal to the forthcoming Colloquium of the Dutch churches in England to find a solution to the quarrel.[57] The Colloquium approved of the London consistory's hand- ling of the case, but it cautioned Austin Friars to act with tenderness before censuring or suspending Salomon vanden Broecke. With this in mind the consistory decided to approach Herbert Palmer, the minister of vanden Broecke's parish, on behalf of the Colloquium, and ask him to intervene. Palmer, who was one of the leading Puritan divines, had become preacher of St James, Duke Place in 1643. Apart from his preaching and writing Herbert Palmer was famous for his financial assistance to refugee students from Germany and Hungary. It is highly probable that it was through this work that some of the ministers and elders of Austin Friars had come to know him well enough to claim to be 'familiaerlyk' with him. One of the people who represented the Dutch community in this case, the minister Cesar Calandrini, had al- ready corresponded with Herbert Palmer in the 1630s and together with the elder, Gillis vander Put, he secured the assistance of Palmer.[58] Palmer's invervention did not produce any results. The consistory was forced to censure vanden Broecke and suspend him from the Commun- ion. The latter's relations with Palmer and his local parish appear to have come under stress too since towards the end of 1646 he began attending the services of the French church; a practice which was imme- diately halted by the Dutch consistory.[59]

During 1643 the political and religious struggle in England also began to absorb members of Austin Friars. Thus when the consistory wrote to one of its elders, then residing in Middelburg, asking him to continue in his eldership because, as it pointed out to him, several of the elders and deacons of the church were leaving office, they informed him that one of the deacons, Jan de Groot, was 'entirely drawn away from us by political affairs'. This was further elaborated in the minutes of the consistory where it appears that de Groot had refused to continue as deacon because he was busy 'inde saken des lants'. Exactly what politi- cal matters he was involved in is difficult to determine, but de Groot had been Master of the Brewers Company from 1641 to 1642 and was to become Alderman of the City in 1651. Since we know that several of the leading brewers were strong supporters of Puritanism there can be no doubt where de Groot was exercising his political talents.[60]

Admittedly the case of Jan de Groot was unique and by itself insignificant, but together with the growing number of cases of members who withdrew themselves from the church it constituted a threat to the continued existence of Austin Friars. The leadership of the church decided to act more vigorously in order to retain members who were drifting away from the community. In March 1644 it was decided that a list of members who were regularly absent from Communion should be drawn up. These members were to be admonished by the elders. During 1644 it became apparent that the congregation was losing control over a substantial number of members. In January the consistory had considered a report concerning one of its most socially important members, Lady Mayerne, the daughter of the Dutch Ambassador, Albertus Joachimi, who was married to Charles I's physician, Theodore de Mayerne.[61] Lady Mayerne had not only recently separated herself from the congregation, neither partaking in the Communion nor the service, but she had also been seen attending sectarian gatherings in the City.[62] This action had caused great offence to members of the church. Lady Mayerne's case was far from being an isolated one. Among the main items on the agenda of the Synod of the foreign churches which was convened in May was the loss of members by the alien communities. It was discussed:

> What course may be taken with such members of our Congregations, who continually absent themselves from the hearing of Gods word and the receiving of the Holy Sacrament, joyning themselves to the private meetings of the Separatists not allowed by the Magistrate: and being admonished by us will not desist, upon pretence that by these meetings they are better edified: also pretending tendernes of consciences, and that our Congregations are full of scandalous members whome they desire not to make knowen unto us. And if such require a Church-Testimoniall to depart, whither it shall be granted them?[63]

The Synod expected 'the chiefest remedie against this grievance' to come from the Long Parliament. This is hardly surprising since Presbyterianism enjoyed its greatest prestige during this period after Parliament had passed the Solemn League and Covenant in September 1643. Further proof that the foreign congregations were well informed about the strength of Presbyterianism can be seen from the fact that the Westminster Assembly recommended Presbyterianism to Parliament in November 1644 as the only fit government for the Church of England.[64] Yet the foreign churches realized that they could not found their hopes solely on some future legislation by Parliament. Immediate action was called for.

II That in the meane time our best indeuors be used to prevent the further growth of this evill viz.

1. That the Discipline be more strictly putt in execution against scandalous persons, whose admission to the H. Communion is the main pretence of their separating from us.

2. That the ministers indeuor both in priuate and in publike to reduce such as begin to stray, to the unity of the church whereof they are members.

3. That fervent prayers be directed to that purpose in our monthly Fasts.

4. That publike warning be giuen to our severall Congregations in the name of this Assembly, That all should take heed of disturbing the peace of the church by such disorderly Separation.

5. That no Testimoniall or Certificate shall be granted unto them, least we should seeme therby to countenance their Separation.[65]

These measures were publicized from the pulpit of Austin Friars. A fortnight later a member of the congregation requested a copy of this document 'against the Separatists'. True to their traditional attitude in matters which could be considered as having political implications the consistory acted with care. The man was informed that the only way he might obtain a copy was by appearing in the consistory and explaining his reasons for wanting one.[66]

The growth of sectarianism in London continued to worry the leaders of Austin Friars. Thus during 1644 when they were recruiting a new, third minister for the church in the Netherlands, they informed the elder, Dirick Hoste, who resided in Middelburg, that he should ensure that the candidates under consideration did not lean 'too much towards the Independents or Brownists'.[67] Likewise the deacon, Timotheus Cruso, who had also been requested to inquire about candidates, informed the minister, Cesar Calandrini, that one of the candidates was not available, 'which causes no difficulty, in my opinion, as I am told that he inclines to the Independents'.[68] In the end the consistory resolved the problem by appointing the minister to the Dutch church in Colchester, Jonas Proost. The loss of members to the Independent congregations in London had obviously forced the Dutch community to revise its opinion of those sections of English Puritanism which supported Separatism and religious toleration. In 1644 it was doubtful whether the consistory would have considered favourably the Leiden professor, Anthonius Waleus's, recommendation of March 1639 of a candidate for the ministry of Austin Friars. Waleus had recommended the candidate as a man whose 'talents are considerable; he is 30 years of age, has a quiet and excellent wife, understands English having lived for some time in England, and imitates the mode of preaching of the faithful English ministers'.[69]

The congregation also felt mounting pressure from the stricter Puritans in other ways during this period. For most Puritans the observance of the Sabbath was of paramount importance. This was not the case for continental, or more specifically Dutch, Calvinists. Austin Friars had already aroused criticism from Puritan circles in London around 1616 because of its merchant members' lack of Sunday observance. It had caused indignation among the English that the Dutch merchants attended business on the Exchange on Sundays after the service. Apparently this practice had continued and in November 1647 the consistory found it necessary to exhort those members who did business on the Exchange on Sundays 'to the great annoyance of pious Englishmen'.[70]

A certain Cornelius Duyts, who had probably been inspired by the Parliamentary ordinances of 1644 ordering the strict observance of the Sabbath and the destruction of all superstitious images, enquired whether or not some of the inscriptions in the windows of the Dutch church were idolatrous and ought to be destroyed. The consistory did not find that the church windows could cause offence. Austin Friars generally appeared, as opposed to the French church, to have persisted in their traditional ways without letting the turbulence of Puritan reform influence them unduly. Thus in May 1644 the Dutch churches did not want to abolish their holy days and the Synod made the following decision:[71]

> That the Brethren of the French Churches, assembled in a Colloque at London, in the years 1644, having made an Act for the utter abolition of all Festivals and Holy-dayes, Have declared that they do not intend thereby to judge or condemn other reformed Churches, whose practise is different in this particular.[72]

However, these incidents were only minor irritations for the consistory of the Dutch congregation. The real problem was still the loss of members which continued increasingly during 1644 in spite of the publication of the Synod's decisions. In August 1644 it was decided that members who attended gatherings of the Separatists should be severely admonished. A week later Cesar Calandrini informed the consistory that he, on the request of a member, Assuerus Fromanteel, had conducted a public debate with the Baptist minister, William Kiffin.[73] Kiffin was one of the most able Baptist leaders of his generation who at the same time managed to become an extremely rich merchant, mainly through the wool trade to the Netherlands. He was not unaccustomed with public disputations having been, for instance, one of the four Baptist representatives opposing Daniel Feastley at Southwark on 17 October 1642.[74] Assuerus Fromanteel, who was behind this incident, had originally been a member of the Dutch church in Norwich, but he had moved to London in 1629. His request for a debate between Kiffin and Calandrini in August was the first indication of his flirtation with the Baptists or Anabaptists. Half a year later, in February 1645, it was reported to the church authorities that he had joined the Anabaptists and had been re-baptized.[75] Shortly afterwards, in April 1645, Fromanteel explained his position in a letter to the consistory. It appeared that he had either joined Kiffin's congregation or another gathering of Particular Baptists.

> As regards the fundamentals of the Christian Religion or Doctrine, I do not know that I differ from you, as the latter is also published by many devout teachers of the public assemblies of England. But I confess that I am unlearned though I take every opportunity to increase my knowledge. Nor do I know any difference between my opinion and the sound doctrine established by the laws of this country, wherefore I consider it my duty to remain in Christian community with all those who confess this belief. But I differ from you in that I consider it uncertain and without command that baptism should be administered to any one but a person who is able to confess his belief in Jesus Christ. As regards the persons whom you call Anabaptists I can say that they never endeavoured to draw me towards them except by the living Word.[76]

Having received an answer from the consistory Fromanteel wanted a public debate in the church about infant baptism. This was denied him and after several exhortations from the consistory he was finally excommunicated in November 1646.[77] The Fromanteel case was accompanied by a host of others. One such was a certain Mrs Wall who also joined the Baptists.[78] Likewise Lady Mayerne continued to create problems for the consistory. She claimed that she did not receive any consolation from fellowship with the Dutch community. She also complained that the consistory allowed scandalous people to partake in the Communion, a complaint not unknown to the consistory since it had been included in the issues raised during the Synod of 1644.[79]

Towards the end of 1644 the problem of absent members had reached such proportions that a whole consistory meeting had to be devoted to discussing it. It was decided in order to stop the decay of the community that the ministers and elders should approach the members in question and try to win them back through friendly persuasion and admonition.[80]

A year later the problem remained unsolved.[81] The pressure on the Dutch church was clearly increasing at a time when the sects were gaining ground, especially in London. This coincided with the evaporation of the hopes for a Presbyterian discipline to be introduced into the Church of England. After the battle of Naseby in June 1645 it was obvious that the need to appease the Scots through a strict Presbyterian solution in church matters had disappeared. From then on the Independents acquired a strong ally in the New Model army under the leadership of Oliver Cromwell.[82]

By the beginning of 1646 the consistory in Austin Friars was increasingly concerned about the Baptist congregations' inroads into its membership. When it became known to the ministers and elders that another of the community's influential members, the wealthy land-reclaimer, Sir Cornelius Vermuyden and his wife, might have joined the Baptists, they immediately called Vermuyden before the consistory. Vermuyden claimed that he had wanted to present his newly born child for baptism in the Dutch church, but that his wife had objected to this. She did not approve of the Dutch practice of particular witnesses or godparents attending the baptism. She had therefore been inclined to have the child baptized in the English Church, 'this being a common custom'. They had, in the end, decided to have the child baptized at home by 'Mr. Symson' which would have taken place had the child not died.[83] Vermuyden also used the opportunity to defend his visits to separatist congregations pointing out that he only went to congregations which agreed on doctrine with all the Reformed churches and then only 'for the sake of being edified'.[84] 'Mr. Symson' clearly referred to the well-known Independent divine, Sidrach Simpson. He appears to have been a natural choice for the Vermuydens having spent several years in exile in Rotterdam where his congregation included both Seekers and Anabaptists. He had returned to London in 1641 where he lectured at St Margaret's Fish Street and Blackfriars, becoming a member of the Westminster Assembly in June 1643. Being one of the five 'dissenting brethren' he was a staunch advocate of religious toleration.[85]

In April 1646 the consistory resolved that the threat which the Independent and Anabaptist gatherings constituted to Austin Friars should be brought up in the approaching Colloquium of the Dutch churches in England. The sects were still drawing members away from the London congregation.

The consistory decided to delegate the minister, Cesar Calandrini, and the elder, Dirick Hoste to visit Sidrach Simpson and William Kiffin. They were instructed to point out to Simpson and Kiffin that their communities were not allowed to receive any members of the Dutch congregation who were under the church's censure. The Dutch consistory referred Simpson and Kiffin to the earlier order, of January 1643, from the House of Lords. Both Simpson and Kiffin proved very forthcoming in this matter. Kiffin even promised to inform the other congregations of Particular Baptists that they were not supposed to accept any members of the Dutch congregation into their communities without prior investigation that the people in question were not under the censure of Austin Friars.[86]

In the meantime Austin Frairs was faced with new dilemmas. In August 1645 Parliament had decided to introduce a moderate form of Presbyterianism in London, and the City had been divided into 12 classes. This system was slowly being implemented in the spring of 1646. In July the Dutch consistory received a letter from the Puritan minister of St Mary-at-Hill, John Ley, who was also a member of the Westminster Assembly, informing them that his parishioners had elected a member of their congregation, Nicolas Corselis, as an elder of their church.[87] Nicolas Corselis had been elected:

> not onely without his consent but against his mind, so farre that without leaue to your selfe and your assistant Elders he is loth to undertake the Eldership whereto hee is elected; I presumed it would not be offensive to you or any of your Associates, that being borne (as I heare) in our Parish and having his dwelling among us, hee bee helpful to us as an officer, when with you, (at least for the present) hee stands in relation of a private Christian.[88]

Ley was obviously well-informed. Nicolas Corselis had been a deacon to Austin Friars from 1632 to 1639 and was later to become an elder to the church in 1647.[89] The Dutch consistory was severely alarmed by the possible effects of this incident on the congregation. It was found that it would prove detrimental to the church if other parishes were to follow the example of St Mary-at-Hill. As so often before it was Calandrini and Hoste who were commissioned to act on behalf of the congregation, and they presented Ley with the church's objections to the election of Corselis. Ley proved receptive of their arguments against the election of Nicolas Corselis and apparently managed to convince his parishioners to select another candidate, since Corselis was able to undertake the eldership in Austin Friars in 1647.[90]

During 1646 and 1647 it had become apparent that the Independents were rapidly becoming the dominant force both politically and religiously. After the army's declarations of June and July 1647 it was obvious to all observers of the political situation that the Presbyterians had lost the struggle, and that some kind of religious tolerance would be allowed. The victory of the Independent party was finalized by Pride's purge of Parliament on 6 December 1648 when all supporters of Presbyterianism were excluded from the House of Commons.[91]

The fifth Synod of the foreign churches, which was to be the last for a considerable number of years, met in London in September 1647. It reiterated the decisions of the previous Synods that Parliament should be petitioned to renew the privileges of the foreign congregations. The alien churches can hardly have considered it a particularly convenient time when they finally went ahead and petitioned the House of Commons in December. By then they had probably exhausted their patience having had to postpone the petition for six years.[92] Not surprisingly they did not receive any response to their petition. Other, more important matters occupied the attention of the House of Commons.

However, from 1647 no more references to the loss of members to the Independent congregations can be found in the minutes of the Dutch consistory. Either the appeal of the different sects, especially Baptists, had started to wane or the close contacts with leading Independents, like Sidrach, Simpson and William Kiffin were paying off. Likewise the good relationship between governors of the church and Puritan ministers within the Anglican Church, as for instance, Hebert Palmer and John Ley, had proved sufficient to contain the threatening loss of members to the local parishes.

The friendships between individual ministers and elders of Austin Friars and Puritan divines and laymen which had grown under the Laudian regime proved invaluable to the Dutch church in London to withstand the difficulties in the 1640s. What Laud had attempted to achieve through his drive for uniformity during the 1630s, namely to undercut the existence and membership of the alien churches through the Injunctions, had proved a total failure. Strangely enough it was the growth of sectarianism following Laud's downfall which came dangerously close to achieving these objectives during the turbulent years between 1640 and 1647.

Notes

1. O. P. Grell, *Dutch Calvinists in Early Stuart London*, Leiden 1989, 7–32.
2. See below, Chapter 7, 'The Schooling of the Dutch Calvinist Community in London, 1550–1650'.
3. J. Strype, *Annals of the Reformation*, 2 vols, Oxford 1824, II, p. 422.
4. *C.S.P. Dom. Charles I*, vol. CXXV, no. 81.
5. See A. H. Dodd, 'Mr Myddelton the Merchant of Tower Street', in S. T. Bindoff, J. Hurstfield, C. H. Neale (eds), *Elizabethan Government and Society: Essays Presented to Sir John Neale*, London 1981, pp. 249–81.
6. Guildhall Library MS 7397/7, fol. 39r.
7. P. Collinson, *The Religion of Protestants. The Church in English Society 1559–1625*, Oxford 1982, p. 249.
8. *Austin Friars*, Appendices I, II and III. See also A. Plummer, *The London Weavers' Company 1600–1970*, London 1970, p. 451. John la Motte was elected Alderman of the City in March 1648, see A. B. Beaven, *The Aldermen of the City of London*, 2 vols, London 1908, vol. 1, p. 170.
9. F. Bellers, *Abrahams Interment: Or the Good Old-Mans Buriall in a Good Age*, London 1656, fols 2r–3r. See also D. A Kirby, 'The Radicals of St. Stephen's Coleman Street, London 1624–1642', *The Guildhall Miscellany*, III, no. 2, April 1970, pp. 112 and 118.
10. Samual Clarke, *The Lives of sundry Eminent Persons in this later Age*, London 1683, pp. 102–4. See also D. A. Kirby, op. cit., p. 112.
11. *C.S.P. Dom Charles I*, vol. CCLXXXVI, no. 355 and W. Prynne, *Canterburies Doome*, London 1646, pp. 391–2.
12. Sheffield University Library. Samuel Hartlib MSS. 50H 11/1/106 and

46/11/3. See also F. Rose-Troup, *John White, the Patriarch of Dorchester*, London 1930, p. 43.

13. J. H. Hessels (ed.), *Ecclesiae Londino-Batavae Archivum*, (Hessels) vols I–III, parts 1–2, Cambridge 1887–1897, vol. III, no. 2535. Cesar Calandrini was examined by the six ministers of the Dutch and French congregations in London on 7 March 1617 before he was accepted as a minister to the Italian church, see 'French Church, Soho Square', MS 5 (Actes 1615–1680), fol. 26r. For Calandrini's studies at the University of Leiden see A. G. H. Bachrach, *Sir Constantine Huygens and Britain: A Pattern of Cultural Exchange in the Seventeenth Century*, Leiden 1962, pp. 58–64.

14. Guildhall Library MS 7424, fol. 49.

15. Peter Heylyn, *Cyprianus Anglicus*, London 1671, p. 218.

16. Hessels, III, no. 2285.

17. Ibid., no. 2288.

18. Ibid., nos 2287–8.

19. Ibid., no. 2288.

20. *C.S.P. Dom. Charles I*, vol. CXXV, no. 81.

21. *C.S.P. Dom. Charles I*, vol. CCLXVI, no. 65. All the foreign congregations had had their privileges confirmed in November 1626, see Hessels, III, no. 1860.

22. Hessels, III, no. 2316 and *C.S.P. Dom. Charles I*, vol. CCLXXVIII, nos 63 and 64.

23. Hessels, III, no. 2316.

24. J. J. van Toorenenbergen (ed.), *Gheschiedenissen ende Handelingen die voornemelick aangaan de Nederduytsche Natie ende Gemeynten wonende in Engeland ende in bysonder tot London*, Utrecht 1873 (Gheschiedenissen), p. 388.

25. Guildhall Library MS 7430, p. 55 and *DNB*.

26. Ibid., and S. R. Gardiner, *A History of England under the Duke of Buckingham and Charles I*, London 1884, vol. 1, pp. 151, 253, 303, 331, 349–50 and vol. 2, pp. 96, 134, 333.

27. *DNB* and Guildhall Library MS 7430, p. 55.

28. P. Heylyn, op. cit., p. 263 and Guildhall Library MS 7411/2, pp. 74–5.

29. Hessels, III, no. 2341.

30. Ibid., no. 2343.

31. Ibid., no. 2368 and *C.S.P. Dom. Charles I*, vol. CCLXXXIX, no. 37.

32. Guildhall Library MS 7430, p. 103 ff.

33. Hessels, III, no. 2361 and *C.S.P. Dom. Charles I*, vol. CCLXXXVI, no. 85. H. Trevor-Roper has mistaken the revised Injunctions for the originals of December 1634, whereby the milder approach appears to be Laud's initial policy, see H. Trevor-Roper, *Archbishop Laud, 1573–1645*, London 1940, p. 199.

34. Hessels, III, no. 2363.

35. Ibid., nos 2370–73.

36. Ibid., nos 2375 and 2378. See also *C.S.P. Dom. Charles I*, vol. CCXCVII, no. 4.

37. Ibid., no. 2380.

38. Ibid., no. 2449.

39. Ibid., nos 2449 and 2387 and P. Heylyn, op. cit., p. 265.

40. P. Heylyn, op. cit., pp. 377–8.

41. J. Rushworth, *Historical Collections*, 8 vols, London 1721, vol. II, pp. 272–3.
42. See Grell, *Dutch Calvinists*, Appendices I and II.
43. Guildhall Library MS 7397/8, fol. 69r.
44. W. Prynne, op. cit., p. 391 and Grell, *Dutch Calvinists*, 224–48.
45. J. J. van Toorenenbergen (ed.), *Acten van de Colloquia der Nederlandsche Gemeenten in Engeland 1575–1624 and Uittreksels uit de Acten der volgende Colloquia 1627–1706*, Utrecht 1872. (Acten), p. 317, and French Church, Soho Square, MS 204, fol. 58v.
46. Anon., *Persecutio Undecima. The Churches Eleventh Persecution*, London 1648, p. 58.
47. Guildhall Library MS 7397/8, fol. 108v. The translation of the Dutch discipline was not printed until the beginning of 1646, see Hessels, III, nos 2828–9.
48. French Church, Soho Square, MS 204, fols 65v–66r and *Acten*, pp. 333–4.
49. Ibid., fols 59r–59v and Hessels, III, no. 2659. See also *Acten*, 319.
50. W. K. Jordan, *The Development of Religious Toleration in England*, 4 vols, Cambridge, Mass. 1932–1940, vol. 3, pp. 34–5.
51. French Church, Soho Square, MS 204, fols 59r, 66r and 85v. See also W. K. Jordan, op. cit., p. 80.
52. Hessels, III, no. 2702. See also Guildhall Library MS 7421, Boek de Kerkelyke Vryheden, II. For the internal strife in the French congregations in London and Canterbury, see R. D. Gwyn, 'A Calendar of the Letter Book of the French Church of London from the Civil War to the Restoration', *Huguenot Society Pub.*, vol. LIV, 1979.
53. W. K. Jordan, op. cit., pp. 38–9 and 452–62.
54. Guildhall Library MS 7397/8, fol. 117v.
55. Ibid., fol. 80r. Franchoys vanden Broecke had left £100 at 6 per cent interest in the hands of the consistory, probably as a security for his old age. The consistory had accepted the money on condition that £30 of this sum should be donated to the church as 'Dienstgeld' after his death.
56. Guildhall Library MS 7397/8, fols 118v, 119v and 124v.
57. Ibid., fol. 128v.
58. Ibid., fols 129v and 136r. See also Guildhall Library MS 7424, fol. 49. For Herbert Palmer see *DNB*.
59. Ibid., fols 167v and 168r. The close liaison between ministers of Austin Friars and Puritan divines is confirmed through other evidence. It appears from the minutes of the consistory of 26 October 1643 that the widow of the Dutch minister, Timotheus van Vleteren, was engaged to the Puritan preacher William Sedgwick, see fol. 126v. See also *DNB*.
60. Hessels, III, no. 2725 and Guildhall Library MS 7397/8, fol. 123v. Jan de Groot generally appears under the English translation of his name, John de Great. See M. Ball, *The Worshipful Company of Brewers*, London 1977, pp. 76–7 and A. B. Beaven, op. cit., vol. 1, p. 94 and vol. 2, p. 77.
61. For Theodore de Mayerne see *DNB*.
62. Guildhall Library MS 7397/8, fol. 125r.
63. Guildhall Library MS 7411/2, fol. 113 and *Acten*, p. 333.
64. W. K. Jordan, op. cit., pp. 47–57.
65. Guildhall Library MS 7411/2, fol. 114 and *Acten*, p. 334.
66. Guildhall Library MS 7397/8, fol. 130r.

67. Hessels, III, no. 2747.
68. Ibid., no. 2752. Timotheus Cruso and Abraham Otger, who were acting on behalf of the consistory in its search for a qualified minister, had already informed the consistory in London that it would be difficult to obtain a good candidate in the Netherlands because of the Civil War in England, see Hessels, III, nos 2748–9.
69. Hessels, III, no. 2512. For Anthonius Waleus see *Nieuw Nederlandsch Biografisch Woordenboeck*.
70. Guildhall Library MS 7397/8, fol. 181v. For the event in 1616 see MS 7397/7, fol. 65v.
71. Hessels, III, no. 2738 and W. K. Jordan, op. cit., p. 54.
72. 'French Church, Soho Square' MS 204, fol. 66r and *Acten*, pp. 332–3.
73. Guildhall Library MS 7397/8, fols 133r–133v.
74. For William Kiffin see W. K. Jordan, op. cit., pp. 533–4 and *DNB*.
75. Guildhall Library MS 7397/8, fol. 139r.
76. Hessels, III, no. 2790. See also no. 2794.
77. Hessels, III, no. 2874 and Guildhall Library MS 7397/8, fol. 141v; see also Hessels, III, nos 2845 and 2862.
78. Guildhall Library MS 7397/8, fols 133v and 141v.
79. Ibid., fols 146v and 147r. Lady Mayerne remained in the congregation, but was repeatedly admonished during the following years; see, for instance, fol. 152r.
80. Ibid., fol. 135v.
81. Ibid., fol. 152r.
82. W. K. Jordan, op. cit., pp. 64–9.
83. Guildhall Library MS 7397/8, fol. 153r and Hessels, III, no. 2840.
84. Hessels, III, no. 2840.
85. See *DNB*.
86. Guildhall Library MS 7397/8, fols. 158v, 159r and 160r. See also Hessels, III, no. 2702.
87. W. K. Jordan, op. cit., pp. 70–80 and *DNB*..
88. Hessels, III, no. 2867.
89. See Grell, *Dutch Calvinists*, Appendix I.
90. Guildhall Library MS 7397/8, fols 161v and 162v.
91. W. K. Jordan, op. cit., pp. 87–118.
92. 'French Church, Soho Square' MS 204, fol. 85v and Hessels, III, no. 2952.

CHAPTER FIVE

Merchants and ministers: the foundations of international Calvinism

The importance of godly merchants and ministers for the success and propagation of Calvinism in the second half of the sixteenth century is generally recognized. Together, these two groups came to dominate the growing number of Reformed communities, exercising considerable social and moral control over the congregations they served as ministers and elders. Their role and significance for the creation and maintenance of contacts between Calvinist individuals and communities across Europe, that is, international Calvinism, has, however, received less attention. In what follows, I shall try to demonstrate how this international network of Reformed ministers and merchants came about and provide some examples of how it operated.

Retrospectively, it can be argued that Calvin's flight in 1536 from France to Basle in Switzerland, and his later move to Geneva, was to set the scene for what became a Reformed diaspora of considerable proportions later in the sixteenth century. What began as a relatively small-scale exodus of primarily Protestant ministers, eventually turned into mass emigration later in the century. However, as opposed to the later mass movement of Reformed emigrants, the early emigration was not unique to Calvinism, but was shared with other Protestants.

Even if the diaspora of the 1530s, 1540s and 1550s was characterized by the part played by the Reformed clergy it has to be emphasized that it also included an important lay and broadly evangelical element. This early emigration was largely a consequence of the growing confessionalization of European states and societies, such as the Habsburg Netherlands ruled by Charles V and France under Francis I, and was primarily targeted on Switzerland, England and Germany.[1]

Among the famous Reformed ministers who like Calvin left France in the 1530s and 1540s and sought refuge in Geneva were Pierre Viret, Nicholas des Gallars and Theodore Beza, while Reformed Italians, such as Bernardino Ochino and Peter Martyr fled to Strasburg via Basle in the 1540s. A few years later Ochino and Martyr found their way to England on the invitation of archbishop Thomas Cranmer. Here they were joined in 1549 by Martin Bucer and Paul Fagius who made

England their new home as a consequence of Strasburg's acceptance of the Augsburg Interim. Their arrival in England at the beginning of the reign of Edward VI was complemented by the return from exile of a number of English Protestants such as John Hooper, who had sought refuge in Bullinger's Zurich. During the short reign of Edward VI England became a safe haven for Reformed Protestants on a par with the Swiss cities of Zurich, Basle and Geneva, harbouring several leading Reformation theologians such as the Pole Johannes a Lasco.[2] Within popular Reformed mythology England, as a place of refuge, was perceived to be second only to Geneva, which was gradually coming to represent the new Jerusalem for the embryonic Reformed movement.

Consequently, Geneva, a city of around 10,000, more than doubled its size because of the arrival of religious refugees of mainly French and Italian origin, from Calvin's recall in 1541 to his death in 1564,[3] while the foundation of the stranger churches in London under the superintendency of Johannes a Lasco demonstrates the importance of England for the Reformed exodus. Whereas the prominence of Geneva within international Calvinism began to fade rapidly less than a decade after Calvin's death, England retained its significance for the Reformed diaspora, in spite of the brief Catholic interlude under Mary (1553–58). It can be argued that without the Marian exile, which saw such leading English Protestants as Christopher Goodman, William Whittingham and Anthony Gilby seek shelter in Geneva, John Jewel in Zurich, John Foxe in Basle and Edmund Grindal in Strasburg, English Protestantism may not have become an integral part of European Calvinism. But by having acquired a stake in the Reformed diaspora these exiles, on their return to England at the accession of Elizabeth, played a prominent part in guaranteeing that the Elizabethan government extended its hospitality to Dutch/Walloon and French Reformed emigrants throughout the sixteenth century. That the Elizabethan government's rationale for welcoming such a substantial influx of Reformed immigrants might have been economically motivated is of little significance in this context. There were, on the other hand, important economic reasons why London especially remained an attractive option for Calvinist merchants fleeing France and the Netherlands in the sixteenth century. As opposed to Geneva which had been a prosperous entrepôt for German and Italian merchants in the fifteenth century, but which by the mid-sixteenth century had witnessed considerable economic and financial stagnation, England, and especially London, had gained constantly in economic importance.

The mass exodus which followed this first stage of the diaspora began in the late 1560s and continued over the next 30 years. It differed from the earlier and religiously diffuse emigration by being predominantly

Reformed in character. It consisted of a small but important number of refugees from northern Italy, especially from the city of Lucca, where Peter Martyr had last been active shortly before his flight to Basle/ Strasburg, of a considerably greater number of exiles from France following the outbreak of the Wars of Religion (1562), and last but not least of huge numbers of refugees from the Southern Netherlands as a result of Alva's repression.

It was a mass exodus of Reformed merchants and highly skilled craftsmen which was primarily brought about by the aggressive Counter-Reformation policies of the governments in these areas, even if it should be borne in mind that economic considerations, especially among the merchant elite, may have played a considerable part in the timing of the emigration. It has been estimated that the Spanish reconquest and re-Catholization of the Southern Netherlands under the Duke of Alva and Alexander Farnese caused around 100,000 people to flee these areas, especially Flanders, Liège, Tournai and Valanciennes, between 1567 and 1590.[4] In the wake of the St Bartholomew Massacre (1572) they were joined by French co-religionists, some of whom had already helped reinforce Calvinism in Flanders by seeking shelter there from the Wars of Religion in the 1560s.

They settled primarily in Germany where they sought refuge in most of the important trading centres such as Frankfurt, Nuremberg, Cologne, Hamburg/Stade, Aachen, Wesel and Frankenthal, and in England, where they demonstrated a clear preference for London and other towns and cities of southeast England, such as Colchester and Norwich, where they constituted between a fifth and a third of the population around 1600; and, of course, especially in the case of the craftsmen, in the United Provinces, where the towns and cities of Holland and Zeeland, such as Leiden and Haarlem became their preferred destination.[5] It should be emphasized, however, that this diaspora was made up of a series of emigrations and hardly ever constituted a simple migration from one place to another. It was a complex affair and would often continue for a couple of generations, not coming to an end until the first decades of the seventeenth century.

The motives and character of this emigration – whether it was mainly religious or predominantly economic in origin – has been a bone of contention among a generation of Dutch and Belgian historians.[6] No doubt motives were mixed, but economic reasons do not necessarily exclude religion or vice versa. There is, after all, nothing contrary to good Calvinism in making a sound choice of where and when to emigrate. As long as one did not compromise one's faith, a sound choice of time and place, making the best use of the resources God had put at the disposal of Man, can, in fact, be interpreted as an obligation for the

Godly. Accordingly, the claim by many economic historians that the significance of economic motives grew when the emigration of wealthy Reformed merchants and entrepreneurs accelerated in the 1580s does not necessarily undermine the religious commitment of this group. In fact, the wholehearted commitment to Calvinism of the merchant elite is underlined by the prominent role it played, serving as elders and deacons, within the exiled Reformed churches which the refugee communities established in nearly all the places where they settled.

Even if questions may be raised about the initial religious commitment of some of the wealthier emigrants the effect of joining the diaspora cannot but have reinforced their sense of belonging. In other words, emigration however diffuse its reasons and causes was a major social experience which can only have served to reinforce the Reformed faith of those who undertook it. When reading the Old Testament these refugees would construe their experience as a direct consequence of God's Providence and see it as evidence of the New Covenant. As these refugees settled in most of the major cities in northern Europe they came to form an international movement, perhaps less through their Calvinism, which often differed in points of doctrine, and their conviction of being God's chosen people, than through their shared experience of displacement and minority existence in foreign and occasionally hostile environments. This social and, in my opinion, most prominent aspect of international Calvinism was reinforced by the tendency of these merchants to intermarry and their reliance on each other for business.[7]

This international dimension of the Second Reformation was further enhanced by the foundation of Reformed academies and universities, starting with the Academy in Geneva in 1559. For the Reformed ministers this development acquired a special significance. Thus Calvin's Academy, which was intended to provide a centre for the education of Reformed ministers, proved a resounding success, attracting more than 300 students from all over Europe in 1560.[8] By the 1570s the Genevan Academy's paramount position in the education of Reformed ministers had been taken over by the University of Heidelberg and a number of newly founded academies, such as Ghent (1578–83) and Herborn (1584). They were later supplemented by the new universities in the United Provinces, of which Leiden (1575) became the most famous, and at the turn of the century by the French Reformed Academies of Sedan and Saumur. By then the *peregrinatio academica*, visiting the most famous Reformed seats of learning, was gradually gaining ground among the more privileged Reformed students of theology. Significantly, however, all these academies and universities continued the Genevan tradition of attracting large numbers of international students, adding another important international aspect to Calvinism, through contacts and friend-ships between individual ministers and their teachers.

Accordingly it is my contention that the social experience of exodus and diaspora, which Reformed merchant endured to an even greater extent than most of their co-religionists, was of paramount importance in providing Calvinism with an international character. This was espe-cially the case since these merchants provided the lay leadership, of elders and deacons, of most of the Reformed churches. A further and significant manifestation of this Reformed internationalism was gener-ated by the common experience of a considerable number of their consistorial colleagues, the ministers, especially through their educa-tional background in an international academic environment.[9]

In order to illustrate how this operated in practice, I shall focus on London, one of the major centres for the Reformed diaspora, and on some of the leading members of the stranger churches in particular.

Undoubtedly, Cesar Calandrini, who became a minister to the Dutch Reformed church in London in 1639, was an archetypal product of international Calvinism. Cesar's family history is closely linked to the Reformed diaspora which began in the 1560s. He belonged to one of three closely connected aristocratic merchant families who had fled the repression of the Counter-Reformation in Lucca. Well in advance of their conversion to Protestantism, which according to family tradition should have been inspired by the preaching of Peter Martyr in the 1540s while he was Prior of the St Frediano monastery, the three families of Diodati, Burlamachi and Calandrini were firmly ensconced among the mercantile oligarchy in Lucca. Considering both the timing of their flight, 20 years after the departure of Peter Martyr, and their trade contacts with French commercial centres, such as Lyon, which were strongly Calvinist, it is, however, highly likely that members of these families did not fully convert to Reformed Protestantism until they encountered Calvinism in France. This was certainly the case of Pompeo Diodati who, while in Lyon, decided to free himself 'from the yoke of Antichrist and to dedicate myself wholly to the pure service of God' and consequently decided to emigrate to Geneva.[10]

Having converted to Calvinism in 1562, Pompeo Diodati had to wait another four years before those of his family who shared his religious belief were ready to leave Lucca. Obviously, considerable time was needed for these merchant/financiers to dispose of their real estate and disengage from business involvements before emigration could be con-templated. When that was achieved, most of the Diodatis, Calandrinis and Burlamachis who were already related, but later used the opportu-nity to reaffirm their family alliances through further marriages, left Lucca between September 1566 and March 1567. They appear to have faced no problems in leaving the city and travelled in style via Lyon, where Pompeo joined them, not to Geneva as originally intended, but to Paris. Here they acquired a country house, Luzarches, seven miles outside the city, and Pompeo married Laura Calandrini, sister to Giovanni. This purchase of a considerable estate, near Paris, is a clear indication that the families must have been able to dispose of, or transfer, considerable parts of their property before leaving Lucca. Thus in June 1567 when they were officially banished and the Lucchese government confiscated their remaining property, the damage must have been limited.

However, the renewal of the French Wars of Religion in the autumn of 1567 meant renewed exile. Initially, in November 1567, they were forced to flee before the advancing Catholic armies, but were fortunate to find another French refuge in Montargis where they were offered protection by the widow of the duke of Ferrara, Renée de France, daughter of Louis XII, who had played host to John Calvin when he was in Italy in 1536. They were unable to return to Luzarches and Paris on a permanent basis until 1570. There they remained until the St Bartholomew Massacre in August 1572, when most of them fled to Sedan. By then the families had begun to split up, some settling in Antwerp, others in Frankfurt, Nuremberg and Stade/Hamburg, Pompeo Diodati, on the other hand, 'resolved to go thence to Geneva, which I had all along desired, and feeling that God had afflicted us in France because we had not gone thither in the first instance, as I purposed'. Still, it took Pompeo and his immediate family another three years before they reached Geneva and one is left with the distinct impression that their arrival was eventually caused more by accident than intent.[11]

Giuliano, the most senior member of the Calandrini family to leave Lucca, died in Sedan shortly after the St Bartholomew Massacre. His two sons, Cesare and Giovanni (the latter was the father of Cesar Calandrini who became a minister to the Dutch Church in London), left France in the years immediately after the massacre and established a merchant house in Antwerp. Here Giovanni married Marie, daughter of the wealthy Antwerp merchant Jean de Maistres, while his brother Cesare married her sister Esther three years later in Frankfurt. The brothers must have moved on shortly before the Spanish siege and recapture of Antwerp in 1584–85 and settled in Frankfurt. Two children were born to Giovani Calandrini during his family's residence here. Gian Luigi, born in 1585, eventually settled in Geneva where he became a shareholder and codirector with his father-in-law, Francesco Turrettini, of the city's most prominent banking/merchant organization, the Grand Boutique.[12] He also became closely involved with one of the leading European financial establishments of the early modern period, the merchant/banking house set up in Amsterdam/London by his father

Giovanni and another brother-in-law, the famous London banker of the Stuart period, Philip Burlamachi. His financial contacts were extensive and he became the Genevan Republic's leading banker until he was ruined by Philip Burlamachi's spectacular bankruptcy in England in 1634.[13] His brother Philip, born two years later, looked after the interests of the Calandrini/Burlamachi firm in Amsterdam after his father and brother-in-law had moved to London at the start of James I's reign. In 1622 Philip collaborated with Sir Henry Wotton in Venice in a Calvinist attempt to raise funds for the recapture of Bohemia.[14]

Shortly after Philip's birth Giovanni Calandrini moved to Stade near Hamburg. In 1589 he became an elder to the Reformed church in Stade and by 1597 he was heavily involved in the English cloth trade exporting over a thousand pieces to Hamburg in late 1597. The Dutch Republic's increasing dominance over world trade must by the 1590s have encouraged Giovanni to move his business to Amsterdam, where he arrived in 1599.[15] In Amsterdam, eight years later, in his mid-sixties, he remarried. The bride, Catherina Pietraviva, was the widow of Assuerus Regemorter, who had been a minister to the Dutch Church in London from 1585 to 1604. Most likely the couple's acquaintance went back to the period 1582–85, when Assuerus Regemorter had served the Reformed Church in Antwerp as a minister. Giovanni and his family would have been likely members of Regemorter's congregation.[16] The marriage appears to have been the Calandrini family's first contact with the stranger churches in London with whom they were to be so closely associated by the second decade of the seventeenth century.

Within a year of his marriage, Giovanni had moved to London together with his son-in-law, Philip Burlamachi, who had married his eldest daughter Elizabeth in February 1608. Apart from the already mentioned sons, who settled in Geneva and Amsterdam, another of Giovanni's sons, Marco, remained on the Continent. He conveniently continued the family enterprise in Stade/Hamburg where by 1633 he was among some of the major lenders to the Danish Crown.[17] With one exception all the other children settled in England. Giuliano and Pompeo joined the merchant house of Calandrini/Burlamachi, Cesar became a minister while Anna-Maria, the other daughter, married the Huguenot military architect and engineer, David Papillon, who together with his mother had fled to London in 1588.[18]

Meanwhile, Giovanni's brother, Cesare Calandrini, had moved from Frankfurt to Nuremberg. Here he was active in the cloth trade from 1597 and established a partnership with another Reformed refugee from Lucca, Ludovico Peiez, who was already among the wealthiest merchants in Nuremberg. Cesare also continued his collaboration with Giovanni and between 1602 and 1609 their operations in Nuremberg received considerable investments from the influential Frankfurt banker, Johann von Bodeck, who was a Reformed refugee from the Southern Netherlands. Cesare's standing within Nuremberg must have been considerable since the city council made him a member of the commission for the improvement of the coinage in 1620.[19] In 1626 Cesare's son, Jeremia Calandrini, was among the originators of the European collections for Calvinist refugee ministers from the Upper Palatinate. This was a relief work which was to continue for the next 20 years and see the close involvement of the Dutch church in London and Jeremia's cousin, Cesar Calandrini.[20]

By the early seventeenth century the prominent financial and commercial position held by Cesare in Nuremberg and Giovanni Calandrini/ Philip Burlamachi in London/Amsterdam helped reinforce the family network. Younger members of the Geneva-based branch of the family, such as Nicolao Diodati, Pompeo's son, and Vincent Burlamachi, Fabrizio's son, came to live with their relations in these mercantile centres in order to learn the trade and the necessary languages.[21]

Cesar, who was born at Stade in 1595, appears to have been the first member of the Calvinist wing of the Calandrini family to have been destined for a scholarly or ecclesiastical career. He commenced his university education when he matriculated at the Academy in Geneva in May 1612. The choice of Geneva for the 17-year-old was undoubtedly influenced by family rather than academic reasons. The presence in Geneva of several influential family members who could provide guidance for the young man, not to mention his relation, Jean Diodati, at the Academy, must have been decisive. Jean Diodati, who had become professor of Hebrew at the early age of 21, had by 1609 been given a Chair in Theology and had served as Rector of the Genevan Academy. When Cesar Calandrini matriculated in 1612, Jean Diodati was already renowned internationally as a leading Calvinist theologian.[22] Thus a tutor of the highest quality was available in Geneva from within the family.

Before he returned to England, where he continued his studies in Oxford, Cesar Calandrini also studied for a while at the newly founded Academy at Saumur (1599). The presence in Saumur of such leading orthodox, Calvinist theologians, as Franciscus Gomarus and Louis Cappel would have been an obvious attraction. Initially, Calandrini's stay in Oxford was short. In November 1616, six months after he had been admitted as a reader to the Bodleian Library, he matriculated in theology at the university of Leiden where only a year later he concluded his studies. During his stay in Leiden Calandrini renewed his acquaintance with the Huygens family, with whom the Calandrinis had been close while living in Amsterdam, and he developed his friendship with

Constantine Huygens, the Dutch poet and diplomat, with whom he shared lodgings in Leiden and kept up a correspondence after his return to England.[23]

Back in London in late 1617 Cesar Calandrini became a 'proponent' or trainee minister in the French church. He was an obvious choice, bearing in mind that this was the community where his brothers-in-law, Philip Burlamachi and David Papillon, had already served as elder and deacon.[24] These early contacts to the French church probably also account for Cesar's marriage in August 1621 to Elizabeth Harderet, a granddaughter of the minister to the French community in London, Robert le Maçon, sieur de la Fontaine, who had died in 1611.[25] Only a few months after his return, in March 1618, Cesar was examined and ordained by the joint body of ministers of the Dutch and French churches.[26] Their support and the backing of the apostate archbishop of Spalato, Marco Anthonio De Dominis, who had become Dean of Windsor and preached occasionally to the small Italian congregation at Mercer's Chapel in 1617, secured Calandrini the appointment of minister to the Italian Reformed church in London. Consequently, the Italian church was reconstituted, elders and deacons once more elected, and the church re-admitted as a member of the Coetus of the stranger churches.[27]

Initially, Cesar Calandrini acquired an influential mentor in De Dominis and lodged with him at the Savoy Hospital. Later, he found it increasingly difficult to reconcile his Calvinism with De Dominis's Catholic syncretism. In this respect Calandrini's personal experience of the synod of Dordrecht may have played a considerable part. He arrived in Dordrecht on 13 January 1619, exactly two months after the start of the Synod, in the company of Archbishop Abbott's chaplain, Dr Thomas Goad, who replaced Joseph Hall in the British delegation. This journey may well have provided the foundations for the continued contacts between the two men in the years to come.[28] Cesar, who for a period at least stayed with his relation and teacher, Jean Diodati, a member of the Genevan delegation, at the house of the headmaster of the French school in Dordrecht, Jean de Grave, appears to have attended the remaining sessions of the Synod.[29]

Jean Diodati, a strong supporter of the Counter-Remonstrant position, was eventually elected as one of the deputies of the Synod entrusted with drawing up the canons. Upon the adjournment of the Synod Diodati appears to have visited Cesar Calandrini in London, after having attended 'a meeting in Cambridge'. Considering that two of the four English delegates to Dort were resident Cambridge academics, namely John Davenant, Lady Margaret Professor of Divinity and Master of Queen's College, and Samuel Ward, Master of Sidney Sussex College, not to mention the single Scottish delegate, Walter Balanqual,

who was a fellow of Pembroke College, a briefing of the British delegation by one of the Synod's deputies in Cambridge seems an obvious
explanation for this visit.[30]

During the Synod Cesar Calandrini appears to have become increasingly hostile towards the Remonstrants. On 24 April 1618 he informed
Constantine Huygens that 'the Remonstrants seem to have appropri-
ated all the tricks of the Jesuits, especially Episcopius' and in another
letter of 17 July 1619 Calandrini concluded by stating that 'you must
cast out the Remonstrants'.[31]

On his return Cesar Calandrini finished his studies in theology at
Exeter College, Oxford, under the guidance of its Rector and newly
appointed Regius Professor of Divinity, John Prideaux. Prideaux's orthodox Calvinism and negative attitude to the Remonstrants would
have proved attractive to Calandrini who appears to have stayed in
contact with his teacher after his student days.[32] Shortly after he had
acquired his BD, on 20 June 1620, Calandrini was instituted to the
well-endowed rectory of Stapleford Abbots in Essex. Since this was a
benefice held by Prince Charles we can safely assume that this was one
of the last favours De Dominis, with his excellent Court contacts, was
able and willing to bestow on his protégé. By then, De Dominis appears
to have developed doubts about Calvinism in general and the validity of
Calandrini's Reformed ordination by the stranger churches in particular. His attempt to get Bishop Thomas Morton of Lichfield, a solid
Calvinist who had already condemned Arminianism as early as 1609, to
reordain Calandrini, was, not surprisingly, unsuccessful.[33] Clearly, De
Dominis had little or no concept of the theological position of at least
one of the leading Jacobean bishops, and when shortly before his departure to Rome he denounced Calandrini as a Genevan and a Puritan he
also took the opportunity to include Thomas Morton. This incident
may well have inspired the two leading English Arminians, Richard
Montagu and John Cosin, to try to have Calandrini ousted from his
rectory and replaced with an Arminian candidate of their own in 1624,
a scheme which eventually came to nothing.[34]

Calandrini's extensive list of English correspondents confirms his
theological position as similar to that of the stricter Calvinists or Puritans within the Church of England. It includes names such as the
ministers Herbert Palmer, John Davenport, Stephen Marshall, Thomas
Gataker, Thomas Edward, Dr Thomas Goad, Dr Walter Balanqual,
James Ussher and John Prideaux. Likewise, the great majority of his
continental correspondents belonged to the orthodox, Counter-
Remonstrant wing of European Calvinism, including such leading figures as Festus Hommius, Henrich Alting, Johannes Polyander, Andreas
Rivet, Maximilian Teellinck and Johannes de Laet in the United Prov-

inces, Benedict Turrettini and Jean Diodati in Geneva and Pierre du Moulin in France.[35]

For some years Calandrini continued to serve the Italian church in London as its minister while simultaneously looking after his parish in Stapleford Abbotts. This was made possible through Stapleford Abbotts geographical position *vis-à-vis* London, being only 'some 3 hours riding' away.[36] Cesar Calandrini resided in the City until 1626, becoming closely involved in James Ussher's great Protestant scheme, the *Bibliotheca Theologica*, an elaborate attempt to write a providential history of the True Church based on the best available sources. This was an enterprise for which Calandrini's many international contacts in the world of trade and Reformed religion must have been useful.[37]

When nearly 20 years later Cesar Calandrini was elected minister to the Dutch church in London the guidance he had received from Ussher in providential history must have proved beneficial. He took over the responsibility for writing the history of the Dutch exile community begun by his predecessor, Simon Ruytinck, who had served the church from 1601 to 1621.[38] Apart from Calandrini's personal interest in providential history which he shared with a number of Reformed Protestants, who held the study of time and history second only in importance to that of the Bible, his family appears to have been deeply concerned with its own history. Several members of the Burlamachis, Diodatis and Calandrinis wrote detailed histories of the exodus from Lucca and their subsequent tribulations in exile, such as Renée/Renata Burlamachi, a sister-in-law of Cesar and his uncle, Pompeo Diodati, just to mention a few. Copies of these manuscripts seem to have circulated within the wider family where in some cases they were translated for the use of later generations.[39] The aim of these family histories, as well as most Reformed works of history from this period was, of course, to work out and understand God's will and plan for the world in general and for the elect in particular.[40]

This preoccupation with providential history which came to characterize late sixteenth and early seventeenth century Calvinism was not only reinforced by, but, in my opinion, closely linked to the experience of exodus and diaspora. Thus, it is no coincidence that the three major martyrologies of Reformed Protestantism – and the first Reformed works to promote providentialism to a wide audience, those of Jean Crespin, Adriaan van Haemstede and John Foxe – all grew out of their authors' personal experiences of persecution, flight and exile.[41]

The history of the Dutch community in London by Simon Ruytinck and Cesar Calandrini, fits neatly into this category of Calvinist historical works. The authors wrote a providential history of the community which thanks to God's Grace and Mercy had survived all the tribulations and tests to which it has been exposed. It is a history, which together with the Bible, would have served to confirm members of the Dutch Reformed church in the belief that they belonged to the elect. Thus, when Ruytinck recorded how the Dutch/Walloon exiles, who had fled London at the start of Mary's reign, arrived in Copenhagen, and how they were expelled, he added 'that they had trusted in God who had preserved them in Copenhagen, where several thousand people had died from the plague while none of the exiles had even been ill'. Similarly, when Calandrini described the aftermath of the trial in 1619 of several of the most prominent members of the Dutch/Walloon merchant community in London for illegal export of bullion, he emphasized how most of the witnesses against the foreign merchants had later fallen on hard times and had been seen begging at their victims' doors. 'Likewise, shortly afterwards several of the judges had lost the King's favour and their offices and been imprisoned in the Tower', where many had later died. King James himself, who was considered heavily involved in the case by the Dutch/Walloon communities, 'had only managed to survive in bad health for a few years'.[42] Clearly, if God did not always protect the elect he could, at least, be counted on to punish their enemies.

Cesar Calandrini may also have had personal reasons for continuing Ruytinck's history. He had been one of Ruytinck's close friends and contributed a poem to the volume of poetry *Epicedia in Orbitum* commemorating Ruytinck's death.[43] Later, when Calandrini was continuing Ruytinck's history, he described his predecessor's death as a colossal loss to the community, 'because he was extremely energetic and active in all good services. He deserves to be given the ornaments of the most outstanding pastors of the soul, whom he truly followed: For zeal for thy house has consumed me (Psal 69:9) and the love of your members (Church) has exhausted me.'[44]

Simon Ruytinck had a lot in common with his younger friend. Like him he belonged to the Reformed diaspora and like the Calandrinis Ruytinck's family had been influential in their place of origin. His father, Jan, had been Secretary of Ghent before the family fled to Norwich in 1573.[45] Like Calandrini, Ruytinck had studied at two of the major Reformed seats of learning, Leiden and Geneva, and like his friend he appears to have mastered a number of languages.[46] Ruytinck's manuscripts and published books show us a man, who in spite of his orthodox Calvinism was characterized by a tolerant, learned and humanist outlook.[47]

Ruytinck may well have introduced Calandrini to the small but influential community of historically inclined merchant/scholars within the Dutch church in London. They were all close to Ruytinck and are probably best described as belonging to the more 'liberal', humanist, strand within the Reformed tradition. Three prominent members of this circle, Emanuel van Meteren, Jacob Cool (Ortelianus) and Johan Radermacher/Rotarius, are likely to have befriended Cesar Calandrini. Jacob Cool contributed together with Calandrini, to the *Epicedia* in commemoration of Ruytinck, having already dedicated his *Paraphrasis ... vanden CIIII Psalm* to Simon Ruytinck in 1617, while Cesar Calandrini's father, Giovanni wrote an entry in Van Meteren's *Album Amicorum*.[48] Simon Ruytinck wrote a biography of Emanuel van Meteren, who died in April 1612, which was added to the 1614 edition of Van Meteren's famous history of the Dutch Revolt. According to Ruytinck, he had written it 'out of love and esteem' for Van Meteren.[49]

Recent scholarship which has been concerned with the merchant/historian Emanuel van Meteren and his two friends and associates, his second cousin, Jacob Cool, named Ortelianus after his famous uncle, the cartographer Abraham Ortelius in Antwerp, and the merchant/scholar Johan Radermacher, have portrayed these men as strongly heterodox Calvinists and members of the freemasons of the late sixteenth and early seventeenth century, the Family of Love.[50] Considering that this view is based on circumstantial evidence it is surprising that it has been left unchallenged.

In the case of Emanuel van Meteren, the Antwerp born and apprenticed merchant, who in 1583 became Consul to the Dutch merchants in London, the perception of him as a heterodox and possible Familist owes much to his involvement in the bitter dispute within the Dutch church in London in 1561. Van Meteren was among the most prominent defenders of the minister Adriaan van Haemstede, who had argued for a tolerant approach to Anabaptists. This politically highly sensitive issue eventually led not only to van Haemstede's excommunication, but also to that of a number of his supporters in the Dutch church, including van Meteren, who did not make his peace with the church until a decade later.[51] Combined with van Meteren's friendship with Abraham Ortelius, who probably was a member of the Family of Love, and his often quoted introduction from 1599 to the first edition of his history of the Dutch Revolt, this has been taken as proof of his Familist leanings.

The fact that Van Meteren became reconciled with the Dutch Reformed Church in London in 1571 and, according to Simon Ruytinck, that the ministers of the church attended him on his deathbed, appears to have been disregarded.[52] Furthermore, the minister Simon Ruytinck's friendship with and biography of Van Meteren seem to contradict the accepted view of Van Meteren as a Familist.[53]

Similarly, much has been made of Van Meteren's history as being unusually pragmatic and uninfluenced by religious prejudice. It is correct that Van Meteren in his introduction to the 1599 edition appeals to both Catholics, strict Calvinists and *politiques*. The introduction clearly demonstrates his distaste for religious persecution and intolerance, but it also, and more importantly, shows him as an orthodox, liberal Calvinist who believed in providential history, stating that he had written his history 'In order that such a History may serve as a mirror of insight for the Netherlanders, and all other nations, of the true knowledge of the wars described, and that they may understand God's just decisions and providential grace'.[54] And below, when recommending his history to the *politiques*, Van Meteren stated his hope that they 'might recognize in the outcome of the various events the wise and righteous judgements of God, and moreover find that He does not give his commandments in vain but that he wants to be served and honoured in this world with body and soul'.[55] Van Meteren, in other words, wanted to write a godly, providential work of history. This was a solidly Calvinist enterprise pursued, as we have seen, by his friends, the ministers Simon Ruytinck and Cesar Calandrini.

Like his relation Emanuel van Meteren, Jacob Cool was born in Antwerp, where his father had briefly returned from London in the early 1560s.[56] He was by trade a silk merchant, but retained a strong scholarly interest throughout his life. In this, he was initially encouraged by his learned uncle in Antwerp, Abraham Ortelius, who expressed his satisfaction over Jacob's interest in history in 1587 and later himself taught his nephew in Antwerp.[57] Cool, who became a good classicist, a learned collector of Greek and Roman coins and medals, a herbalist and an author of a number of religious books, retained his interest in history in later life. Thus, when his protégé and nephew, Abraham vanden Bossche, informed him about his educational progress in 1623, he stressed that 'Theology attracts me, and after that I long for the study of History.'[58]

Cool's devotional authorship confirms him as a staunch Calvinist. Before printing his works, he often circulated them among friends within the Reformed churches in England and the Netherlands. His tract, *Of Death, a true Description*, which was published in Dutch in 1624 and in English in 1629, was forwarded to the minister of the Dutch community in Colchester, Jonas Proost, the minister in Grijpskerke near Middelburg, Wilhelm Thilenius, who was elected a minister to the Dutch community in London and Willem Teellinck in Middelburg, all of whom belonged to the Counter-Remonstrant wing of the Reformed churches. They all praised the godly qualities of Cool's tract and Proost replied:

> I wish to pray unto God, and to imitate you in this respect, that in the serenity of prosperity and health, I may have like thoughts of death and a similar preparation of mind, as a splendid testimony of

that spiritual life, which the Author of life, Jesus Christ, works in those that belong to him.[59]

Thirty years earlier, Cool's Reformed faith appears to have caused him some problems with his Familist/spiritualist uncle.[60] But in spite of his association with his uncle and a considerable number of scholars who did not belong to the Reformed faith Cool remained firmly anchored within the Reformed tradition. He eventually served the Dutch community in London as an elder from 1624 until his death in 1628. This was undoubtedly a capacity where his many international contacts would have proved useful.[61]

Cool and Van Meteren's friend and correspondent, Johan Radermacher, is yet another Reformed merchant/scholar with a strong Antwerp connection. Born into a patrician family from Aachen in 1538, Radermacher spent some of his early years in London, where he lived with his parents when the Dutch Church in Austin Friars was established in 1550.[62] After his father's death in 1554 Radermacher was apprenticed to the wealthy Antwerp merchant Aegidius Hooftman, and it is from this period that his friendship with Emanuel van Meteren dates.[63] Five years later Radermacher was back in London where he was actively involved in obtaining the church in Austin Friars for the use of the Dutch community.[64] In 1561 he was elected a deacon to the Dutch church.[65] A few years later Radermacher appears to have returned to Antwerp, from where he once more emigrated to London after the 'Wonderyear' (1566).[66] He took up membership of the small Italian church in London on his return, but cannot have remained a member for long.[67] By August 1571 he had been elected an elder of the Dutch church, a position he kept until he re-emigrated to Antwerp in December 1580.[68]

In Antwerp, Radermacher joined the Reformed community on his arrival and reported back to his consistorial colleague, the minister Gotfried van Winghen, that the Reformed church in Antwerp was prospering and the 'number of followers of Christ was increasing'.[69] At this stage Radermacher was seriously contemplating joining those of his lay consistorial colleagues in London who had decided to serve 'the churches under the cross' during the great apostolic age of the London community in the 1570s. Eventually, he decided against becoming a minister and settled for an eldership within the Antwerp community.[70]

Radermacher who was instrumental in recruiting the London community's student, Assuerus Regemorter, as a minister for the Reformed church in Antwerp, played an active role within the Antwerp community until the city's surrender to the Spaniards in 1585.[71] He then returned to Aachen, his birthplace, where he was elected an elder to the Dutch church in 1589. In 1598 he was made 'Weinmeister' of Aachen, but when shortly afterwards the city returned to Catholicism

Radermacher moved via Hamburg, where he was actively importing cloth from England in 1599, to Middelburg. By 1602 he had become an elder in the Reformed church in Middelburg.[72]

Undoubtedly, Johan Radermacher had some unusual interests, not least in hermeticism and the philosophy of John Dee, but his life and career can hardly be described as heterodox. To make him a member of the Family of Love would make a mockery of the overwhelming evidence of his Calvinism.[73]

Like his associates Radermacher had a strong interest in history as can be seen from his involvement in Philip Marnix's plans for a history of the Dutch Revolt which was promoted by the National Synod which met in Dordrecht in 1578. The Colloquium of the Dutch exiled churches in England which met that year commissioned Radermacher to be responsible for all the relevant material about the English communites to be included in Marnix's history.[74]

Of far greater significance, however, was Radermacher's role in the world of international Calvinism. Together with his friends and colleagues within the Dutch community in London, Radermacher constituted an important link in the chain of international Calvinism, which had been strung together in the Reformed diaspora and reinforced through its complex web of emigrations. It was merchants and ministers like him and his friends who through emigration, education and trade created a European Calvinist network which incorporated most of the leading trading centres, such as Hamburg, Frankfurt, Nuremberg, Amsterdam, Middelburg, London, and briefly in the 1570s and 1580s Antwerp. Their social experience of exodus and displacement served to reinforce their feeling of election and sense of belonging to the New Covenant. For such exiles providential history became the mortar which kept the 'faithful' together, providing them with both identity and purpose. It served to actualize biblical time, transporting it into the present, thus reinforcing their sense of election. Among the Reformed exiles gathered in London this is strongly in evidence in the community's long-term concern for providential history, starting with Emanuel van Meteren, Johan Radermacher and Jacob Cool and continued by Simon Ruytinck and Cesar Calandrini.

Notes

1. For the early emigration from the Netherlands, see A. Pettegree, *Emden and the Dutch Revolt. Exile and the Development of Reformed Protestantism* (Oxford 1992), pp. 1–25. For France, see M. Greengrass, *The French Reformation* (Oxford 1987), pp. 24ff.

2. See A. Pettegree, *Foreign Protestant Communities in Sixteenth-Century London* (Oxford 1986), pp. 133–81.

3. See W. Monter, *Calvin's Geneva* (New York 1967), pp. 165–6 and W. Monter, 'Historical Demography and Religious History in Sixteenth-Century Geneva', *The Journal of Interdisciplinary History*, 9 (1979), 435–51, especially 402–4.

4. J. G. C. A. Briels, *De zuidnederlandse immigratie, 1572–1630* (Haarlem 1978). It should be borne in mind that the mobility of the refugees makes any accurate estimate of the size of the emigration difficult. See also H. Schilling, 'Innovation through Migration: The Settlements of Calvinistic Netherlanders in Sixteenth- and Seventeenth-Century Central and Western Europe', *Social History,* 16:31 (1983), 7–33, especially 9–10.

5. For England, see O. P. Grell, *Dutch Calvinists in Early Stuart London* (Leiden 1989), pp. 7–32 and above, Chapter 3, 'A Friendship Turned Sour: Puritans and Dutch Calvinists in East Anglia. For Germany, see H. Schilling, *Niederländische Exultanten im 16. Jahrhundert* (Gütersloh 1972), and H. Schilling, 'Innovation'. For craftsmen settling in the United provinces, see J. I. Israel, *Dutch Primacy in World Trade 1585–1740* (Oxford 1989), pp. 35–7.

6. See especially the works by J. A. van Houtte and H. van der Wee. For a summary of this debate, see H. Schilling, 'Innovation', 10–11.

7. Undoubtedly Calvin's and other Reformed leaders' refusal to tolerate 'nicodemism' among their followers served to reinforce emigration. For 'nicodemism', see R. Stauffer, 'Calvin', and A. Duke, 'The Ambivalent Face of Calvinism in the Netherlands 1561–1618', in M. Prestwich (ed.), *International Calvinism 1541–1715* (Oxford 1985), pp. 15–37, especially pp. 23–4 and pp. 109–33, especially pp. 117–18. For Johannes a Lasco's writings against 'nicodemism', see Pettegree, *Foreign Protestants*, pp. 124–5. See also H. A. Oberman, 'The Impact of the Reformation; Problems and Perspectives', in E. I. Kouri and T. Scott (eds), *Politics and Society in Reformation Europe* (London 1987), pp. 3–31, especially 15–20.

8. G. Lewis, 'Calvinism in Geneva in the Time of Calvin and Beza, 1541–1608', in Prestwich (ed.), *International Calvinism*, pp. 39–69, especially p. 64.

9. For the Calvinist academies, see R. Stauffer, 'Calvinism and the Universities', in L. Grane (ed.), *University and Reformation* (Leiden 1981), pp. 76–98. For an example of the *perigrinatio academica*, see Grell, *Dutch Calvinists*, pp. 139–44.

10. Quoted from 'Narrative of Pompeo Deodati' printed in A. F. W. Papillon, *Memoirs of Thomas Papillon of London, Merchant, 1623–1702* (Reading 1887), p. 412.

11. 'Narrative of Pompeo Deodati', pp. 411–21. See also W. Monter, 'The Italians in Geneva: A New Look', *Genève et l'Italie: Etudes publiées a l'occasion du 50e anniversaire de la Société genevoise d'études italliennes par Luc Monnier* (Geneva 1969), pp. 53–77, especially p. 69, 71–2.

12. For The Grand Boutique, see W. Bodmer, *Der Einfluss der Refugianteneinwanderung von 1550–1700 auf die schweizerische Wirtschaft* (Zurich 1946), pp. 41–9, 82–3, 151.

13. A. Pascal, 'Da Lucca a Ginevra', *Revista Storica Italiana*, 2 (1935), 253–315, especially 262–3. For Philip Burlamachi, see R. Ashton, 'The Disbursing Official under the Early Stuarts: The Cases of William Russell

and Philip Burlamachi', *Bulletin of the Institute of Historical Research*, 30 (1957), 162–74. See also R. Ashton, *The Crown and the Money Market 1603–1640* (Oxford 1960), pp. 20–22.

14. D. C. Dorian, *The English Diodatis* (New Brunswick 1950), pp. 312–13; for Wotton's contacts to Jean Diodati, see p. 99.

15. For Giovanni Calandrini, see W. Baumann, *The Merchant Adventurers and the Continental Cloth-Trade (1560s–1620s)* (Berlin 1990), pp. 262, 271–2 and Dorian, *English Diodatis*, p. 310. For Dutch Republic, see Israel, *Dutch Primacy*, p. 42.

16. For the marriage, see Grell, *Dutch Calvinists*, p. 124. From the late 1570s until the fall of Antwerp in 1585 several members of the Calandrini/ Burlamachi/Diodati/Turrettini clan settled in Antwerp, among them the later founder of The Grand Boutique, Francesco Turrettini, who served the French Reformed church in the city as an elder for a couple of years between 1579 and 1585, see Bibliotheque publique et universitaire de Geneve, MS Suppl. 438, f.66r.

17. See Dorian, *English Diodatis*, p. 310 and J. T. Lauridsen, *Marselis Konsortiet* (Århus 1987), pp. 32–3.

18. For Papillon, see *Dictionary of National Biography*.

19. For Cesare Calandrini in Nuremberg, see G. Siebold, 'Zur Situation der italienischen Kaufleute in Nürnberg während der zweiten Hälfte des 17. und der ersten Hälfte des 18. Jahrhunderts', *Mitteilungen des Vereins für Geschichte der Stadt Nürnberg*, 71 (1984) 186–207; L. Bauer, 'Die italienischen Kaufleute und ihre Stellung im protestantischen Nürnberg am Ende des 16. Jahrhunderts', *Jahrbuch für Fränkische Landesforschung*, 22 (1962), 1–18 and W. Bauman, *The Merchant Adventurers*, 271–2.

20. Grell, *Dutch Calvinists*, pp. 176–9.

21. MS Suppl. 438, f. 58r, 74r.

22. Grell, *Dutch Calvinists*, p. 63 and Dorian, *English Diodatis*, 98–9, 248.

23. For Saumur, see Stauffer, 'Calvinism & Universities', 87–8; for Calandrini, see A. G. H. Bachrach, *Sir Constantine Huygens and Britain 1596–1687* (Leiden 1962), pp. 58–62 and Grell, *Dutch Calvinists*, pp. 62–5.

24. French church, Soho Square, London, MS 4, consistory book 1588–1615, f. 483r, 503v and MS 5, consistory book 1615–1680, f. 10r, f. 46r, f. 74v, 77r.

25. Grell, *Dutch Calvinists*, p. 63. Elizabeth was also the daugher of a leading elder of the French church in London, see P. R. Sellin, 'Caesar Calandrini, the London Dutch, and Milton's Quarrels in Holland', *Huntington Library Quarterly*, 31 (1968), 239–49, especially 245, n. 25.

26. French church MS 5, f. 26r.

27. J. J. van Toorenenbergen (ed.), *Gheschiedenissen ende Handelingen die voornemelick aengaen de nederduytsche Natie ende gemeynten wonende in Engeland ende in bysonder tot Londen* (WMV, 3, 1, 1873), pp. 416–17.

28. J. A. Worp, *Constantijn Huygens Briefwisseling 1608–1687*, 6 vols (The Hague 1911–17, RGP vols 15, 19, 21, 24, 28, 32), Letter no. 60. See also Guildhall Library MS 7424, f. 49ff. and C. R. Elrington (ed.) *The Whole Works of James Ussher*, 17 vols (Dublin 1847–64), vol. 16, p. 214. For the English delegation, see N. Tyacke, *Anti-Calvinists. The Rise of English Arminianism c. 1590–1640* (Oxford 1987), pp. 99–100.

29. *Huygens Briefwisseling*, nos 60, 64. Vincent Burlamachi, another mem-

ber of the family, also stayed with Jean Diodati at the same lodgings in Dordrecht at this time, see MS Suppl. 438, f. 75v.

30. *Huygens Briefwisseling*, no. 66; Dorian, *English Diodatis*, pp. 100–101; Tyacke, *English Arminianism*, pp. 44–5.

31. *Huygens Briefwiseling*, nos 64, 66; compare with the neutral letter of August 1617, no. 35.

32. See J. Foster, *Alumni Oxoniensis* 4 vols (Oxford 1891–92), I, p. 230; Guildhall Library MS 7424, f. 49ff and Tyacke, *English Arminianism*, pp. 72–4.

33. Grell, *Dutch Calvinists*, pp. 63–6; see also Tyacke, *English Arminianism*, p. 71 (for Thomas Morton) and p. 122 (for Bishop Neale's interview with De Dominis).

34. *The Correspondence of John Cosin, D. D. Lord Bishop of Durham*, part 1 (Pub. of the Surtees Society, L11, 1869), pp. 27–30.

35. Guildhall Library MS 7424, f. 49ff.

36. See Guildhall Library MS 7397/7, f. 102v and *Cosin Correspondance*, p. 27.

37. See H. Trevor-Roper, *Catholics, Anglicans and Puritans* (London 1987), pp. 124–39.

38. For Calandrini's contribution, see *Gheschiedenissen*, pp. 389–483; see also his draft in MS, Guildhall MSS 9622/1 and 2.

39. See MS Suppl. 438 (in Italian); 3 copies in English of Pompeo Diodati's Memoirs in Papillon of Acrise Place MSS U1015, F 8, Kent County Archives; 1 copy in French of Pompeo Diodati's Memoirs and 1 copy in French of Renata Burlamachi's Memoirs in Trinity College, Dublin, see T. K. Abbott (ed.), *Catalogue of the Manuscripts in the Library of Trinity College, Dublin* (London 1900), no. 1152, VIII.

40. There is a considerable literature on Protestant providential and apocalyptic history, see among others J. W. Thompson, *The History of Historical Writing*, 2 vols (New York 1942), especially I, pp. 520–645; K. R. Firth, *The Apocalyptic Tradition in Reformation Britain 1530–1645* (Oxford 1979), pp. 1–31, and A. Zakai, *Exile and Kingdom, History and Apocalypse in the Puritan Migration to America* (Cambridge 1992), pp. 12–55.

41. Exile has been recognized as being of paramount importance for the development of the apocalyptic tradition in Britain, see Firth, *Apocalyptic Tradition*, p. 69; for the general significance of migration within ecclesiastical history and the way Puritan emigrants to America viewed their own situation, see Zakai, *Exile*, p. 8 and *passim*. For Adriaan van Haemstede, see A. J. Jelsma, *Adriaan van Haemstede en zijn martelaarsboek* (The Hague 1970); for Jean Crespin, see J. Gilmont, *Jean Crespin* (Geneva 1981); for John Foxe, see Firth, *Apocalyptic Tradition*, pp. 69–110.

42. *Gheschiedenissen*, pp. 23, 393. Ruytinck wrote two accounts of his history: Guildhall MS 9621 which was used by Toorenenbergen for *Gheschiedenissen*; and Guildhall MS 9620, which differs on a number of points and is divided into headed chapters, often of a providential nature. Further historical notes by Ruytinck can be found in Guildhall MS 10,055.

43. *Epidecia in Orbitum* (Leiden 1622).

44. *Gheschiedenissen*, 395.

45. *Nieuw Nederlandsch Biografisch Woordenboeck* (hereafter *NNBW*), IV, 1181–2.

46. See Simon Ruytinck's two theses, *Theses Physicae de Elementis* (Leiden 1597) and *Disputationum Theologicarum Repetitarum. Decima quinta de Creatione Homines. Leiden ad Imaginem Dei* (Leiden 1598). Ruytinck received his first degree in Leiden under the auspices of the famous French Reformed theologian, Pierre du Moulin, who was then professor of philosophy at the University of Leiden. For Ruytinck's languages, see *Gheschiedenissen*, p. 395.

47. For Ruytinck, see below, Chapter 9, 'Calvinist *Agape* or Godly Dining Club?'. In his extensive coverage of the Hampton Court Conference in 1604 Ruytinck's sympathy was evidently with those Puritan ministers who were dismissed, but it was tempered by the observation that a good cause had been damaged through the rashness of some of those ministers who, wanting to carry the Reformation further, had acted without common consent, *Gheschiedenissen*, pp. 187, 179.

48. See Jacob Cool, *Paraphrasis vanden CIIII Psalm* (Middelburg 1626), and J. A. van Dorsten, '"I. C. O.": The Rediscovery of a Modest Dutchman in London', in J. A van Dorsten, *The Anglo-Dutch Renaissance* (Leiden 1988), pp. 8–20. For Giovanni Calandini's entry, see Emanuel van Meteren, *Album Amicorum*, Bodleian Library MS Douce 68, f. 110 (signed as 'Lucensis', dated Leiden, 20 August 1607) and Bachrach, *Constantine Huygens*, p. 61.

49. See *Gheschiedenissen*, p. 274 and L. Brummel, *Twee Ballingen's lands tijdens onze opstand tegen Spanje: Hugo Blotius (1534–1612), Emanuel van Meteren (1535–1612)* (The Hague 1972), pp. 119, 125.

50. This view was launched by J. A. van Dorsten, *The Radical Arts* (Leiden 1972), pp. 32–7; it was accepted by Brummel, *Twee Ballingen*, pp. 127–8, N. Mout, 'The Family of Love (Huis der Liefde) and the Dutch Revolt', in A. C. Duke and C. A. Tamse (eds), *Britain and the Netherlands, VII. Church and State since the Reformation* (The Hague 1981), pp. 76–93, especially p. 84, and E. M. Janssen, 'A "Trias Historica" on the Revolt of the Netherlands: Emanuel van Meteren. Pieter Bor and Everhard van Reyd as Exponents of Contemporary Historiography', in A. C. Duke and C. A. Tamse (eds), *Britain and the Netherlands, VIII, Clio's Mirror. Historiography in Britain and the Netherlands* (Zutphen 1985), pp. 9–30, especially p. 15.

51. For a recent analysis of this episode, see Pettegree, *Foreign Protestant Communities*, pp. 173–5.

52. See Simon Ruytinck's Levensbericht in the 1614 edition of Emanuel van Meteren's, *Commentarien Ofte Memorien Vanden Nederlandtschen Staet, handel, Oorloghen ende Gheschiedenissen van onsen tyden* ..., f. 672ff and Brummel, *Twee Ballingen*, p. 125; for the reconciliation, see Pettegree, *Foreign Protestant Communities*, p. 180.

53. Furthermore, Emanuel van Meteren's son-in-law, Abraham der Kinderen, served the Dutch church in London as a deacon, see Grell, *Dutch Calvinists*, pp. 263, 274. See also J. H. Hessels (ed.), *Ecclesiae Londino-Batavae Archivum*, I–III (1–2) (Cambridge 1887–97), I, no. 224.

54. The introduction to the 1599 edition is quoted in Brummel, *Twee Ballingen*, p. 123.

55. Cited in Janssen, 'Trias Historica', p. 17.

56. His father might well have belonged to the pro-Haemstede wing within the Dutch church in London, since his first wife was a sister of Adriaan

van Haemstede, see Hessels, I, no. 47; see also Van Dorsten, *Radical Arts*, p. 23.

57.   Hessels, I, nos 149, 161.
58.   Ibid., no. 364.
59.   Hessels, I, nos 366, 370, 371.
60.   Ibid., nos 228, 229.
61.   See below, Chapter 10, 'Plague in Elizabethan London: The Dutch Response'.
62.   For Radermacher's birthplace and date of birth see H. Kellenbenz, *Unternehmerkräfte im Hamburger Portugal- und Spanienhandel 1590–1625* (Hamburg 1954); for his presence in London in 1550, see Hessels, III, no. 1660. See also entry *s.v.* Radermacher in *Nationaal biografisch Woordenboek* 13 (Brussels 1990) col. 674–80.
63.   Hessels, I, no. 330.
64.   Ibid., III, no. 1657.
65.   A. A. van Schelven (ed.), *Kerkeraads-Protocollen der Nederduitsche Vluchtelingen-Kerk te Londen 1560–1563* (Amsterdam 1921), p. 202; like so many other Dutch/Walloon exiles he also had ties to the French Church in London, see Van Dorsten, *Radical Arts*, p. 37.
66.   Hessels, I, no. 331.
67.   See R. E. G. Kirk and E. F. Kirk (eds), *Returns of Aliens Dwelling in the City and Suburbs of London under James I*, 4 vols, Publications of the Huguenot Society of London, X (London 1900–8), I, p. 388; see also K. Bostoen, 'Kaars en Bril: de oudste Nederlandse Grammatica', *Archief. Medelingen van het Koninklijk Zeeuwsch Genootschap der Wetenschappen* (1984), especially 11. (I should like to thank Dr O. Boersma for drawing this article to my attention.)
68.   W. J. C. Moens, *The Marriage, Baptismal, and Burial Registers 1571 to 1874 and Monumental Inscriptions, Dutch Reformed Church, Austin Friars* (Lymington 1884), pp. 146, 209; for Radermacher's continued activity as an elder, see Hessels, III, nos 223, 231, 535, 675, and II, no. 185.
69.   Hessels, II, no. 185.
70.   See Hessels, II, nos 188, 189, 190, 194, 197, and III, no. 722 (by 15 July 1581 Radermacher had become an elder in Antwerp); see also Grell, *Dutch Calvinists*, 120–28.
71.   Radermacher was given a gift by the city of Antwerp for negotiating the city's surrender, see *National Biografisch Woordenboek* 13, col. 675.
72.   J. Reitsma and S. D. van Veen (eds), *Acts der provinciale en particuliere synoden gehouden in de noordelijke Nederlanden gedurende de jaren 1572–1620*, 8 vols (Groningen, 1892–9), V (Zeeland), p. 50.
73.   See Hessels, I, no. 334; see also Radermacher's entry in Abraham Ortelius's *Album Amicorum*, where he quotes Jeremiah 18, 6 and Paul's Letter to the Romans 8, 28, both places expressing strong providentialism, see Abraham Ortelius, *Album Amicorum*, f. 94, in Pembroke College, Cambridge.
74.   See Brummel, *Twee Ballingen*, pp. 148–9 and J. J. van Toorenenbergen (ed.), *Acten van de Colloquia der Nederlandsche Gemeenten in Engeland 1575–1609* (WMV, 2, 1, 1872), pp. 49–50. Radermacher was the owner of a considerable library. It contained over 1,500 volumes and was predominantly theological in orientation, comprising more than 560 works

in Latin and many more in Spanish, Italian, French, English, German and Dutch. His taste appears to have been typically Reformed with the works of Calvin, Beza, Bullinger, Bucer, Zanchius, Ursinus and Oecolampadius especially well represented in several languages. It also comprised a considerable number of historical works which was only matched by his interest in medicine. Radermacher's interest in providential history is clearly indicated by his ownership of a copy of Bullinger's sermons on the Apocalypse and folio-copies of Crespin's and Foxe's martyrologies, not to mention a copy of John Bale's, *The Image of Both Churches*. See *Catalogus Miscellaneus Variorum Ac Insignium Imprimis Latinorum, Italicorum, Hispanicorum, Gallicorum, Anglicorum, Germanicorum, & Belgicorum Librorum Doctissimi viri D. Ioannis Radermacheri Senoris, Mercaturae & literarum studiosi qui obijt Middelburgi Anno 1617* (Middelburg 1634), J4r (Bullinger), G1v (Crespin), H2r and v (Foxe and Bale), and K. Bostoen, 'Kaars en Bril', 12.

CHAPTER SIX

From persecution to integration: the decline of the Anglo-Dutch communities in England, 1648–1702

The revolution of 1688 and William of Orange's acquisition of the English Crown appear to have generated little interest among the Anglo-Dutch communities in England. The Dutch congregation in London, which had made a habit of greeting the new rulers of England since the Church's re-foundation under Elizabeth in 1560, did not make any reference either to William's arrival or to his and Mary's later coronation in its consistory books or correspondence.

Only in the minutes of the Coetus, the joint body of the French and Dutch communities in London, can any references to William be found. This body had obviously appreciated the Prince's political importance early on, since it had taken the opportunity to pay its respects on three occasions prior to 1688. It had saluted him in October 1670 during his visit to England and twice in 1677 – in October on his arrival and again in November when it congratulated William on his marriage to Mary, wishing him a happy return to Holland. We can safely assume that the initiative behind these actions originated from within the leadership of the French congregation; as opposed to the Dutch, the French church in London was still a dynamic community towards the end of the seventeenth century, having recently received a considerable influx of new, Huguenot immigrants in connection with the Revocation of the Edict of Nantes in 1685.

During a meeting of Coetus on 23 December 1688 it was decided to wait on 'the Prince of Orange'. This meeting and its decision was remarkably well timed, considering that James II had fled to France only the previous night. It is evident that the leaders of the stranger churches were well informed about the political developments and surprisingly enough were prepared to act before the Lords, on 24 December, had officially requested William of Orange to take charge of the interim administration and issue circular letters for parliamentary elections.

A deputation consisting of four ministers and four elders from the two churches was consequently received by William on 14 January 1689 – 'very gratiously in his bedchamber'. The deputies praised the

Lord for having chosen William as his instrument and added that 'they acknowledged and honoured His Princely Highness holding him in their highest esteem and gratitude, as the most illustrious champion and unique protector and redeemer of God's oppressed Church and People'. They fully realized that William had disregarded any personal dangers to which he might have been exposed 'by sea and by land' in order 'that he could save the British Israel from invading Popery and everlasting slavery'.

The speech was delivered by one of the Dutch ministers, Samuel Bischop, and requested William to continue the Crown's protection of the stranger communities. The discourse of the address bears all the hallmarks of the more radical Whigs, among whom a number of the leading members of the Dutch and French communities could be counted. Leading City Whigs such as James and John Houblon and Christopher Lethieullier were all closely associated with the French church, where several of their ancestors had served as elders and deacons, and Sir John Lawrence, a former Lord Mayor, was equally closely associated with Austin Friars. Likewise, the striking similarity in style and content between the Address of 11 December 1688 from the Lord Mayor and Corporation of the City of London to William and the speech delivered by Samuel Bischop was hardly accidental, but can be taken as proof of their mutual political and religious origin.

William, who must have been pleased with the speech, nevertheless offered the deputies a characteristically non-committal answer: 'Ick bedancke de Nederlantsche en Fransche kercken, en sy mogen staet maecken, dat Ick haer sal Dien to Doen, wat ick kan.'[1] On this occasion, as on many others, William certainly did not promise more than he could guarantee. The representatives from the French and Dutch churches might well have found the response of their first co-religionist ruler disappointing, especially if they bore in mind the more straightforward answer they had received in 1685 upon the accession of the Catholic, James II, who had promised in no uncertain terms to continue his brother's protection of the foreign congregations. In June 1660 Charles II had informed the stranger churches that 'he would protect them as belonging to the Reformed religion, which he professed himself, and would protect all Reformed Churches together with them'.[2]

That a King, who was nicknamed 'Dutch William' by the English and who felt more comfortable in the company of Dutch than Englishmen, should have shown so little interest in, and attracted so little attention from, the Anglo-Dutch communities should, howeverr, not surprise us.[3] None of the members of the Anglo-Dutch congregations was among the many strangers whom William was accused of favouring. Moreover, only a minority of those Dutchmen who settled in England as a consequence of William's accession were to join the Anglo-Dutch churches. Prominent exceptions were the banking brothers, Gerard and Joshua van Neck, who both served the Dutch church in Austin Friars as elders in the early eighteenth century.[4]

By 1688 the congregation in Austin Friars was culturally far more English than Dutch in its outlook. Most of its members were by then four or five generations removed from the original immigrants who had founded the church in 1550. As distinct from its French sister-church in Threadneedle Street, the community had not received a significant number of new members from the Continent for more than a century. As a consequence, Austin Friars had seen a gradual decline of its membership, from a peak of around two thousand towards the end of the 1580s to below a thousand in the second half of the seventeenth century.

The leaders of the congregation in London had attempted to halt or delay the growing tendency among the membership to abandon their Dutch roots when, during the late 1630s, they decided to employ a schoolmaster who could teach Dutch to the community's children. It was probably a hopeless cause from the outset, and the implementation of the policy eventually left much to be desired. The richer members who were supposed to have financed the cost of hiring a schoolmaster proved unwilling to pay, at the same time as they appeared to prefer the services of one of the many independent English schoolmasters who operated in London.

Towards the middle of the seventeenth century the Dutch language in which the church conducted its affairs was at best only passively understood by a large proportion of the community. In this context it is of significance that from at least as early as 1649, on the occasion that one of the consistory members of Austin Friars chaired the monthly Coetus, the minutes would be taken down in English whereas the French continued to use their mother tongue.[5]

During the 1650s an increasing number of members requested the consistory of Austin Friars to provide them with an attestation in English since they did not understand Dutch. Likewise, a growing number of ministers' and elders' children had to be examined in English in the main tenets of the Reformed faith before they could be confirmed as members of the church.[6]

A number of the smaller, provincial Anglo-Dutch congregations had folded well before the Williamite Revolution. The Colloquia of the Dutch churches in England, which had been instituted in 1575 as a less formal structure than the Classis and especially geared to the Dutch churches' exposed political situation, came to an end in 1706, at a time when only four congregations were still in existence.[7] Apart from London, the other three surviving communities had by then been struggling for most of the second half of the seventeenth century.

Austin Friars had to contribute considerable sums of money to keep a growing number of the provincial congregations in existence from the start of James I's reign. In retrospect it is slightly ironic that Austin Friars, which had been instrumental in fostering Dutch communities in a number of provincial towns, thereby helping to regenerate their declining economies in the reign of Elizabeth, now found its initiatives had created financial liabilities.

In 1561 Austin Friars had provided the first 25 households to found the Dutch congregation in Sandwich. From the 1620s, however, the London community was called upon to provide occasional financial assistance to this church. In 1645 the leaders in Sandwich informed London that, owing to the great troubles in Flanders – a reference to the renewed military campaign against Spain by the Dutch Stadholder, Frederick Henry – more than a hundred poor fugitives had arrived. The Sandwich community pointed out that it was unable to help these refugees because of the decline in the community's fortune and membership. It is evident from the letter that the refugees had left their homes primarily because of the devastation caused by the war and not, like the founding fathers of the Dutch community in Austin Friars, because of their faith. A number of the fugitives attended services in the Dutch church, but the elders in Sandwich had observed that 'some show sufficiently that they care little for it'. In spite of this cautionary note, Austin Friars offered to provide financial assistance and added that 'in these fugitives from Flanders we may behold the condition of our ancestors and the foundation of our churches in this country'. The elders in London, disregarding the effects of the English Civil War, suggested that the refugees should be persuaded to join the other Dutch communities, where their skills could be of use, adding that: 'Agriculture flourishes at Maidstone; weavers of wool have now a very good trade at Colchester, and they want workmen. Those who work in stuffs find employment at Norwich and also at Canterbury if they understand French.'[8]

A number of the refugees appear to have followed the advice of Austin Friars. The following year the community in Maidstone, which Austin Friars had helped establish in 1567, pointed out to the elders in London in connection with their now regular request for economic support that it was important to maintain a Dutch church in their town since a number of 'wandering papists' who had fled the war in Flanders could 'be gained for the true knowledge of Christ' through their congregation.[9]

The term 'wandering Papists' was probably a correct one; few of these refugees intended to stay in England and, if the effects of the

English Civil War had not already encouraged them to return to Flanders, then the peace treaty of Münster on 30 January 1648 certainly did. Thus they were never to experience the accelerating decay of the provincial Anglo-Dutch communities during the late 1640s and 1650s.

In 1650 – five years before the church collapsed – the Dutch community in Maidstone begged the congregation in London to assist it. It had been without a minister for 18 months and assistance from Austin Friars was essential if its members should not be tempted to abandon the church and 'content themselves with the English'.

> Hitherto we have kept the Church open in the forenoon, and in the afternoon read two or three chapters, singing one of the Psalms, praying the customary prayers and reading a sermon. But we see that the people show little inclination to come to Church, and there are often not more than eight persons present, who are most of the time asleep. Hence the Reader gets discouraged and we should like to have your help and advice.[10]

Austin Friars had too many problems of its own during the 1650s to offer much assistance, and a few years later the community in Maidstone came under further pressure from the local population, who wanted them to allow an English minister to preach in their church every Sunday – a practice apparently already introduced in other Anglo-Dutch congregations. The Maidstone community felt unable to refuse this request, since they could not manage to keep the church open on their own. Many of its wealthier members had already left the congregation, more likely than not following the general demographic trend and moving to London, where they would have joined Austin Friars. Others had left for the local English churches and of those who remained a majority understood English as well as Dutch.[11]

Disregarding the brief existence in Halstead and Thetford in the late sixteenth century of offshoots of the Colchester and Norwich congregations, Maidstone became the first Dutch church to disintegrate. In March 1655 the community responded to the invitation for the approaching Colloquium of the Dutch churches in England by informing the church in London that the community had now totally decayed – the door of the church was locked and 'the people of any quality had gone over to the English'.[12]

The collapse of Maidstone was closely followed by the dissolution of the community of tapestry weavers in Mortlake, originally organized by Sir Francis Crane and established under the aegis of Austin Friars in 1621–22. The Civil War had undermined the livelihood of this community, which had primarily supplied the royal palaces with tapestries under the guidance of the German painter, Francis Cleyn. In November 1645 the weavers informed Austin Friars that they had petitioned

Parliament for financial assistance, but in the meantime they requested the London community to commission six tapestries depicting the Acts of the Apostles at a cost of £357.

Austin Friars assisted the Mortlake community, though not by ordering the suggested tapestries, which the church considered unsuitable because of the amount of work involved in their production, and unsaleable with regard to the subject-matter. Instead, the church commissioned a set called the 'Hunters' Chase' at the considerably higher cost of £450.[13] If the change of theme – from a religious to a secular one – was intended to improve the tapestries' market possibilities, then the elders in London were gravely mistaken. The money to finance the enterprise had come out of the Austin Friars poor-box and, despite desperate attempts to sell the tapestries between 1647 and 1652, they proved nearly impossible to get rid of.

The timing was obviously unfortunate, coinciding with the sale of the royal collection of tapestries which took place from 1649 to 1653 on the order of the Council of State. Finally, however, in March 1652, the consistory gave in and dropped the idea of a minimum price. It decided that the tapestries had to be sold immediately in order to minimize the loss of interest to the poor-box and to avoid the danger of the tapestries losing their colour in storage. A couple of weeks later they were sold to the elder, David Otger, for £300, thus, apart from the interest, causing a loss of £150 to the community's poor-box.[14]

Mortlake collapsed four years after the Restoration, but not before its trainee minister, Peter Tessemaker, had caused great anxiety among the leaders of Austin Friars. In January 1664 they received a complaint about him from the English minister in Mortlake. According to the latter, Tessemaker, while preaching in English, had criticized Charles II and the way the Church of England had been restructured after the Restoration. This was clearly a highly inauspicious subject to comment upon and Austin Friars immediately dispatched the elder, Willem Ruyshout, with a letter to Tessemaker. In it he was ordered to stop preaching in English henceforth. Tessemaker was forbidden to meddle with affairs concerning 'the State of Church-government of England' in his sermons, as well as his prayers, in Dutch and English. The London consistory informed him that he had acted against his instructions and might have caused great misfortune to the foreign churches in England. The dispatch of Willem Ruyshout was not only intended to provide guidance to the Dutch community in Mortlake and to call Tessemaker to order, but was also an attempt to contain the damage caused among the local, Anglican clergy and to guarantee that the incident did not lead to a formal inquiry. Ruyshout therefore paid a visit to the English minister who had complained about Tessemaker's sermon and assured him that the Anglo-Dutch congregations did not approve of the Non-conformists. This was an obviously opportune statement, but self-contradictory, since the Reformed, Anglo-Dutch churches, at least by Anglican definition, inhabited the domain of Nonconformism in 1664. Nevertheless, Ruyshout succeeded in his mission, and informed his colleagues in London that the English minister 'promised me to let bygones remain in oblivion'.[15]

The smallest of the Dutch communities in England – Yarmouth – survived until 1680, in spite of having seen its membership fall to 28 male members as early as 1635. The church, which had been founded in 1569, had been receiving regular financial support from Austin Friars since at least 1609. This assistance – between £12 and £20 p.a. – was obviously justified by the Yarmouth community's importance to visiting sailors and fishermen from the Netherlands, who arrived twice a year for the herring fisheries. They used Yarmouth as their base to dry and repair nets and to take in supplies, and on Sundays a number of them attended service in the Dutch church. In the 1630s the Yarmouth community had argued for their financial support to be continued on the basis that, without a Dutch church in Yarmouth, these sailors and fishermen were likely to spend their Sundays drinking in the local inns. Such a practice might, in the church's opinion, reflect badly on all the Dutch communities in England.[16] From 1645 the church in Yarmouth had to make do with young ministers – *proponenten* – who generally came over from Zeeland to serve the community for two-year stints in order to learn English before returning to the Netherlands to take up a permanent position. Without their service the church in Yarmouth would have been unable to survive, but the inexperience of these young Zeelanders, especially with regard to English church policy, could give cause for anxiety in London.

In September 1664 the then minister in Yarmouth, Johannes Beverlandt, informed the London consistory that English people fre-quently requested him to baptize their children in their homes, adding that they would rather leave them unbaptized than bring them to their parish churches. Obviously members of the Nonconformist communi-ties in Yarmouth were trying to circumvent the Act of Uniformity by having their children quietly baptized in accordance with the ritual of the Dutch Reformed communities in England. Austin Friars told Beverlandt to stay clear of these people, warning him that 'neither we nor our Churches would give authorisation in this respect and it might tend greatly to prejudice the foreign churches in England'.[17]

The value of the Yarmouth congregation *vis-à-vis* visiting Dutch fishermen was recognized by the town's magistracy. When, during the mid-1640s, 'the Independents' tried to take over the Dutch church, they were prevented from doing so by the local authorities, who wanted to preserve the church 'which is necessary, not only for the maintenance of our poor, but for all the Dutch strangers who arrive here and require assistance'. After the Restoration, however, the Yarmouth congregation barely managed to continue. Its principal members had died and their children had nearly all joined the local, parish churches. The church had only 36 members left – male and female – who were all natives and understood English. The resources of Austin Friars had by then diminished considerably and the church felt unable to help; instead an attempt was made to raise money for Yarmouth across the sea through the Dutch ambassador. But times had changed in 1660, and it was impossible to generate any interest in the Netherlands in contributing towards the maintenance of the Dutch communities in England.[18]

The larger Dutch churches in Norwich and Colchester were still active communities in 1688, but they were pale shadows of their former selves. The Civil Wars in England proved especially detrimental to the church in Colchester. The Royalist rising in Essex and the start of the Second Civil War led to the occupation of Colchester by Royalist forces. Shortly afterwards General Fairfax laid siege to the town and starved and bombarded Colchester into surrender in August 1648. The town, as well as the Dutch community, was totally devasted and Austin Friars was asked for urgent assistance in September by its brothers in Colchester. A month later the London community was able to forward the considerable sum of £523.[19]

The new balance of religious forces which came into existence during the Civil Wars and Interregnum made life exceedingly difficult for the elders in Colchester. The sects and gathered churches proliferated and the Dutch church lost members to these communities, as it did during the late 1650s to the Quakers. In 1652 the leaders of the church were far from happy about the prospect of having to host the next Colloquium of the Dutch congregations in England. They wanted the venue moved, pointing out that such an unusual gathering might prove counterproductive 'in a town where the Magistracy and its Minister and most of the inhabitants are great Independents, who hate and despise even the name of Presbyterian Government'. They had also heard about the recent attack on Presbyterianism by Peter Sterry, preacher to the Council of State, in a sermon entitled: *England's Deliverance from the Northern Presbytery, Compared with its Deliverance from the Roman Papacy*. They were, therefore, forced to conclude that, since 'our Church government is in bad odour in this country, and in this town consisting mostly of Independents, Anabaptists and Separatists, such an assembly would not be welcome'.[20]

The experiences of the Civil Wars and Interregnum convinced the Dutch church in Colchester that it had had enough of the free-for-all in the religious domain. In March 1659 the elders in Colchester informed London that they looked to the present Parliament for improvement: 'we hope that the Lord will bless this Assembly for the purpose of restoring a good government and discipline in the Church, whereby the unbridled liberty of heretics and sectarians may be restrained and our discipline the more confirmed, *as in the time of the Bishops*'. This was a remarkable conversion for a Reformed community which, together with the other Dutch churches, had fought a rearguard action in the 1630s against Archbishop Laud's Injunctions to the foreign churches. By 1659 they looked back nostalgically to the period prior to the Civil Wars when the bishops had been firmly in control of the Church of England.[21]

Norwich was by far the largest of the provincial Dutch churches and it always cherished its independence from London, refusing, for instance, to accept that the Coetus of the foreign communities in London held any authority over it. As late as 1647 Norwich attempted to exercise its independence. Austin Friars wanted to call a special Colloquium in 1647 in order to assist the French communities in solving their internal difficulties. The elders in Norwich were far from keen to attend, since they had been disappointed with the treatment of their 'gravamina' during the last Colloquium in May 1646. It is probably no coincidence that, when the Colloquium met in September, Norwich chose not to send any delegates of its own, but instead commissioned a minister and an elder from Austin Friars to represent it.[22]

By 1687, however, the community in Norwich was close to dissolution: its membership had declined considerably and its minister had been absent in the Netherlands for nearly a year. The Catholics in Norwich, led by Sir Henry Benefield or Bedingfield, a leading member of a well-established recusant Norfolk family, who had no doubt been encouraged by James II's promotion of Catholicism, petitioned the town council in order to acquire the Dutch church, which they claimed was now without a lawful minister. The situation was serious enough for Austin Friars to contact the Dutch ambassador, Aarnout van Citters, and ask him to use his influence with James II in order to prevent the Norwich community from losing its church to the 'papists'.[23]

The Dutch kept their church in Norwich, and it is possible that they benefited from James's recent ambition to win political support from Dissenters, as demonstrated by the Declaration of Indulgence issued in April 1687. Even if doubt remained in Presbyterian circles as to James's motives, a number of people, like Austin Friars' newly recruited minister from Holland, Adriaen van Oostrum, considered the Declaration to be sincere:

> Moreover, many of my friends ask me what has induced me to go
> to such a country; what the fate of the Church will be; whether I
> know that the king belongs to the Roman Religion; how I would
> pray if there came war and other questions inspired by fear and not
> by reason, as his Majesty's favourable declaration sufficiently dem-
> onstrates their idleness.[24]

It was, in other words, the cumulative effect of anglicization and integration, combined with the lack of renewed waves of immigration to
mitigate these trends, that had watered down or obliterated the provincial Anglo-Dutch communities well in advance of William's and Mary's
arrival.

As I have argued elsewhere, it was not Archbishop Laud's Injunctions, issued to the foreign churches in 1635 as part of the Archbishop's
general drive for uniformity – ordering their members of the second
descent to join their parish churches – that accelerated the process of
disintegration. No evidence can be found to support John Rushworth's
and Clarendon's claims that many members and ministers of the foreign
churches returned to the Continent. In retrospect it is far more likely
that Laud's Injunctions benefited the Dutch congregations rather than
harming them. The Injunctions, therefore, served to sharpen the community's consciousness of its Reformed religion and Dutch culture, thus
giving it an extra lease of life and reinforcing its position as a 'model
community' for the Puritan opposition.[25]

By contrast, it was the chaotic years during the Civil Wars and the
Interregnum which proved detrimental to a number of the provincial
churches and harmful to the rest, including the mother-community in
Austin Friars.

The relief and optimism among the leadership of Austin Friars caused
by the convention of the Long Parliament and the fall of Laud did not
last long. The foreign churches in England met in Synod in September
1641 to discuss what actions should be taken in order to have the
Injunctions nullified and their privileges renewed. Grand designs were
drawn up for the French and Dutch churches to co-operate more closely
in future. It was decided that their triennial Colloquia should take place
at the same time, in order that the churches might consult each other.
Their Disciplines should be revised and collated into one, which should
then be translated into English. apart from the consultations, nothing
came of these plans, and, when another Synod assembled in May 1644,
it was decided to postpone the initiatives 'in regard of the sad distractions of this Kingdome, and that Parliament itself is now about a
Reformation'.[26]

Parliament's abolition of bishops, deans and chapters and the call of
the Westminster Assembly must have seemed very promising

developments from the Dutch churches' point of view. But already by
the autumn of 1642 the elders of Austin Friars had strong indications of
the mounting problems they would have to tackle during the next two
decades.

Apart from their French sister-churches, which were already embroiled in a dangerous internal conflict with strong political implications which threatened to involve the Dutch communities, their most
immediate concern was with the loss of important members to the
English parish churches.[27] Without the traditional support of the Bishop
of London, Austin Friars found it increasingly difficult to stop members
who were being disciplined by the congregation from joining their local
parish churches. Many of these churches had, of course, become far
more Reformed in character and accordingly more appealing to members of Austin Frairs. The Dutch elders could no longer rely on any
central ecclesiastical authority for assistance in these cases, but depended on their contacts with individual, English ministers. Admittedly
their connections were often excellent, but the consistory could hardly
expect to be on as close terms with every preacher in London as they
were with the Puritan divine, Herbert Palmer, minister of St James,
Duke Place.

The proliferation of independent or gathered churches in London
complicated life further for the elders in Austin Friars. Trying to recruit
a third minister for the church from the Netherlands between August
1643 and June 1644 proved difficult enough because of the Civil War,
but attempting to ensure that the candidate should not lean too much
towards the Brownists or Independents while simultaneously being reasonably 'precise' proved impossible. The consistory resolved the difficulties by choosing Jonas Proost, minister to the Dutch church in Colchester, who was a well-known and trusted preacher.[28]

In the search for a qualified minister in the Netherlands, Austin Friars
had been able to draw on the advice of three merchant members, the
elders, Adam Lawrence and Dirick Hoste, and the deacon, Nicholas
Corselis, who were already in the Netherlands as Commissioners for
Parliament. Together with the radical London merchant Maurice
Thompson, whose wife had been a member of the church since the
1630s, they were promoting a public collection in the Netherlands for
the relief of 'the Protestant Cause' in Ireland.[29]

However, not all officers of the church were able to find the time to
serve Parliament as well as Austin Friars during these years, and for
some the Dutch church no longer took first place. The deacon, Jan de
Groot, or John Great as he was known among the English, retired in
1643 because of his political involvement. He was a member of the
Brewers Company and had served the Company as a Master from 1641

to 1642 and later, in 1651, he was elected an Alderman of the City. Bearing in mind the Puritan leanings of many of the leading brewers, it is hardly surprising that Jan de Groot decided to spend all his energy in the Parliamentary cause.[30]

It was, however, not the members who became involved in politics who constituted the major problem for the Dutch church in London. They were relatively few, as compared with those who separated themselves from the community because they felt more at home within the Independent churches. Austin Friars lost a considerable number of members to the sects between 1644 and 1646, especially to the Baptists. The ministers and elders constantly had to remonstrate with leading members who defected, such as Theodore de Mayerne's wife, a daughter of the Dutch ambassador, Albertus Joachimi, and the wealthy land-reclaimer and drainage specialist, Sir Cornelius Vermeyden.

The minister, Cesar Calandrini, felt obliged to conduct a public debate with the Baptist preacher William Kiffin, in an attempt to stop members from joining the Baptists. In 1646 Calandrini, together with the elder Dirick Hoste, visited both the well-known Independent divine Sydrach Simpson and William Kiffin, requesting them not to accept any members from Austin Friars in their congregations who did not carry an attestation from the consistory. Both Simpson and Kiffin, who had spent time in exile in Holland, proved exceptionaly amenable to the Dutch position and promised not to accept anyone who was under censure.[31]

The mid-1640s were hectic years, and the consistory hardly managed to solve one problem before it had to face the next. But Austin Friars was not only on the defensive. The church entered the war of religious pamphlets in an obvious attempt to promote the Presbyterian cause, and published the Middelburg minister Wilhelm Appolonius's caution against religious radicalism, forwarded to the Westminster Assembly in October 1644. Entitled *A Consideration of Certaine Controversies at this Time Agitated in the Kingdom of England, Concerning the Government of the Church of God*, it had been written on the request of the Classis of Walcheren. At the same time, Austin Friars also attempted to further the Presbyterian cause by publishing 800 copies of its Discipline printed in English.[32]

For a while Presbyterianism appeared to have carried the day. In August 1645 Parliament decided to introduce a moderate form of Presbyterianism in London, and the City was divided into 12 classes. The system was gradually being implemented in the spring of 1646 and already in July the consistory in Austin Friars realized the possible dangers to their community inherent in the new set-up. The minster of St Mary-at-Hill, John Ley, a member of the Westminster Assembly, informed Austin Friars that his parishioners had elected one of its leading members, Nicholas Corselis, as an elder of their church. The consistory was alarmed by the possible effects of Corselis's election. It might set a precedent for other parishes keen on recruiting elders with prior experience of Presbyterian church government. Eventually the damage was contained and Corselis, who had been a deacon from 1632 to 1639, remained within the Dutch community and was later, in 1647, elected an elder.[33]

The deteriorating economic climate of the 1640s presented the Anglo-Dutch community in London with further difficulties. The cloth trade especially was faced with problems generated by the Civil Wars, and in 1649 Dutch and French weavers in the City once again found themselves under attack from the Weavers' Company, which wanted to restrict their trading. In May the Coetus decided to try to reach a negotiated settlement with the Weavers' Company before contemplating a petition to Parliament, even if the precaution of consulting a 'learned Counsell in the law' was taken. Protracted and unsuccessful negotiations with the Weavers' Company ensued until the former Commissioner for Parliament in the Netherlands, and elder to Austin Friars, Dirick Hoste, managed to procure a letter in favour of the 'Stranger-Weavers' from the Speaker of the House of Commons, William Lenthall. Hoste's excellent relations with Lenthall, who was an adherent of Presbyterianism, and a number of other members of Parliament, such as the radical London mercer, Colonel Edmond Harvey, proved rewarding in this situation. The work Hoste had undertaken in 1643, together with another couple of elders from Austin Friars, on Parliament's behalf in promoting the collection in the Netherlands for Irish Protestants now paid off.

When the Dutch craftsmen finally petitioned Parliament in December 1649, Dirick Hoste forwarded a copy of the petition to William Lenthall for 'his approbation'. The Dutch community used the opportunity to emphasize the considerable service several of its members had tendered Parliament:

> And whereas your petitioners cheerfully and willingly performe any imployement or seruice that may tend, either to the safety or prosperity of this State, and many of them have not only emptyed their purses, but hazarded their persons in the Parliaments seruice for these 7 or 8 yeares last past, and their zeale hath bin always conspicuous in the execution of any office, that might advance the tranquillity and glory of this State ...[34]

William Lenthall and Colonel Harvey obviously belonged to those 'friends in Parliament' who used this opportunity to advise the stranger communities and Coetus to forward the craftsmen's petition to Parliament through the newly established Council of State. This change of strategy made Coetus request the assistance of the radical parliamentarian minister to the French congregation in Threadneedle Street, Jean de la Marche, who just four years earlier had agitated the consistory of Austin Friars and distressed Coetus by calling for the execution of Charles I. Now, less than a year after Charles's execution, Jean de la Marche proved a man with extremely useful connections. In spite of the Council of State's decision to return the petition to the House of Commons, de la Marche was able to use his influence with the President of the Council of State, John Bradshaw, who had pronounced the death sentence on Charles I. Bradshaw recommended the petition to 'some prime men of the Parliament for promoting it'.

Meanwhile Coetus decided that, for the petition to succeed, it was necessary 'that there should need one of the Members of the Parliament to move it in the House and to call upon Mr Speaker for recommending the Peticion whereof the Originall rests by him'. Once again, Dirick Hoste used his influence with William Lenthall, who promised to recommend the petition, while another elder to Austin Friars, David Otger, approached Major-General Philip Skippon, who had already on his own account offered to move the petition in the House of Commons. Skippon's offer can hardly have come as a surprise to the members of Coetus. He was a Presbyterian who for over a decade had served under Dutch colours in the Thirty Years War and who in 1622 had married Maria Comes, a member of the Dutch community in Frankenthal. When Skippon returned to England in 1638 and became Captain-General of the Honourable Artillery Company in London, he appears to have been on friendly terms with several of the leaders of the Dutch communities, especially the brethren John and Timotheus Cruso. The former was an elder to the Norwich congregation and captain of the Walloon–Dutch regiment in Norwich, while writing extensively on military matters; the latter was a deacon to Austin Friars and a lieutenant in the Artillery Company.[35] No doubt these contacts proved crucial in warding off the attack from the Weavers Company in 1650, even if similar problems on a smaller scale reoccurred during the 1650s.[36]

Towards the end of 1646 it had become obvious that the Presbyterians, who had major backing only in London, were losing the political and religious struggle with the Independents who controlled the army. Austin Friars itself managed to stand aloof from the confrontation between the City and the army in the summer of 1647, though one of the church's recent and more exotic members, Sydenham Poyntz, played a central part in the events. The sympathy of the leaders of the Dutch community obviously rested with the Presbyterians, as can be seen from the minister Cesar Calandrini's 'Memorandum of past Events', where he, under 20 August 1647, referred to the leading Presbyterian members of Parliament who had fled the country after the army had occupied London, by stating that the 'Best members desert Parliament'.[37]

Sydenham Poyntz, who had left England in the 1620s to become a soldier in the Netherlands, had risen to the rank of sergeant-major in the Imperial army during the Thirty Years War. On his return to England his service in Germany forced him to defend himself against accusations of being a Papist. Poyntz, who must have joined Count Johan Maurits of Nassau's expeditionary force for Brazil which left the Netherlands in August 1636, claimed to be of the Reformed religion. On his return to England towards the end of 1644 or the beginning of 1645, Poyntz and his wife, Elizabeth Baijart, joined the Dutch church in London. Their attestation informs us that both had been members of the Dutch Reformed Church in Paraíba in Brazil. The date of issue, 3 May 1644, guarantees that Sergeant-Major Poyntz and his wife must have joined Count Maurits's retinue, taking ship from Paraíba in order to return to the Netherlands.

Back in England, Poyntz, like many other experienced soldiers, was warmly welcomed by Parliament. In May 1645 it gave him command over a regiment of horse and one of foot before making him Commander-in-Chief of the Northern army with the title of Colonel-General. He quickly became one of the few leading figures within the army who was trusted by the Presbyterians and, when the open breach occurred between the City and the army towards the end of July, he was given a command in London under Major-General Edward Massey by the Presbyterian leadership. That the ministers and elders in Austin Friars recognized his importance can be seen from the fact that Poyntz was included in the list of dignitaries who received free copies of the recently printed English version of the church's Discipline. When the Presbyterian resistance collapsed, Sydenham Poyntz fled to the Netherlands, from where, in October 1647, he requested the consistory of Austin Friars to provide him with an attestation.[38]

A few years later Austin Friars attracted yet another colourful character, Sir Balthazar Gerbier, military engineer, diplomat, art-agent and architect, who had probably become a member of the church already in 1617, shortly after he had originally arrived from his native Middelburg in the company of the Dutch ambassador, Sir Noel de Caron, who was a long-standing member of the London community. In 1617 Gerbier, who was newly married, lived with his father-in-law, the jeweller and engraver William Kipp, in Coleman Street. Kipp was a member of Austin Friars and this probably explains why Gerbier, who was trained as a calligraphic artist, is said to have painted the ten commandments in the Dutch church in London, 'his first rise in preferment'. On his return to England in 1649 Sir Balthazar immediately tried to establish his Reformed credentials with the elders in Austin Friars by sending them a copy of a pamphlet in which he distanced himself from his daughters, who had turned Catholic, adding, 'as I am a native Vassal of the United Netherlands, I considered it advisable to send a copy to you as my countrymen and co-religionists'. This was clearly a gesture intended to pave the way for the substantial loan Gerbier wanted to obtain from Austin Friars for his continental-style academy for the sons of gentlemen. The consistory informed Gerbier that it was in no position to lend him the £150 he needed, but added that he was welcome to approach individual members of the community. In consideration of Gerbier's good services to 'the Dutch Nation' and in gratitude for his two books, the elders decided to give him £10 as a present.[39]

The outbreak of the First Anglo-Dutch War in 1652, which made the Anglo-Dutch churches postpone their approaching Colloquium, saw Sir Balthazar Gerbier back in action. This time he claimed he was approaching the ministers and elders on behalf of Hugh Peters, in order to solicit from the Anglo-Dutch communities a petition to Parliament for peace with the United Provinces. The time and energy Gerbier spent over a fortnight in August attempting to coerce the consistory of Austin Friars into submitting this petition would indicate that he was doing his best to ingratiate himself with the Cromwellian faction for personal purposes. After consultations with their friends in Parliament, the consistory, however, decided to let the matter rest – a decision which did not spoil the church's relations with Hugh Peters, who was still counted among the community's friends a year later.[40]

Initially the First Anglo-Dutch War caused some anxiety, especially among the provincial communities. They advised Austin Friars to postpone the forthcoming Colloquium, being afraid that 'such a meeting of our Dutch communities might be misinterpreted especially by those who hold our communities in no favour'. Their worries, however, turned out to be unfounded and the Dutch congregations were never faced with anything like the hostility which the English communities in the Netherlands encountered as a consequence of the war. The fact that the Anglo-Dutch churches by 1652 consisted primarily of English people of Dutch origin undoubtedly helps to explain that. They were considered a legitimate part of the population, as opposed to the English communities in the Netherlands, which were considered alien elements and primarily consisted of recent immigrants.

This favourable position made it possible for the deacons of Austin Friars to involve themselves in charitable assistance of Dutch prisoners of war. This activity was not only appreciated but encouraged by the English government. Hugh Peters obtained £400 from the Council of

State, which was forwarded to Austin Friars, requesting the church to assist 'all Netherlanders captured during the present war and wanting travelling money'. Besides this sum Austin Friars advanced £600 from the community's own poor-box for the assistance of Dutch prisoners of war. The consistory later found it difficult to be reimbursed by the States General and was still negotiating for the repayment of the last £200 in April 1655. Austin Friars repeated its charity during the Second and Third Anglo-Dutch Wars, in 1665–67 and 1672–74, but only with the greatest reluctance. The hesitation of the leaders of the community was not caused by any negative reactions to the enterprise from either the English government or the population, but by the difficulties the church repeatedly encountered when attempting to get reimbursed by the States General.[41]

In February 1655, with the First Anglo-Dutch War concluded, the Dutch churches finally managed to organize their Colloquium. It was obviously badly needed, since Austin Friars claimed that:

> the uniformity and purity of doctrine, and the unanimous exercise of the Discipline, begin to suffer greatly from the general inroad of pernicious heresies and corruption of morals, so that the Churches of Jesus Christ will not be able to dispense longer with their spiritual intercourse and mutual assistance, without great disadvantage and injury.[42]

However, Austin Friars, like the Dutch community in Colchester, was still to face some problems with the Quakers. In May 1657 a certain Pieter Cornelisz Plockhoy, newly arrived from Holland, offended members of the church by keeping his hat on during the public prayers. Plockhoy was admonished and subsequently threatened with being reported to the magistrate, but that did not discourage him and he persisted in his behaviour. Eventually he was allowed to state his case in the consistory. He presented the ministers and elders with a document containing a number of questions, the first three being: 'Is Scripture the light or a proclamation of it? Is Scripture the Word of God or a proclamation of it? What is the Gospel?'

Plockhoy rounded off his documents by requesting the consistory to answer his queries in writing and forward them 'to some of those who the World ridicule with the name "Beeuenaers" [Quakers]'. He also used the opportunity to add a small note, this one in English, as if to underline his bilingual abilities. In it, in the best Quaker tradition, he admonished the leadership in Austin Friars to conducts its affairs in a more sober and honest fashion:

> If it is that the poor among you suffer so much want, as your pitiful cry (remember the great need of the poor) indicates, it would become you, who are aware of it (instead of being an

example of excess) first of all to lay down your ornaments in dress (against the saying of Peter: I Petr. 3, vers 3) so that your abundance may supply the want. But if it is untrue, as I believe it to be, you do wrong in exciting the people to benevolence when there is no wont.[43]

A month later the ministers and elders appear to have been able to rid themselves of Plockhoy's disturbing presence at the services in Austin Friars and his name does not reoccur in the minutes. Undoubtedly the consistory was correct when labelling him a Quaker in 1657. But what about Plockhoy's religious position a couple of years later when he published his two pamphlets, *The Way to the Peace and Settlement of these Nations* (24 January 1659) and *A Way Propounded* (May 1659)? To judge from them, Plockhoy remained close to Quakerism, even if social and co-operative schemes of a Utopian nature appear to have become his prime concern from 1658 onwards.

His first pamphlet consisted of two letters forwarded to Oliver Cromwell, probably during the summer of 1658, in which he argued strongly for a general toleration.

> which cannot be except there be a good publik-minded, and godly Magistrate, that will suffer all sorts of people (of what Religion soever they are) in one Countrey, as God (the great Magistrate) suffers the same in all Countreys of the world; which I expect first in England and so from thence to break forth (as a light) to all other Countreys and Nations.

Furthermore, Plockhoy claimed to have presented his ideas personally to the Lord Protector on several occasions, having been introduced by some members of the Council of State. His story would appear to confirm George Thomason's note in the latter's copy of *A Way Propounded*, where he points to Hugh Peters as the promoter of Plockhoy.

In this, his second pamphlet, Plockhoy fully developed his scheme for a co-operative society. As opposed to the Levellers and Diggers, he was not concerned with agriculturally based societies but, having received his inspiration from the Quakers, he wanted to create a crafts-based, mercantile co-operative society on a voluntary basis, where honesty and plain dealing were to be adhered to. In religion Plockhoy still favoured toleration, with the following proviso:

> All things wherein the Kingdom of God doth not consist (not contradicting Scripture or reason) are to be left free, as the outward form of Baptisme, the Lords supper and the like, because in the omitting of such things there seems to be more danger than in performing them.

However, in order to combat superstition and 'any human forms of Religion', the societies were to build 'a great meeting place, not onely for our family or Society, but also for all rationall men', providing seating and desks for everyone to write and read at. Here the Scripture should be read and everyone should be at liberty 'to propound somewhat for mutuall edification' – Plockhoy's roots in Quakerism had not been repudiated.[44]

At the time of the Restoration, Pieter Cornelisz Plockhoy must have realized that he had no future in England. Consequently he returned to his native Netherlands. In 1662 he managed to obtain permission from the magistracy in Amsterdam to put his ideas to the test. Together with 23 associates he was granted the right to establish a settlement in New Amsterdam (later New York). The experiment, however, turned out to be short lived. In 1664 English immigrants conquered the colony, thus bringing an end to Plockhoy's hopes of realizing his ideas.[45]

By the Restoration Austin Friars, like the rest of the Anglo-Dutch communities, had faded and lost most of its original vigour. Still, it was the ministers and elders of Austin Friars who suggested to Coetus in the autumn of 1660, that the two churches in connection with the Restoration settlement might be able to reactivate the charter granted them by Edward VI in 1550 and elect their own superintendent. Whether the leaders of Austin Friars seriously considered it possible to elect a superintendent from among themselves, as had originally been done with Johannes a Lasco, after having been under the authority of the Bishop of London for a hundred years, is questionable. But the two communities took the opportunity to exercise the right to choose. In a situation which was not without political dangers, their election of the new Bishop of London, Gilbert Sheldon, could hardly have been more sensible.

Coetus's choice of the French Royalist minister Louis Hérault, who had been recalled by the congregation in Threadneedle Street in connection with the Restoration to act as spokesman for the deputation sent to greet Sheldon, was yet another example of its considerable diplomatic skill. Gilbert Sheldon, however, an episcopalian churchman moulded in the Arminian tradition, did not take kindly to his election by the stranger churches. He desired to see the charter for himself, and, by the time the deputies returned, a couple of days later, Sheldon had obtained an order from Charles II, placing all the stranger churches under the authority of their bishops:

> In which respect he thought it unnecessary to present our election to the King, but promised in ample terms to maintaine our Churches in their priuiledges. The Coetus thought good, to lett it rest there for the present and if any of us had occasion to speake with the Bishop, in case the Bishop should first speake of it, that we then should take the opportunity to informe him more fully about it.

Thus Sheldon quickly quashed what slender dreams the stranger churches had nourished about renewed independence of the English bishops. In 1663, however, when Sheldon had been appointed Archbishop of Canterbury, Coetus appears to have been prepared to raise the issue once more with the new Bishop of London:

> It hath been proposed whether or no in our speech to the Bishop of London we should say to his Lordship any thing that should intimate that wee doe acknowledge him for our superintendent. The Company hath thought fit to suppose that as a thing granted and to expresse it in smooth words as a thing supposed.

Eventually members of Coetus had second thoughts when they examined the speeches prepared for the bishops. The title of superintendent was left out: 'The brethren thought safest for this time not to have it mentioned att all.' Considering the less tolerant climate in the wake of the Act of Uniformity, which had sent scores of Presbyterian ministers into exile in the Netherlands, among them Cesar Calandrini's son, Lewis, who had succeeded his father as rector of Stapleford Abbots in Essex, this was probably a wise decision.[46]

Later, in July 1683, Coetus found itself in a similar dilemma. The revelation of the Rye House Plot in June had seen the Protestant Whigs, among whom, as we have seen, the stranger churches were strongly represented, fall into great disfavour with the Crown. Several Whigs went into exile in the Netherlands, among them the naval contractor Thomas Papillon, a member of the French church in London and a nephew of the former minister to Austin Friars, Cesar Calandrini. The leadership of the stranger churches obviously felt a need to disassociate itself from the plot and contemplated congratulating 'his Majestie upon his happy deliverance of the late horrid conspiracie'. Initially, however, caution forced Coetus to withhold its congratulation:

> considering noe English churches have done it before, [they] thought it too great a presumption and a matter of too high a moment for our churches to addresse themselves to his Majestie on that account. But to giue most hartie thankes to Almightie God for his Majesties most happy & most signal deliverance, and shall continue earnestly to pray for his majesties long peaceable government, and to exhort our churches to continue loyall & faithfull to the same.

Later, on the advice of Henry Compton, Bishop of London, the address was formally presented to Charles II.[47]

For Austin Friars the Restoration was the last occasion on which its leaders attempted to show a measure of independence, but by 1660 the church, led by its two great but ageing ministers, Cesar Calandrini and Jonas Proost, appears to have travelled too far down the road of decline.

It was a sad but inevitable development for a congregation which had originally served as a model community for the Church of England when it was founded in 1550, and later, until the outbreak of the Civil War, had provided a working example of a truly Reformed community for English Puritans. The complex religious developments of the 1640s and 1650s had gradually exhausted and depleted the Anglo-Dutch community in London.

Apart from inroads into the community's membership generated by the sects, it was the general influence of anglicization which was making itself felt by the 1650s. At the time of the Restoration Austin Friars still had a considerable, albeit smaller, number of wealthy merchants as members. The eldership of the church, however, had changed. It no longer comprised leading City merchants and money-lenders, as it had during the reigns of both James I and Charles I, when rich financiers and operators like John de Moncy (business partner of Sir William Courten), Giles vander Put, Peter van Loor and John la Motte had served the Dutch community as elders. For these men, the church had always taken first place, as can be seen from the example of the first member of Austin Friars to be elected to the Aldermanic bench in 1648, John la Motte, who excused himself and paid the fine, while retaining his eldership in Austin Friars. His example was not followed, as we have seen, by John de Groot, who was elected an Alderman in 1651. Neither was it followed by two leading City Whigs, Sir John Frederick, who was elected Alderman in 1653, Sheriff in 1655, and who served as Lord Mayor in 1661, after having been elected to Parliament, nor by Sir John Lawrence, who acquired fame when he, as opposed to most other people in authority, stayed in London honouring his civic duties as Lord Mayor during the plague of 1665. Both Frederick and Lawrence contributed generously to collections in Austin Friars but never served the church as elders or deacons.[48] Before the Civil War that would have been unthinkable. By the 1650s they clearly felt that their obligations to the wider community in London were of greater importance than were those to the church.

Small wonder that the Toleration Act which received William's and Mary's assent in May 1689 was unable to generate much interest among the weakened Anglo-Dutch churches in England. The stranger churches had fared well during their first century, having had their privileges granted and renewed by royal prerogative and having only experienced difficulties in the brief reign of Mary and during the Laudian quest for uniformity. In the Civil War period the attempts of the Synods to have their privileges recognized by statute had failed and the stranger churches had to be content with a partial confirmation of their Disciplines from the House of Lords in January 1643.[49]

Normality for the churches, in the form of privileges granted by royal prerogative, returned with the Restoration. The religious confrontation, however, which grew out of the lack of comprehension and the accompanying hostility of Anglicanism towards Non-conformity presented the Dutch and French churches with serious problems as early as 1662. The churches were forced to mobilize their political allies in Parliament in order to be exempted from the Act of Uniformity. When William died in 1702 and the High Anglicans commenced their campaign against Occasional Conformity – the action whereby Dissenters, taking the Anglican Communion once a year, had managed to evade the effects of the Corporation Act – the Anglo-Dutch communities once again found themselves directly embroiled in English Church policy.

In the autumn of 1702 news reached the consistory in Austin Friars that a bill against Occasional Conformity was about to be passed by the House of Commons. A meeting of Coetus was called and the churches consulted the Attorney-General and their own solicitor about the possible effects on their communities should the bill go through. They were informed that the bill would put the Dutch and French churches on a par with conventicles. Consequently they decided to petition the House of Commons through a Member of Parliament. John Ward, one of their Whig friends in the Commons, advised them against this avenue. Instead they had their petition printed and distributed among members of the House in order to lobby as many as possible for their cause. In spite of Ward's assistance, they failed in their attempt to secure a majority in the House of Commons for the insertion of a clause in the bill which would exempt members of their churches. Faced with defeat, Coetus decided to take its campaign to the House of Lords – a redrafted petition was printed and distributed. This time it was successful and a clause which exempted the Dutch and French churches was among the amendments of the Lords which eventually caused the bill to fail.[50] The threat of Tory reaction, and with it the bill against Occasional Conformity, however, did not disappear. In 1711 the Occasional Conformity Act was finally passed by Parliament. This time the Dutch and French churches did not succeed in getting a clause inserted which exempted their communities.[51] The political deal struck by the Earl of Nottingham, the Tory champion of the Church, and the Whigs might well have taken the Dutch and French churches by surprise and prevented Coetus from taking appropriate action. Three years later, when the Schism Act was passed, Coetus proved itself more equal to the situation and secured the insertion of an exempting clause.[52] Thus the Anglo-Dutch communities were able to register success in what proved to be their last active involvement in English Church policy.

Notes

1. For the greeting of new rulers, see O. P. Grell, *Dutch Calvinists in Early Stuart London* (Leiden 1989), 91. For Coetus's greeting of William and Mary, see Guildhall Library (henceforth GL) MS 7412/1, fos 119–22; Coetus also greeted William and Mary a few months later at Hampton Court after their coronation (see fos 122–5). For Sir John Lawrence, James and John Houblon, and Christopher Lethieullier, see J. R. Woodhead, *The Rulers of London, 1660–1689* (London 1965). For Lawrence's connection to Austin Frairs, see GL MS 7397/8, fo. 255v. His uncle, Adam Lawreyns, was an elder in the Dutch church in London and John married the daughter of another elder, Abraham van Ceullen/Cullen (see GL MS 7397/8, fo. 98r); for the elders, see Grell, *Dutch Calvinists*, pp. 259, 263, 269. For James and John Houblon and Lethieullier, see R. Beddard, *A Kingdom without a King* (Oxford 1988), 40, 52; see also R. D. Gwynn (ed.), *A Calendar of the Letter Books of the French Church of London from the Civil War to the Restoration, 1643–1659* (Huguenot Society of London, 54; London 1979), 92–3. For the Address to William from the Lord Mayor and Corporation of London, see Beddard, *Kingdom*, p. 173, App. 4. See also J. R. Jones, *The Revolution of 1688 in England* (London 1972), 311–12.
2. J. H. Hessels (ed.), *Ecclesiae Londino-Batavae archivum* (Cambridge 1887–97) (henceforth Hessels), iii, no. 3517.
3. H. H. Rowen, *The Princes of Orange: The Stadholders in the Dutch Republic* (Cambridge 1988), 144.
4. C. Wilson, *The Dutch Republic and the Civilisation of the Seventeenth Century* (London 1968), 237–40.
5. Grell, *Dutch Calvinists*, 106–19, and GL MS 7412/1, for minutes taken down in English.
6. GL MS 7397/8, fos 200v, 207r, 215v.
7. J. J. van Toorenenbergen (ed.), *Acten van de Colloquia der Nederlandsche Gemeenten in Engeland, 1575–1609,* together with the *Aanhangsel, Uittreksels uit de Acten der volgende colloquia, 1627–1706* (Werken der Marnix-Vereeniging Serie II – Deel I; Utrecht 1872), 387–8 (henceforth *Acten, Aanhagsel*).
8. Grell, *Dutch Calvinists*, pp. 11–12; Hessels, iii, nos 2817, 2820.
9. Ibid., no. 2876.
10. Ibid., no. 3082; J. Lindeboom, *Austin Friars: History of the Dutch Reformed Church in London, 1550–1950* (The Hague 1950), 107.
11. Hessels, iii, no. 3170.
12. Ibid., no. 3225; I have not included the often short-lived and insignificant communities in Dover, Coventry, Canvey Island, King's Lynn and Ipswich.
13. Hessels, iii, no. 1807, for Archbishop Abbot's permission to establish a Dutch church in Mortlake; for tapestries, see nos 2821 and 2827. The price was lowered by £90 from the original £540. See also W. G. Thomson, *Tapestry Weaving in England, from the Earliest Times to the End of the XVIIIth Century* (London 1914), 72, 86, 88–9, and GL MS 7397/8, fos 151r–v.
14. GL MS 7397/8, fos 182r, 200r, 201v, 208v. See also Hessels, iii, nos 2797, 2872, 3117, and Thomson, *Tapestry Weaving*, 98–100, 109–10.

15. Hessels, iii, nos 3638, 3639, 3641.
16. Grell, *Dutch Calvinists*, 84; Lindeboom, *Austin Friars*, 107–108.
17. Hessels, iii, nos 2827, 3267, 3273, 3544.
18. Ibid., nos 3503, 3521. The Yarmouth church came close to dissolution in 1670 (see no. 3736).
19. Ibid., nos 3010, 3013; R. W. Ketton-Cremer, *Norfolk in the Civil War* (Norwich 1985), 351–2. Half of the £12,000 fine imposed on Colchester was paid by the Dutch community (see L. F. Roker, 'The Flemish and Dutch Community in Colchester in the Sixteenth and Seventeenth Centuries', *Proceedings of the Huguenot Society of London* (Henceforth *HSP*), 21 (1966), 15–30).
20. Hessels, iii, no. 3130; Roker, 'The Flemish and Dutch Community', 29. Peter Sterry's sermon was published in Leith in 1652; for Peter Sterry, see *Biographical Dictionary of British Radicals*, eds R. L. Greaves and R. Zaller (London 1982–84) (henceforth *BDBR*).
21. Hessels, iii, no. 3475 (my italics).
22. Ibid., no. 2908; *Acten, Aanhangsel*, 345.
23. Hessels, iii, nos 3949, 3955. For Sir Henry Bedingfield, see Ketton-Cremer, *Norfolk in the Civil War*, 170–71, 303–304, and J. T. Evans, *Seventeenth-Century Norwich* (Oxford 1979), 311.
24. Hessels, iii, no. 3955. A considerable number of pamphlets discussing James's Declaration of Indulgence and the King's true commitment to toleration were quickly translated into Dutch and published in The Netherlands during 1687 (see W. P. C. Knuttel, *Catalogus van de Pamfletten Verzameling berustende in de Koninklijke Bibliotheek* (The Hague 1889–1970), ii. 2, pp. 395–8). R. D. Gwynn thinks that the legal guarantees offered by the Declaration encouraged French Huguenots to come to England, but indicates that the refugees simultaneously mistrusted James II (*Huguenot Heritage: The History and Contribution of the Huguenots in Britain* (London 1985), 136, 140–41).
25. See above, Chapter 4, 'From Uniformity to Tolerance: The Effects on the Dutch Church in London of Reverse Patterns in English Church Policy, 1634–1647'. See also Grell, *Dutch Calvinists*, 224–48.
26. See above, Chapter 4.
27. See Gwynn, 'Introduction', in Gwynn (ed.), *Calendar*, 1–20.
28. See above, Chapter 4.
29. *Commons Journal*, iii. 184; for the three members of Austin Friars, see Grell, *Dutch Calvinists*, app. 1. For Maurice Thomson, see *BDBR*. For his wife's membership of Austin Friars, see GL MS 7390/1, under 1632 and *passim*.
30. See above, Chapter 4. Jan de Groot/de Great appears to have lost faith in the Parliamentarian cause at the time of the Second Civil War. He was fined for having equipped 'an armed foot soldier' to serve under the Royalist General, Lord Goring, in the Essex insurrection (see *Calendar of the Proceedings of the Committee for Advance of Money, 1642–1656*, ed. M. A. Everett Green (London 1888), ii. 1015).
31. See above, Chapter 4.
32. Hessels, iii, nos 2828, 2829, 2865. For Appolonius, see *Nieuw Nederlandsch Biografisch Woordenboek* (henceforth *NNBW*).
33. See above, Chapter 4.
34. GL MS 7412/1, fos 10–12, 14, 16–20, 25; Hessels, iii, no. 3067. For

Dirick Hoste, see Grell, *Dutch Calvinists*, app. 1. For William Lenthall and Edmond Harvey, see *BDBR*. For Lenthall's enthusiasm for Presbyterianism, see Evans, *Seventeenth Century Norwich*, 155–6.

35. GL MS 7412/1, fos 20–22, 25. For Jean de la Marche, see Gwynn, 'Introduction', pp. 9, 11. For John Bradshaw, see *DNB*. For Philip Skippon, see *BDBR* and Grell, *Dutch Calvinists*, 244. Nicholas Abeels and Abraham Otger, both merchant members of Austin Friars, the latter serving the London congregation as both deacon and elder during the 1640s and 1650s, were both members of the Honourable Artillery Company (see G. Gold Walker, 'Huguenots in the Trained Bands of London and the Honourable Artillery Company', *HSP* 15 (1933–37), 302–13). For John Cruso's friendship with Skippon, see above, Chapter 3, 'A Friendship Turned Sour: Puritans and Dutch Calvinists in East Anglia 1603–1660'.

36. GL MS 7412/1, fos 40–41, 63–5. See also Hessels, iii, nos 3179, 3180.

37. Hessels, iii, no. 3041; C. Russell, *The Crisis of Parliament: English History, 1509–1660* (Oxford 1981), 381. See also I. Gentles, 'The Struggle for London in the Second Civil War', *Historical Journal*, 26/2 (1983), 277–305, and V. Pearl, 'London's Counter-Revolution', in G. E. Aylmer (ed.), *The Interregnum: The Quest for Settlement, 1646–1660* (London 1987), 29–56.

38. For Sydenham Poyntz's early career, see *DNB* and J. Maclean, *Memoir of the Family Poyntz* (London 1886). No information about Poyntz's activities between 1636 and 1644 can be found in these publications, nor, for that matter, in Sydenham Poyntz's vindication of himself: *The Vindication of Colonel-General Poyntz against the False and Malicious Slanders Secretly Cast forth against Him* (London 1646). In this pamphlet Poyntz claimed that 'My constant Profession which from my first years according to the Instruction of this my native Country have been of the Reformed Protestant Religion, and accordingly have for some years been an elder of the Dutch church as is very well known' (see extract from *The Vindication* printed as Appendix B, p. 145, in *The Relation of Sydenham Poyntz, 1624–1636*, ed. A. T. S. Goodrick (Camden Society, 3rd ser. 14; London 1908)).

Poyntz must have taken up his eldership while serving in Brazil with the Dutch forces under Johan Maurits, count of Nassau-Siegen, between 1636 and 1644; see the attestation issued for him and his wife (J. H. Hessels (ed.), *Register of the Attestations or Certificates of Membership, Confessions of Guilt, Certificates of Marriages, Betrothals, Publications of Bans etc. Preserved in the Dutch Reformed Church, Austin Friars, London 1568 to 1872* (London 1892), no. 696); see also a similar attestation from Brazil for Sydenham's brother, William, and his wife (no. 693). For the Dutch in Brazil, see C. R. Boxer, *The Dutch in Brazil, 1624–1654* (London 1973), esp. 68–70, 156–7.

Poyntz received two copies in 1647 of the recently printed English translation of the Discipline of the Dutch churches in England (see Hessels, iii, no. 2896). He requested the consistory to issue him with an attestation for him and his wife in October 1647 (see GL MS 7397/8, fo. 181r; 28 Oct. and 31 Oct.)

39. For Sir Balthazar Gerbier, see *DNB*, *NNBW*, H. Ross Williamson, *Four Stuart Portraits* (London 1949), 26–60, and H. Colvin, *A Biographical Dictionary of British Architects, 1600–1840* (London 1978). Gerbier, a

native of Middelburg, who had arrived in England in 1616 or 1617 in the company of the Dutch ambassador, Sir Noel de Caron, must have married Debora, daughter of the Dutch jeweller, William Kipp, soon after his arrival. The newly married couple lived with William Kipp in Coleman Street in 1618 (see R. E. G. Kirk and E. F. Kirk (eds), *Returns of Aliens Dwelling in the City and Suburbs of London under James I* (Huguenot Society of London, 10; London 1900–08), 160, 177, and esp., 198). For William Kipp's membership of Austin Friars, see Hessels, iii, nos 2500 (320), 2868, 3341; for his activities as an engraver, see A. M. Hind, *Engraving in England in the Sixteenth and Seventeenth Centuries* (Cambridge 1952–64), ii. 210–11. For Gerbier's training as a calligraphic artist, see H. Colvin, *The Canterbury Quadrangle, St John's College, Oxford* (Oxford 1988), 51.

For Sir Balthazar Gerbier's appeal to Austin Friars, see Hessels, iii, nos 3045, 3051, 3052, and GL MS 7397/8, fo. 195r. Gerbier had also corresponded regularly with Samuel Hartlib, who had close links with the leadership of Austin Friars (see G. H. Turnbull, *Hartlib, Dury and Comenius* (London 1947), 57–61 and Grell, *Dutch Calvinists*, 245–6). The former Grand Pensionary of Holland and West-Friesland, Jacob Cats, who headed the special Dutch embassy to England in 1651–52, found Gerbier a useful contact during his stay in England (see Lodewijk Huygens, *The English Journal*, eds A. G. H. Bachrach and R. G. Collmer (Leiden 1982) 144).

40. Hessels, iii, nos 3145, 3148. For Hugh Peters, see R. P. Stearns, *The Strenuous Puritan: Hugh Peter, 1598–1660* (Urbana 1954). When the leaders of Austin Friars wanted to have some Dutch prisoners of war released in April 1653, the consistory decided to contact Hugh Peters, 'die is wel geaffectioneert en vermach veel' (GL MS 7397/8, fo. 215r).

41. Hessels, iii, nos 3133, 3134, 3157, 3161. For money received via Hugh Peters, see ibid., no. 3145. For Austin Friars's assistance to Dutch prisoners of war, see ibid., nos 3172, 3186, 3675, 3681. For Austin Friars's attempts to get reimbursed by the States General, see ibid., nos 3239, 3679, 3682, 3708. For Dutch hostility to English communities in The Netherlands, see K. L. Sprunger, *Dutch Puritanism: A History of English and Scottish Churches of the Netherlands in the Sixteenth and Seventeenth Centuries* (Leiden 1982), 391–2. Even the special Dutch embassy, which had been in England since late December 1651 in order to attempt to revoke the Navigation Act, did not encounter any hostility from the English population after hostilities had broken out between the two countries (see Lodewijk Huygens, *The English Journal*, 28, 135–6). The embassy had been greeted on its arrival by the leaders of Austin Friars, who had requested its members to attend service in the Dutch church in London, where it was given special place of honour on Sunday, 7 January 1652 (see ibid., 48); it was a communion service, which was attended by 500 people, a little below half the church's membership, according to Lodewijk Huygens.

42. Hessels, iii, no. 3225.

43. See GL MS 7397/8, fos 241r–v, 242r; Hessels, iii, no. 3388. For the full text of Plockhoy's document, see GL MS 7428/20.

44. See Peter Cornelius (Plockhoy), *The Way to the Peace and Settlement of these Nations* (London 1659), especially 3 and introduction. For George

Thomason's note, see *A Way Propounded* (London 1659) (British Library copy E. 984 (7)), 19; I owe this reference to Professor G. E. Aylmer; for Plockhoy's view on toleration see p. 11. See also C. Hill, *The World Turned Upside Down: Radical Ideas during the English Revolution* (Harmondsworth 1975), 346, and G. P. Gooch, *English Democratic Ideas in the Seventeenth Century* (repr. New York 1959), 177–8.

45. R. B. Evenhuis, *Ook dat was Amsterdam* (Amsterdam 1967), ii. 356.

46. GL MS 7397/8, fo. 257r (15 Nov. 1660); GL MS 7412/1, fos 82, 87–8. For Gilbert Sheldon, see *DNB* and R. Hutton, *The Restoration: A Political and Religious History of England and Wales, 1658–1667* (Oxford 1985), 145, 200–1; for Louis Hérault, see Gwynn, *Huguenot Heritage*, 56–7. For Lewis Calandrini, see T. A. Davids, *Annals of Evangelical Nonconformity in the County of Essex* (London 1863), 474–5.

47. For Thomas Papillon, see I. Scouloudi, 'Thomas Papillon, Merchant and Whig, 1623–1702', *HSP*, 18 (1947–52), 49–72, esp. 53–60. For Coetus's reaction to the Rye House Plot, see GL MS 7412/1, fos 112–13.

48. For Frederick and Lawrence, see below, Chapter 10, 'Plague in Elizabethan and Stuart London: The Dutch Response'.

49. See Gwynn, *Huguenot Heritage*, 96–7.

50. See GL MS 7397/9, fo. 148r; Hessels, iii, nos 4039, 4045, 4046.

51. *Statutes of the Realm* (London 1810–28), ix. 551–2.

52. Hessels, iii, no. 4137; *Statutes of the Realm*, ix. 916.

CHAPTER SEVEN

The schooling of the Dutch Calvinist community in London, 1550–1650

In 1550 the Dutch congregation in London was officially established and received its Charter. The permission of the government of Edward VI to allow the Dutch in London to form a separate *corpus corporatum et politicum* under their own superintendent, Johannes a Lasco, had been prompted by a desire of leading Protestants within the government to create a church which could serve as a model for the Church of England.[1] Given the implied emphasis of Reformed Protestantism on the ability of its followers to be capable of reading the Bible one would expect at least primary education to have been given considerable attention in this new model community.

All indications confirm that the church did its utmost to fulfil these obligations of a truly Reformed congregation. It established its own school in the precincts of the church and employed a schoolmaster, a certain Hermes Backerel. This was done primarily to secure the children of the community the proper religious instruction, as can be seen from Marten Micron's *De Christelicke Ordinancien der Nederlantscher Gemeinten te Londen*, published during the Emden exile in 1554. It recommended public examinations twice a year for children who had reached the age of five in order to make sure that parents and schoolmasters were fulfilling their obligations in catechizing them. Likewise the afternoon services on Sundays were limited to half an hour in order to provide the ministers with time to examine the older children in the articles of faith.[2]

The early death of Edward VI brought the existence of this alien, model congregation to a halt. The accession of Edward's Catholic half-sister, Mary, forced most of the leading members of the Dutch church into exile during the autumn of 1553. When the church was re-established in 1560 under Elizabeth it was not allowed to continue as a separate Reformed community with its own superintendent, outside the Church of England. The Dutch community in Austin Friars was placed under the jurisdiction of the Bishop of London, but it was still allowed to retain its own Discipline. Elizabeth and her chief adviser and Secretary of State, Sir William Cecil, saw the re-settlement of the Dutch immigrants as beneficial in economic terms only. They had no need for any model, Reformed community. In practice this limitation of the

congregation's freedom was more or less nullified through the appointment of Edmund Grindal as Bishop of London. Grindal, who had spent
five years in exile on the Continent and had befriended many leading
Protestants, believed that the Reformed churches represented the ideal
towards which the Anglican Church should strive.[3]

The re-foundation of the Dutch church in Austin Friars did not see
the continuation of the congregation's own school, nor the employment
of another schoolmaster. The extensive costs of restoring the buildings
of Austin Friars in addition to the assistance which had to be given to
members who re-settled after their exile on the Continent probably
swallowed most of the community's resources. Later the wars in the
Netherlands in the late 1560s and the 1570s meant that any resources
the congregation could spare had to go towards helping the Dutch and
Walloon who sought refuge in London.

In this situation the members of the church had to rely on the services
of free schoolmasters of whom there were many, including some of
Dutch origin in and around London. Initially this situation was not too
disagreeable, especially to the wealthier members, since this type of
education was more adaptable to individual requirements.[4] In the long
term, however, the arrangement turned out to be a disappointment to
the Dutch church. The religious instruction provided by these free
schools proved to be particularly dissatisfactory. By 1576 these shortcomings were of sufficient significance to be on the agenda of the
Colloquium of the Dutch churches in England. The attendants were
informed that several of the schoolmasters were not even members of
the Dutch churches and the religious instruction they provided was
suspect. In addition, some of the masters led an ungodly life, which
might easily corrupt the children and infect them with false teachings.
The Colloquium decided that the congregations should do their utmost
to bring to a halt the activities of these masters within the communities.
Likewise the churches were requested to maintain a stricter control over
the schoolmasters who were members of their flocks. They were specifically reminded that it was their duty to make sure that the masters were
well-grounded in the teachings of the church and able to instruct their
pupils in the fundamentals of the Christian doctrine. It was emphasized
that the elders, occasionally assisted by the ministers, were to carry out
examinations and find out which books were used for the instruction of
the children. They were also to admonish the schoolmasters to escort
their children to services every Sunday. It appears that the religious
instruction of the congregations' progeny was in disarray.

It was probably these problems in finding suitable schoolmasters for
members' children which encouraged a former elder of the church in
Austin Friars, Franciscus Marquinus, to become a schoolmaster and

open his own establishment. Marquinus, a silkworker born in Italy, had settled with his family in London around 1559 and had been among the first elders of the congregation after its re-establishment.[5] He was still making a living as a silkworker in the 1570s, but around 1580 he changed his occupation to that of schoolmaster. In 1583 he had 24 strangers' children as pupils and employed another member of Austin Friars, Peter Hurblocke, as usher.[6] About a year later Hurblocke died while trying to save the life of a pupil with whom he had gone swimming. His death created serious problems for Marquinus since he had been in charge of the teaching of Latin, a language with which the former silkworker was unfamiliar. This threatened to disrupt the teaching in Marquinus's school as he immediately informed the consistory of Austin Friars. The ministers and elders considered the matter serious enough to order one of their alumni, Livinius Cabeliau, who had returned from the University of Leiden to receive his practical training before ordination by the congregation's ministers, to help Marquinus, teaching Latin for one month while still preaching once a week to the congregation; a clear indication of the value placed on Marquinus' school.[7] The curriculum seems to have been very similar to that offered in grammar schools of the period. Marquinus operated a free school, but had in many ways extended the normal curriculum for this type of school, which would prepare its pupils for apprenticeship to a merchant, by adding some Latin instruction to the customary reading, writing and arithmetic, with a special emphasis on the teaching of accountancy.[8]

The Dutch congregation appears to have been well satisfied with the services rendered by Marquinus and was not tempted to re-establish a school under the auspices of the church during the reign of Elizabeth. This attitude endured during the first years of James's reign and accordingly only a small paragraph in the Corpus Disciplinae of 1609 dealt with the education of children. It was only laid down that the consistory should decide which books and prayers the schoolmasters were to use and that they should encourage the schoolmasters to accompany their pupils to church.

Marquinus's position as the leading free Dutch schoolmaster vis-à-vis the congregation in Austin Friars was taken over by Abraham de Cerf during the early seventeenth century.[9] Abraham de Cerf appears to have offered a standard free school curriculum in his school, including reading, writing and arithmetic, which was also typical for the so-called French schools in the Netherlands. He does not seem to have touched upon any of the classical subjects which characterized the grammar schools in England and the Latin schools in the Netherlands. As a consequence his own son, Johannes, had to go elsewhere for instruction in Latin.[10] A number of de Cerf's pupils were boarders as can be seen

from a letter he wrote to the consistory in Austin Friars in April 1634.
Life was certainly not without its problems for an ageing schoolmaster
in the early Stuart period:

> I wish to thank you for all the friendship and love which you have
> shown me these thirty-six years since I came to London, assisting
> me with your advice, and sending me your children, which enabled
> me to gain my living and educate my children honestly. You also
> enabled my son Johannes to study, so that he is now an honest
> man. And as you have done so much for me in my youth, I hope
> that you will not forsake me in my old age, otherwise I shall be
> obliged either to go across the sea to seek a better position, or to
> become a burden to the Church. The last eight years so many
> misfortunes have befallen me, that I had to spend all my means and
> to incur debts, as some of you, whom I am unable to pay, know. I
> do not as yet ask for any gifts, but hope that you will produce me
> some pupils, either boarders or ordinary schoolboys, from London
> or other places as Sir Godtschalch, Sir Lamot and others have done
> before. You might also recommend me to merchants who come
> over here from across the Sea and require lodgings either with or
> without board, or to some old men or women. Please show my
> letter to the Deacons.[11]

Abraham de Cerf had to survive on what income he could make from
his school. Obviously this task could become increasingly difficult for a
schoolmaster like de Cerf who was well advanced in years and had not
been able to afford to employ an assistant or usher. De Cerf had to find
the majority of his pupils within the Dutch community. This, together
with the fact that as an elderly immigrant to England, competition with
native schoolmasters for English pupils was severe, only served to make
his life more difficult than that of many English schoolmasters.[12] It
should, however, be added that de Cerf's close relations with the
consistory of Austin Friars guaranteed him at least a minimum of social
security. As a free schoolmaster Abraham de Cerf only received money
for the time his pupils actually spent in his school. The lowest fees were
paid for the smaller children who were only supposed to be taught to
read. This group probably included pupils who were either orphans or
whose fees were being paid by the deacons out of the church's poorbox.
This would help to explain de Cerf's insistence that the consistory
showed his letter from 1634 to the deacons. Fees for the older pupils
would have been considerably higher, according to how many of the
other subjects, writing, arithmetic and accountancy, they were to be
taught. The number who received this further education was obviously
far smaller than that of those who were only taught basic reading
skills.[13]

How exposed a free schoolmaster was to the vicissitudes of life can
be seen in de Cerf's case when in 1636 London suffered another serious

outbreak of the plague. Abraham de Cerf was forced to close his school because all the wealthier members of the London Dutch community stayed in the countryside with their families, thus removing his livelihood and forcing him to ask the deacons of the church for assistance.[14]

When de Cerf died early in 1642 it was obvious that for him like many of his English contemporaries, schoolmastering had proved unprofitable in economic terms. His death highlighted a problem which the consistory in Austin Friars had seen coming for some time: for the first time in its existence the Dutch community in London was left without a qualified Dutch schoolmaster. The deacons pointed out to the consistory that members were inquiring with some persistence where to send their children to school as there was evidently no Dutch schoolmaster capable of filling the gap after the death of de Cerf. Instead the consistory referred the deacons to an English schoolmaster, Richard Dafforne, who could teach the children Dutch.[15] Dafforne was bilingual, having kept a school in Amsterdam during the 1620s where he had also married a Dutch schoolmistress, Vroutie Jacob.[16] His proficiency in Dutch had been proved with the publication of his Dutch reader, *Grammatica ofte Leez-Leerlings-Steunsel* in 1627.[17] Later he returned to London with his family:

> After many years residence at Amsterdam in Holland, I (upon the often Importunate Letters of some Merchants, my very good Friends) resolved to pitch the Tent of my abode in London, which being effected in Anno 1630.[18]

Dafforne was certainly a man who knew the value of advertising as can be seen from the preface of his second book, published in English:

> for the generall Advancement of those that affect Commerce, by Richard Dafforne, Author of the Merchants-Mirrour, Practitioner and Teacher of this Famous and Never Dying Art of Accomptantship; as also Arithmetick, with great facility in English, or Dutch.[19]

Both Dafforne's books were written on the catechistical principle whereby an imaginary pupil asked questions and the professor answered. Should any of his pupils require further instruction, Dafforne made sure that his address was clearly indicated throughout his books. The titles of his English publications are enough in themselves to reveal the market for which Dafforne was writing. He was probably the most commercially oriented of all the schoolmasters who were in contact with the Dutch community in London during the late sixteenth and early seventeenth century, and can be said to have constituted the peak in a development within the Dutch community in London which tended to place more and more importance on the instruction of children in the skills necessary for commerce.

Parallel to this growing emphasis on a schoolmaster who could teach the children the necessary commercial skills a downgrading of the importance of religious instruction seems to have taken place. Thus the original detailed instructions for the catechizing of the smaller children from the age of five, and the older ones through the small and large catechisms respectively, were replaced in 1609 by far shorter instructions, only pointing out the general responsibilities of parents and schoolmasters.[20]

However, the services offered by the free schools did not satisfy all the needs of the Dutch congregations in England. During the Colloquia of 1621 and 1624 it was decided that where the communities possessed sufficient means, schoolmasters should be employed by the churches.[21] Without doubt the Dutch church in London was by far the richest Dutch community in England, but the church did not act on the Colloquia's decisions. In Austin Friars nothing happened until the spring of 1638, when the consistory found that the congregation urgently needed a good schoolmaster who could in particular teach Dutch to the younger generations.[22] This interest in guaranteeing that the offspring were taught Dutch should be seen in the light of the fact that by the late 1630s it was more than 50 years since the church in Austin Friars had been reinforced by an influx of a substantial number of new refugees from the Netherlands. The community in London was slowly being dominated by members who were born in England and who found it increasingly difficult to uphold not only their own Dutch identity but especially that of their children.[23]

Two additional factors made the consistory start looking for a schoolmaster to be employed by the church. Firstly, Abraham de Cerf was getting old and the church could not expect to benefit from his services much longer. Secondly, the position of precentor ('voorsinger') had fallen vacant during the spring of 1638. On 8 April the ministers, elders and deacons of Austin Friars decided to try to find a candidate who could fill this situation and at the same time act as schoolmaster to the community. This combination was common in the Netherlands. The three offices decided that the prospective candidate would be paid £20 per year for his church duties alone, whereas they clearly expected him to operate his school as a free school financed by fees from individual pupils. This was certainly not an insignificant salary when compared with known salaries of contemporary English schoolmasters.[24] It was also decided that the candidate should have a good clear voice in order to fulfil his obligations as precentor. Apart from that he should be able to teach both Dutch and French, presumably reading and writing in both languages, as well as arithmetic. The governors of the church were not only emphasizing the need for someone to teach in the Dutch tongue, but they also wanted a schoolmaster who could cope with the curriculum suitable for a merchant community. The Middelburg schoolmaster, Mattheus de Coninck, who for some time appeared the most likely candidate, fulfilled these demands as can be seen from his application for the position in May 1638.

> I, your suppliant, having heard from the Rev. Mr. Asman, residing in this town, that he thinks me fit for the post of reader (voorlezer) and clerck (voorzinger) now vacant in your Community, beg to offer you my services, being versed in the French and Dutch language, a Musician, and Schoolmaster, able to instruct the old and young according to the talents which God has granted me. I am a member of the Community, married and have one child. If you think that I would suit you, please inform me of the stipend and other emoluments connected with the post.[25]

Later another good candidate from Flushing, Johannes Engelaer, offered his services to the London congregation:

> I am thirty-two; my wife is thirty-eight years of age. I have kept a school for ten years, namely six years in the Parish of Cadsant, where I also served the Church as reader and precentor, and here in Vlissingen four years as schoolkeeper. I teach reading, writing, cyphering, and as much of music as the singing of all the Psalms. But I am especially experienced in the art of writing. My wife is able to teach the girls various manual occupations, as 'lynnen nayen, spellewerck, steken, cammen ende clavesingel spelen', besides reading and writing.[26]

None of these excellent gentlemen was employed. De Coninck probably missed his chance of employment because of his unwillingness to come across for an interview, but the whole scheme most likely failed because of hesitation among the church's leading members about the advisability of accepting further economic liabilities at the time. Archbishop Laud's drive for uniformity and the restrictions placed on the alien communities through his Injunctions must have caused the leaders of the church further procrastination.[27]

The plans appear to have been shelved until the old independent Dutch schoolmaster, Abraham de Cerf died in 1642. It was the lack of educational facilities for the poor of the congregation which reactivated the demand for a schoolmaster to be employed by the church. It is evident that the services of Richard Dafforne, the English schoolmaster recommended by the consistory around this time, could only be afforded by the wealthier members of the congregation.[28] During February the consistory of Austin Friars started to negotiate in earnest with a schoolmaster from Rotterdam, Cornelius van Ram.[29] The consistory wanted to interview Cornelius van Ram before appointing him. Apparently this was the normal procedure and, as mentioned earlier, had proved a stumbling block in 1638. Naturally the consistory offered to pay van Ram's travel expenses; he was even tempted with the promise of a gift should he decide to come across from Rotterdam. In April the consistory informed him that he would be guaranteed a salary of £30 per annum for a period of three years.[30] At the beginning of June Cornelius van Ram informed the leadership of Austin Friars that he could not accept their offer because, as he wrote, he did not find it advisable to move to England during the present disturbances there.[31] On the eve of the English Civil War Cornelius van Ram preferred the relative safety of Rotterdam to the insecurity of London.

After this second unsuccessful attempt to employ a schoolmaster, another four years elapsed before the church resumed its search for a candidate. Thus when a certain Abraham Boville applied for the position of schoolmaster in 1644 the consistory informed him that the congregation had no intention of employing a schoolmaster for the present.[32] Two years later though, in 1646, the demand for a schoolmaster to be employed by the church was reiterated:

> At the earnest request of various members of this congregation. The three offices have met and discussed the need for a good schoolmaster and they have unanimously decided that it is absolutely necessary to employ a schoolmaster. That a qualified candidate should be found and that he should receive a salary of £50 per annum for three years.[33]

It was also decided that the elders should approach the wealthier members, those who had children as well as those who did not, in order to discover what funds the church could expect to have at its disposal. In the meantime the brethren were allowed to act individually in the search for a qualified candidate. Six weeks later, on 8 March 1646, the elder, Dirick Hoste, had received several letters from Middelburg recommending two good candidates.

> Mr. Ouerbeke, a talented man but not very able in French; likewise Mr. Minet, a man (according to the letters) of such excellent qualifications that his equal can hardly be found in the Provinces. This Minet, above-mentioned, stipulates the following conditions. 1 A convenient house always free of charge. 2 The costs of his removal paid. 3 An extraordinary payment of £30 for giving up his position. 4 £30 for the first year and £20 per annum for as long as he should continue as schoolmaster to the congregation.[34]

These four demands were more than the congregation in Austin Friars could meet and on 12 March the three offices informed Minet that they were not able to pay him a regular salary, but that they could offer him a choice of £50 per annum or free accommodation plus £20 per annum for the first three years and £20 for the following three years. Besides that they could offer him £20 towards his travel costs.[35] However, it took some further bargaining before the consistory and Andries Minet reached an agreement about the emoluments of the position. Minet was to receive £50 per year for the first three years and £25 per year for the following three years. Moreover he was given £20 towards his travel expenses, and in case of his death his wife was to receive the rest of his salary for the current year. The consistory also promised to find him a suitable house and prepare it for his arrival.[36]

Andries Minet arrived in London with his family around the beginning of August 1646 and presented himself to the consistory. During the consistory meeting on 6 August it was decided that the community should be informed about his arrival and his address from the pulpit the following Sunday. The congregation should also be exhorted to send children to his school.[37]

In 1646, after two serious attempts, in 1638 and again in 1642, when the consistory had still insisted on interviewing prospective candidates, Andries Minet was employed without having been through this formality. His predecessors' unwillingness to collaborate on this issue appear to have spared him the ordeal. For the first time since its foundation the congregation had taken the significant step of employing its own schoolmaster. Minet moved into the house which the church authorities had rented on his behalf in Fenchurch Street, for an annual rent of £20. Here he was able to offer his services, teaching 'the children of Dutch parents the Dutch language, as well as writing, ciphering, and French'.[38] Andries Minet, however, was not satisfied with the house the consistory had found him. Already in November he informed the consistory that it was too small to house all his boarders. He therefore wanted to find a larger house outside the City, a suggestion with which the consistory was far from happy. The leaders of the church preferred a house in the vicinity of the church in Austin Friars. Two elders and two deacons were commissioned to help Andries Minet in his search for new and better accommodation.[39] These four gentlemen reported to the consistory on 3 December that they had found a suitable house for Andries Minet in Little Moorfields. The rent was £36 per annum. This new location of the school outside the City did not satisfy all the members of the congregation. It was argued that the school was too far out for the children who had to walk to school. Since the consistory had already rented the house, provisionally for half a year, the dissatisfied members were asked to be patient until a better place could be found.[40] Either it turned out to be impossible for the elders to find a new and more central location for Minet's school or the dissatisfaction died down, since Minet was still living in the house in Little Moorfields two years later.

Obviously the salary Minet received from Austin Friars was not enough to support him and his family. When they had paid for their accommodation they had only £14 left. This sum clearly had to be augmented by pupils who paid fees. The salary of £50 per annum for the first three years and £25 for the following three years can only have been a basic salary paid for teaching the poor children the skills neces-sary for reading. The deacons, for instance, had to pay separately for the meals Minet provided for the children who were in their care. The other children had to pay fees according to the level of instruction they requested, French and accountancy tuition obviously being the most expensive. Moreover, the pupils who boarded with the schoolmaster must have provided a substantial and most welcome supplement to his salary.[41]

Andries Minet's financial circumstances were already far from perfect less than half a year after his arrival in London. In December 1646 he tried to talk the consistory into paying the remaining rent for the house in Fenchurch Street until he could move into the larger house in Little Moorfields. He claimed that his departure from Middelburg had caused him greater loss than he had anticipated.[42] He received a negative answer to his request, but later in September 1647 the consistory granted him some money towards the repairs which had to be done on the house in Fenchurch Street.[43] The financial problems appear to have been only forerunners for the economic difficulties Minet was to find himself in from 1649 onwards. During April 1649 it was evident that Minet was unreliable when it came to paying the rent for the house in Little Moorfields, and the consistory decided to withhold his salary until he produced the proper receipts, proving to the ministers and elders that he had settled the matter with his landlord. Since it was the consistory of Austin Friars which had rented the property on behalf of its schoolmaster, the church was in the last instance legally responsible for the payment of the rent. Accordingly, during the summer of 1649 it was decided in the consistory to terminate the lease of the house in Little Moorfields in order not to be held responsible for further out-standing rent. This decision made sense since the first three years during which Minet received £50 per annum had come to an end. For the next three years he would only be guaranteed £25 per year, £11 short of the annual rent of his house in Little Moorfields. After negotiations with the landlord it was agreed that Andries Minet could take over the lease of the house.[44]

However, Minet did not remain much longer in Little Moorfields. Sometime during the spring of 1650 he moved back into the City to a house in Lime Street where his annual rent increased by £4 to £40. Fifteen months later he moved yet again, to an even more expensive house in Broad Street. This was a curious development when it is borne in mind that he was already in financial difficulties before his annual stipend decreased from £50 to £25.[45]

It was not only Andries Minet who was faced with financial difficulties. The consistory in Austin Friars already had problems collecting the money for the schoolmaster's salary before the first three years of his contract had expired. Some members refused to continue their contributions as early as January 1649, and later the same year when the first three years of the schoolmaster's contract had run out, several members refused to pay any more towards his salary.[46] In spite of friendly admonitions by the consistory these members appear to have been hesitant in their contributions and the collections for the schoolmaster's salary were regularly behind schedule during the next three years.[47] Satisfaction with Minet was apparently not the greatest within the congregation and many members chose to dispense with his services.[48]

A couple of months after the arrival of Andries Minet the elder, Dirick Hoste, suggested that the consistory elect some 'Curateurs' who should inspect the school quarterly. According to Hoste such inspections were used in Zeeland in order to get an impression of the children's progress. The consistory decided to adopt this system, but it opted for inspections only twice a year. The inspections were to be carried out by one minister and two elders in rotation, starting with the elder minister and the two most senior elders. These deputies were to form an impression of the children's knowledge of the articles of faith besides their general progress in learning and good manners.[49] In January 1649 the consistory requested the Curateurs to inspect Minet's school immediately. Rumours, apparently coming from Andries Minet's usher, a certain Martinus, had it that Minet neglected his school. During the next meeting of the consistory the Curateurs reported that they were satisfied with Minet's management of the school and the children's progress. On the suggestion of Andries Minet it was decided that for the rest of the year the school should be inspected quarterly in order to stimulate the children to make an extra effort.[50]

Only two further incidents involving Minet are mentioned in the consistory book for this period. In February 1652 the minister, Cesar Calandrini, informed the rest of the consistory that the French church in London had complained that preaching in French took place in the house of the Dutch schoolmaster. A week later it was reported by the two deputies, Calandrini and Otger, that they had spoken to Mrs Minet who had promised that these activities would be stopped.[51] Later, in November of the same year, another rather curious entry can be found. Even in the seventeenth century children were difficult to keep totally in control:

> Mr. Minet, the schoolmaster, shall be given notice through the
> elder of the 'wijk' that henceforth he shall bring his pupils out of
> the church while the Communion is distributed so that they will
> not be found yawning during the ceremony.[52]

Andries Minet appears to have managed to evade economic disaster
while he received his basic salary from Austin Friars. Six months after
payments from the church had ceased his financial position was unten-
able. He was forced to appeal to the consistory for help to repay his
debt, at the same time begging the ministers and elders to pay him a
yearly pension. His debts amounted to £239 of which £139 were what
he termed bad debts. He took the opportunity to state his case in
writing:

> But apart from the loss caused by my moving from one place to
> another, I had, after having found a convenient house for my
> pupils, to go outside the town, which some found too far, others
> too pleasant in summer, while in winter many absented themselves.
> I was then forced to look for another house in town, which I found
> still worse, as I got no Dutch, and had to depend on English pupils.
> I had also to rely upon special favours received from Englishmen,
> to prevent further misfortunes, and to obviate my troubling your
> flourishing Community with my family. Yet all was of no avail, but
> if I could have had Dutch pupils, I should have been encouraged,
> trusting that you, as lovers of study and well-disciplined instruc-
> tion, would keep up my school, and relieve me in my great neces-
> sity, burdened as I am with debts, while I have to support my wife
> and seven children.[53]

Minet's major complaint against the consistory was that it had failed to
fulfil its original promise of sending the community's progeny to his
school. It appears that only few members made use of his establishment.
The ministers and elders requested Minet to prove that such promises
had been made. The schoolmaster was unable to produce any evidence,
and it was pointed out to him that it had always been members' free
choice where to send their children to school. The elders informed him
that they had loyally fulfilled their duty towards him encouraging members to use his school. Likewise the ministers had announced his arrival
from the pulpit. Doubtless Minet had no case against the consistory, but
in order to show their compassion the elders decided to give him £100
on condition that he reached an agreement with his creditors and left
England. Clearly the consistory did not want the situation to be repeated.[54]

A month later the elders omitted the condition that Minet should
leave the country in order to receive the £100; instead they insisted that
he should provide them with security, as a guarantee that neither he, his
wife, nor his children would burden the church in the future. Eventually

Austin Friars was given security in Minet's house in Middelburg, rather ostentatiously named 'Hemelryck', but he himself was never to benefit from the assistance. He died early in January 1654, but the consistory honoured its promise and paid the £100 to his widow at the same time offering 'eenen goeden reyspennink' if she would leave for the Netherlands with her children. Two months later it was reported in the consistory that the widow Minet had left for Middelburg.[55] The ministers and elders in London could breathe a sigh of relief, having saved themselves from further trouble.

The decision to re-employ a schoolmaster by the church in the seventeenth century proved a minor disaster. Economically it turned out to be an expensive affair. At the same time the actual educational gains for the church by having its own schoolmaster appear to have been minimal. The wealthier members always preferred independent or free schoolmasters, like Richard Dafforne, while others found the location of Minet's school inconvenient, especially during the period when it was situated outside the City gates in Little Moorfields. The real benefit, if any, can only have been reaped by children of poor parents or orphans, whose education was paid by the deacons. They, at least, were secured a minimum of free education of a certain quality through the employment of the church's own schoolmaster.

Originally the congregation had started its own school in 1550 in order to improve the religious instruction of the children and 'for a wider reformation of our congregation'.[56] The individual skills acquired and subjects taught in the school were secondary to religion. When Andries Minet was employed in 1646, nearly a hundred years later, the emphasis on religious instruction had disappeared. Now the community primarily wanted a schoolmaster who could teach the younger generations Dutch. Children and grandchildren of Dutch immigrants were finding it increasingly difficult to understand and speak their 'mother tongue'. A Dutch schoolmaster employed by the congregation was thought to be the proper remedy against this tendency to become anglicized within the church. Naturally the schoolmaster also needed the skills to teach reading, writing, arithmetic and French, all considered useful within a mercantile community like the Dutch congregation in London. Back in 1550 the schoolmaster's tasks within the community had been defined primarily in religious terms; in 1646 his role had been secularized. Admittedly he still had to teach his pupils the articles of faith, but the emphasis was now on the secular aspects of the subjects taught.

Free schoolmasters, as well as those employed by the church were struggling economically during the early seventeenth century. It does not appear to have made any difference whether they, like Andries

Minet, received a basic salary or, like Abraham de Cerf, had to survive on fees alone. They were both affected enormously by fluctuations in the attendance at their schools. Falling attendance meant an immediate decrease in their income and without the occasional support from the church authorities in Austin Friars they would never have been able to continue.

It will remain an enigma why a considerable yearly salary during six years did not secure Minet a financially sound start in England. He ought to have done considerably better economically than his predecessor, de Cerf. His failure to attract children of the richer and influential members of the community paired with the financial headache he caused the church guaranteed that the consistory had no ambition to re-employ a new schoolmaster in the foreseeable future.[57]

Notes

1. See: A Pettgree, *Foreign Protestant Communities in Sixteenth-Century London*, Oxford 1986, especially Chapter II. For the Charter see: J. H. Hessels, *Ecclesiae Londino-Batavae Archivum*, Vols I–III, parts 1–2, Cambridge 1887–97. (Hessels). Dl. III, nr. 14. See also J. Lindeboom. *Austin Friars*, The Hague 1950, p. 5 and 10.
2. Marten Micron. *De Christelicke Ordinancien der Nederlantscher Gemeinten te London* (1554), ed. W. F. Dankbaar, The Hague 1956, pp. 37, 67–9.
3. P. Collinson. 'The Elizabethan Puritans and the Foreign Reformed Churches in London.' in *Huguenot Society Proceedings* 20 (1958–64), p. 537 and P. Collinson, *The Elizabethan Puritan Movement*, London 1971, pp. 66–7.
4. R. O'Day, *Education and Society 1500–1800*, London 1982, p. 35. See also W. K. Jordan, *The Charities in London 1480–1600*, London 1974, p. 219.
5. Hessels, Dl. III, no. 92. For the Colloquium of 1576, see J. J. van Toorenenbergen (ed.), *Acten van de Colloquia der Nederlandsche Gemeenten in Engeland 1575–1609* and *Uittreksels uit de Acten der volgende Colloquia 1627–1706*, Utrecht 1872; (Acten), p. 23.
6. R. E. G. and E. F. Kirk (eds). *Returns of Aliens Dwelling in the City and Suburbs of London under James I*, (The Huguenot Society of London, Publication 10), vols I–IV, London 1908, (Returns), Dl. II, p. 18 and 370.
7. Hessels, Dl. III, no. 945.
8. L. Stone. 'The Educational Revolution in England, 1560–1650', in *Past and Present*, 28 (1964), p. 44. See also O. P. Grell, *Dutch Calvinists in early Stuart London*, Leiden 1989, 108–109.
9. Hessels, Dl. III, no. 2291. At least another four schoolmasters were members of the Dutch church in London around 1617: Arnold Greve, Jacob de Pré, Conraet de Wyse and Daniel Six, see *Returns*, Dl. III, pp. 148, 166, 174–6, 183, 224.
10. Guildhall Library MS 7397/7, f. 70r. See also *Algemene Geschiedenis der*

Nederlanden, vols 1–15, Haarlem 1977–83, vol. 7, eds J. Craeybeckx, J. A. Faber, A. M. van der Woude and others, pp. 285–8.

11. Hessels, Dl. III, no. 2291.
12. See P. Orpen. 'Schoolmastering as a Profession in the Seventeenth Century: the Career Patterns of the Grammar Schoolmaster', in *History of Education* 6, no. 3 (1977), p. 186. Orpen points out that the low salary and prestige of the seventeenth-century schoolmaster guaranteed that very few young scholars saw teaching as a life profession.
13. See *Algemene Geschiedenis der Nederlanden*, vol. 7, pp. 264–5 and E. P. de Booy. *Kweekhoven der Wijsheid*, Zutphen 1980, pp. 136 and 139.
14. See R. Finlay, *Population and Metropolis. The Demography of London, 1500–1650*, Cambridge 1981, p. 111 and J. F. D. Shrewsbury, *A History of Bubonic Plague in the British Isles*, Cambridge 1971, p. 372. See also Guildhall Library MS 7397/8, f. 43v, and Grell, *Dutch Calvinists*, 110–12.
15. Guildhall Library MS 7397/8, f.105v.
16. Public Record Office, State Papers 16/305/11 XIV.
17. E. P. de Booy, 'Naar school. Schoolgaande kinderen in de Noordelijke Nederlanden in de zeventiende eeuw', in *Tijdschrift voor Geschiedenis*, 94 (1981), p. 433.
18. Richard Dafforne, *The Merchants Mirror*, London 1636.
19. Richard Dafforne, *The Apprentices Time-Entertainer Accomptantly*, London 1640.
20. *Acten*, pp. 138 and 145.
21. For these colloquia see also Guildhall Library MS 7411/2, ff. 38r and 47r.
22. Guildhall Library MS 7397/8, f. 65v.
23. Grell, *Dutch Calvinists*, pp. 111–20.
24. P. Orpen, op. cit., p. 186.
25. Hessels, Dl. III, no. 2473. The consistory, however, pointed out to de Coninck: '...But (we have) no proof of your ciphering, though we doubt not that you know the art sufficiently for all those who apply themselves to commerce.' Hessels, Dl. III, no. 2474.
26. Hessels, Dl. III, no. 2492 and Guildhall Library MS 7397/8, f. 70r.
27. See Grell, *Dutch Calvinists*, pp. 227–78.
28. Guildhall Library MS 7397/8, f. 106v.
29. Guildhall Library MS 7397/8, f. 107v. Another schoolmaster, Erastus Cleer een Cammer, living in Southwark but not a member of the church, offered his services to the church, Guildhall Library MS 7397.8, f. 106v.
30. Guildhall Library MS 7397/8, ff. 107v, 108r and 110r.
31. Ibid., f. 111r.
32. Ibid., f. 127r.
33. Ibid., f. 153v.
34. Ibid., f. 156r.
35. Ibid.
36. Ibid., ff. 157v, 158v, 159r; see also f. 159v.
37. Ibid., f. 162v.
38. Hessels, Dl. III, no. 3155.
39. Guildhall Library MS 7397/8, f. 166v.
40. Ibid., ff. 166v, 168r, 169v, 171r.
41. Hessels, Dl. III, no. 3155 and Guildhall Library MS 7397/8, f. 170r.
42. Guildhall Library MS 7397/8, f. 168v.

43. Ibid., f. 180r.
44. Ibid., ff. 192r, 192v, 193v, 194v, 195r.
45. Hessels, Dl. III, no. 3155. In August 1650 a certain Paulus vanden Velde tried to recover £10 owed him by Minet through the consistory, Guildhall Library MS 7397/8, f. 199r.
46. Guildhall Library MS 7397/8, ff. 191r and 193r.
47. Ibid., ff. 193v, 209r, 213r.
48. Hessels, Dl. III, no. 3155.
49. Guildhall Library MS 7397/8, ff. 165r and 166r.
50. Ibid., f. 189v.
51. Ibid., f. 207r.
52. Ibid., f 212r.
53. Hessels, Dl. III, no. 3155; see also Guildhall Library MS 7397/8, f. 213v.
54. Guildhall Library MS 7397/8, f. 213v.
55. Ibid., ff. 214r, 215v, 217r, see also 219r.
56. Marten Micron, op. cit., p. 37.
57. In 1674 Andries Minet, a son of the former schoolmaster to the church applied for his father's position, but the consistory was not tempted to employ him, see: Hessels, Dl. III, no. 3770.

CHAPTER EIGHT

Tribute and triumph: Dutch pageants and Stuart coronations

The foreign Reformed communities in England were particularly exposed to the religious and political uncertainties which accompanied the accession of a new sovereign in the sixteenth and early seventeenth centuries. Having been granted a Royal Charter in 1550 by Edward VI which allowed them to become an independent Reformed church under their own superintendent, Johannes a Lasco, these Reformed refugees from the Continent had been given an auspicious start. This positive reception owed much to leading Protestants within the government of Edward VI who wanted to establish a Reformed church which could serve as a working model for further reform of the Church of England.[1] However, the foreign communities' total dependence on royal patronage turned out to be a somewhat mixed blessing. Since they relied on no other legal protection, times of succession could prove particularly fraught and problematic for these communities, and the stranger churches did not need any reminder of how tenuous their situation could become at such times. Most of their members retained clear memories of the troubles and the considerable exodus which had followed the accession of the Catholic Queen Mary in 1553, only three years after the foundation of their churches. Obviously it was of the utmost importance for the exiled communities to retain royal patronage at such occasions. Accordingly, they were meticulous in petitioning new rulers for a renewal of their Charter and privileges by dispatching a deputation of leading ministers and elders from the two dominant Dutch and French/Walloon communities in London.

Apart from doing their best to retain royal patronage the foreign communities were also careful to maintain the best possible relations with the changing leadership of the Church of England and their local government. The London communities always greeted the new Lord Mayor with an oration and a considerable gift, such as an embroidered damask tablecloth with 24 matching napkins to the value of £30. Considering that a fair number of the immigrant craftsmen were engaged in the more luxurious areas of the cloth trade this was evidently not only a valuable gift but simultaneously served as a reminder of the value of the refugee craftsmen to the economic life of the City. The leaders of the foreign Reformed communities performed a similar duty when they greeted new Archbishops of Canterbury and Bishops of London. This latter duty had become essential, after the re-foundation of the foreign churches following the accession of Elizabeth when they no longer were allowed their own superintendent, but had come under the jurisdiction of the Bishop of London.[2] These occasions, however, were of minor importance as compared with the coronation of a new sovereign.

The succession of a new monach offered the foreign Reformed communities, especially the wealthy Dutch community, an important opportunity to impress and influence the new ruler in connection with her/his coronation entry into London. This was the first occasion for the new monarch to be officially presented to the population of the metropolis. In a great procession the newly crowned sovereign would set out from the Tower of London, march through the City, and finish at Westminster. Simultaneously, this was an event which provided the City of London with an opportunity to emphasize its importance to the kingdom and its loyalty to the new sovereign. At considerable expense the City would erect impressive triumphal arches decorated with allegorical paintings and statues, like those created for similar occasions in major European cities such as Antwerp, and organize dramatic tableaux and orations.[3] For the foreign communities it was of the greatest significance to be represented at such occasions in order to demonstrate their loyalty and value to the new ruler, while simultaneously emphasizing their loyalty and economic importance to the Lord Mayor and Aldermen in particular and the citizens of London in general.

In 1559, when Elizabeth undertook her coronation entry into London, most of the Dutch and Walloon merchants who had been based in the City during the reign of Edward VI still remained in exile on the Continent. Thus the Dutch community was unable to offer the leadership and financial commitment necessary for the exiles to contribute to these festivities. Accordingly, James I's coronation provided the Dutch community with its first chance to take an active part in London's celebrations in honour of a new monarch. The wealth and importance of the Dutch community in London at this time is evident from the fact that it decided to erect its own triumphal arch – one of a total of only seven – and among the most opulent on this occasion. This was an even more significant achievement when it is borne in mind that, in architectural terms, this pageant contained the finest examples of triumphal arches ever to be built in Britain.[4]

James I's coronation entry

As early as the spring of 1603 the Dutch community must have offered its services to the committee which had been established by the City a month or two earlier to take charge of the forthcoming celebrations.[5] We know from the history of the Dutch communities in England written by the minister to Austin Friars, Simon Ruytinck, who served the community from 1601 until his death in 1621, that the two most important 'inventeurs' of the Dutch triumphal arch of 1604 were a certain Christopher de Steur[6] and the minister, Assuerus Regemorter. The latter was never to see it finished since he fell victim to the plague and died on 10 September 1603.[7] Likewise, Ruytinck also informs us that the poetry for the occasion had been written by himself, Jacob Cool and 'Monsieur Thorius'.

Jacob Cool, who later served the Dutch community as an elder from 1624 to 1628, was a wealthy silk merchant. He appears, however, to have spent most of his time engaged in more learned activities, evidently encouraged by his uncle, the famous Antwerp geographer Abraham Ortelius. Cool, who was a self-taught classicist and a numismatic expert on Greek and Roman coins and medals, had already made a name for himself as a poet with the publication of his narrative poem, *Den Staet van London in hare Groote Peste*, which had been published in Middelburg by Richard Schilders in 1606. He was a member of the international republic of letters as can be seen from his correspondence, and his particular interests in Roman triumphs is demonstrated by his unpublished work, *Fasti Triumphorum et Magistratuum Romanorum Ab V.C. ad August. obitum. Additis nummorum descriptionibus Ex Hub. Golzio, opera I.C.O. conflati, anno 1588, Antuerpiae 1589.*[8]

Raphael Thorius was a refugee physician from Flanders, who had studied in Oxford before taking his medical degree in Leiden in 1591. Thorius, who practised medicine in London before he was licensed by the College of Physicians in 1596, was, according to Anthony Wood, 'no vulgar poet'. Most of his poetry was not published until after his death in 1625, including his famous Hymnus Tabaci.[9] Together with Jacob Cool, Thorius contributed a verse to the elegy for Simon Ruytinck published in Leiden in 1622 by the printer Isaac Elzevier.[10] Raphael Thorius eventually included some of the poetry he wrote for James's coronation entry into London in his continuation of his father, Franciscus Thorius's, poetry book under the titles *Italorum verba ad Regem Anglia Londini Triumphantem* and *Sermo ad Regem Angliae, halitus nomine Belgicae nationis, cum triumphans ingrederetur Londinum.*[11]

The main creative force behind the triumphal arch built by the Dutch community in 1603–04 must, however, have been the architect Conraet

Jansen who later joined Ben Jonson, Thomas Dekker and Stephen
Harrison in publishing a description of his part in this royal entry: the
triumphal arch built and financed by the Dutch community. Jansen's
pamphlet was entitled *Beschryvinghe vande Herlycke Arcvs Trivmphal
ofte Eerepoorte vande Nederlantshe Natie opgherecht in London* and
was published in 1604–05 for Jansen by the Anglo-Dutch printer in
Middelburg, Richard Schilders.[12] The pamphlet, having been written in
Dutch, was obviously aimed at the London Dutch community and their
friends in the United Provinces, and Conraet Jansen clearly expected to
sell the work himself since the front page announced that it could be
bought at his house with the pair of golden compasses in
Southwark.[13] Jansen, who describes himself as a royal servant and may
well (as has been suggested) have worked for the Office of Works,[14]
informs us that the Dutch in London decided to erect their own triumphal arch in order to 'honour the King and show their gratitude to God
and the City'. This statement is in accordance with that of the Dutch
merchant-historian Emanuel Van Meteren, who claims that it was the
Dutch merchants in London, primarily trading on Brabant, Flanders
and the Walloon areas, who were responsible for the Dutch triumphal
arch in order 'to honour the King, the Queen, the Prince and the City'.[15]

Jansen had been commissioned by a committee of 12 members of the
London Dutch church and he proceeded by appointing three experienced joiners to assist him in supervising the work; they were all members of the Dutch church in Austin Friars, among them Joos Otger who
had been a deacon to the church since 1595.[16] The architect, however,
was dissatisfied with the position the City had allocated the Dutch
community for their arch near the Royal Exchange. He found that
Cornhill Street was too narrow and hampered him in his design. Besides, the whole enterprise had to be done with the utmost haste since
the coronation and the royal entry into London was planned for 25 July
1603. The Dutch had started work on their arch on 12 April. Conraet
Jansen hired a total of 62 people, 6 carpenters, 23 cabinetmakers or
joiners, 4 timber handlers, 14 carvers, 1 turner and 14 painters.[17] Speed
was of the essence and the Dutch community appears to have been
somewhat slower off the mark than their English and Italian counterparts
who had by then already managed to hire the best painters in the City.[18]
Consequently, the Dutch were forced to seek assistance from Antwerp,
where – at a considerable cost – they managed to hire the painters
Daniel de Vos and Pauwels van Overbeke, who immediately crossed
over to London together with their apprentices and took charge of the
canvas-paintings for the arch. Both were undoubtedly painters who
could match the best to be found in London during this period and they
were assisted by another couple of Dutch painters resident in the City,

Adriaen van Sond from Breda, 'painter to the King', and Marten Droeshout. The latter was an uncle to the engraver of the same name who gained immortality for the portrait of Shakespeare prefixed to the folio edition of his works published in 1623, which also included some famous lines by Ben Jonson. The 'M.D.' who did the engravings of the Dutch triumphal arch for Jansen's pamphlet is undoubtedly the same Marten Droeshout who worked on the arch as a painter.[19] The Dutch community appears to have been well provided with good engravers. Thus, the engraver employed by Stephen Harrison to depict the arches in his work celebrating James's entry into London was another member of the Dutch church in London, William Kip.[20]

At least one of the two Antwerp masters, Daniel de Vos, who had been trained by his father the famous Antwerp painter Marten de Vos, had considerable experience in the type of work required for pageants. His father's workshop had been responsible for all the decorative works in connection with the entries into Antwerp of Francis, Duke of Anjou and Ernest, Archduke of Austria in 1582 and 1594.[21] Moreover, both Daniel de Vos and his father would have been well known to several of the leading Dutch merchants in London, especially Jacob Cool, whose uncle, Abraham Ortelius, had been recommending Marten de Vos to his merchant friends in Antwerp.[22] Another two craftsmen/artists, Daniel Papeler and 'Master Roelant Poquet, an Englishman', who is identical with Rowland Bucket, were employed to paint the woodwork on the triumphal arch.[23] Bucket was a highly esteemed and versatile painter who was later employed by Sir Robert Cecil for the decorative work in the interior of the chapel and other parts of Hatfield House.[24]

Plague, however, forced James I to postpone his entry into London and the Dutch accordingly halted work on their arch on 3 June. Like the Italians and the Corporation of the City of London, the Dutch appear to have left their arch unfinished until the epidemic subsided. In his narrative poem, *Den Staet van London in hare Groote Peste*, written in 1604, Jacob Cool informs us that seven arches had been erected 'after the Roman manner', five by the citizens of London, one by the Dutch and one by the Italians. Cool took the opportunity to point out that the Italian arch was on the small side ('hoopken cleen'), but more significantly he informs us that all the arches were left in place, unfinished until the following year.[25] We can assume, as was the case for the Dutch community in a similar situation in 1625, that watchmen were employed by the City authorities as well as the Dutch and Italians in order to secure their investments against vandalism and theft.

Cool's scathing remark about the Italian arch, which, as is evident from Stephen Harrison's *The Archs of Triumph* was on a more modest scale than the other six arches, serves not only to underline Dutch pride and rivalry with the Italians but also the chauvinism of the Venetian ambassador's statement, namely that the Italian arch 'came first, both for the excellence of its design and for the painting which adorned it'. The Dutch merchant-historian Emanuel van Meteren demonstrated greater diplomacy than his compatriot Cool when he stated that 'the Italian merchants or nation erected a beautiful arch in spite of being so few'.[26]

More than eight months later on 13 February 1604 Conraet Jansen and his collaborators were finally able to resume their work, despite the fact that some of the workmen had died from the plague, and they eventually managed to finish the triumphal arch on 14 March 1604 with very little time to spare since James's entry into London took place the following day.[27] No cost had been spared, as pointed out by Emanuel van Meteren, and the Dutch community had spent over £1,000. An impressive figure which compares well with the £4,100 the City and the Livery Companies had raised for their five arches.[28]

It is worth taking a closer look at this, the first triumphal arch erected by the Dutch community in London. Most descriptions of it have hitherto depended totally on Dekker and Harrison who both differ in some important aspects from Conraet Jansen and Simon Ruytinck.[29]

The Dutch triumphal arch was one of the largest in 1604, being 87 ft high, 37 ft broad and 22 ft long. On top of its central gable stood a figure of Providentia on a pedestal supported by the tails of two dolphins. A little lower, on both sides of a small gallery, were the statues of two boys, five ft high, each holding an orange, blue and white striped banner with the inscription 'Vivat Rex' (see Figure 8.1).[30] Its two side gables had, on the right, a statue of Fortitude and on the left one of Justice, both flanked by two obelisks each 13 ft high. Below the figure of Providence there was a picture of James I, sitting on a throne in full royal splendour, flanked by Pietas on the right and Religio on the left with the inscription: 'who has got these guards lives in safety and protection'.[31] Immediately below this picture was the main gallery which had room for the 12 trumpeters, 4 drummers and 4 flautists which the Dutch had employed for the royal entry.[32]

Beneath the main gallery were lifesize figures of Faith and Love, on the left, flanking a painting of David and Josiah. On the right were figures of Hope and Peace, the latter being an addition to the three Christian virtues, flanking a painting of Lucius and Edward VI. These virtues were obviously represented by the two Old Testament kings, as well as the English monarchs.

The pictures of the four kings flanked the main, square gallery at the front of the arch which contained a stage on which sat 17 young ladies from the Dutch community symbolizing the 17 provinces of the

8.1 Front of Triumphal Arch erected by Dutch community in London to celebrate the coronation of James I in 1604. Engraving from *Beschryvinghe vande Herlycke Arcvs Triumphal ofte Eerepoorte vande Nederlantshe Natie opgherecht in London*, Middelburg 1604

Netherlands, each elegantly dressed in the colours of the province she represented and holding its coat of arms. Immediately below this stage was a sculpture of the phoenix, an image commonly applied to James as Elizabeth's successor. Finally, flanking the main passage through the arch, which was decorated with scenes in bronze paint from the story of Solomon, were two paintings. The one on the left portrayed domestic animals revelling in green fields and clear air, with the inscription: *Venit alma cicurubus aura*. The one on the right showed scenes of wild animals such as leopards, wolves and serpents being scared by thunder and lightning coming from the phoenix with the inscription: *Sequitur gravis ira feroces*. Thus, the expectations of the godly and peaceloving subjects were represented together with the new King's expected treatment of the godless and rebellious. Considering that the allegory of Solomon was particularly popular with James, who considered himself to be the British Solomon, it is surprising that only the Dutch community seems to have chosen to apply it on this occasion.[33]

The columns at the front of the arch were painted by Papelar and Buckett to look like black marble, those at the back to look like red marble and all were topped with golden capitals. The back of the arch was totally dedicated to the expression of the old and mutual friendship between the Dutch and English as found in the crafts, navigation and trade between the two countries (Figure 8.2). On top of the central gable stood a sculpture of *Prudentia* whose pedestal rested on the tails of another two large dolphins and underneath carried the inscription *Sine Caede & sanguine*. That peaceful Prudence served to promote crafts and trade, on which the Dutch community in London depended, is further emphasized by the two statues of *Sinceritas* and *Tempus* on the side-gables and the text: *Sincera durant*. This theme was further underlined by the painting of *Diligentia*, *Industria* and *Labor* underneath the statue of *Prudentia* including the inscription: *Artes perfecit, Sedulitate Labor*.

The whole theme was illustrated by the paintings inserted above the three gates leading through the arch. The largest painting, placed over the main gate, showed the coast of England from Dover to the mouth of the River Thames with the sea full of ships from different nations, while the foreground of the picture was taken up by different fishing boats with fishermen catching all sorts of fish in their nets. This, and not the dolphins, was a reference to the fishing trade which was so important to the Dutch economy and possibly to the Dutch merchant community in London. A somewhat smaller picture above the right gate portrayed the customs-house and customs-quay in London, while another painting above the left gate showed part of the harbour of Middelburg in the Netherlands, thus underlining the importance of Anglo-Dutch trade. The inscription pointed out,

8.2 Back of Triumphal Arch erected by Dutch community in London to celebrate the coronation of James I in 1604. Engraving from *Beschryvinghe vande Herlycke Arcvs Triumphal ofte Eerepoorte vande Nederlantshe Natie opgherecht in London*, Middelburg 1604

that through the fortunate government of James the whole of
Britain would see peace and the seas would be opened and liber-
ated in order that this famous City in her wisdom might send her
merchants all over the world and receive her strangers most courte-
ously while she added to her fame and honour abroad and augmented her wealth at home. Likewise, trade would be promoted,
the courage of the craftsmen and skippers increased, idleness banished and mutual friendship maintained'.[34]

Another two smaller paintings were inserted above the side-gates, one
showing people involved in all sorts of needlework, sewing, stiching,
crocheting and so on, the other depicting spinning and weaving 'in the
Dutch manner' and other crafts associated with the cloth trade.[35] These
were, of course, all areas in which the Dutch immigrants had made
significant contributions to their host community.

The front of the Dutch triumphal arch was, in the words of the
architect Conraet Jansen, designed to show James I that he owed everything to God's providence: the unification of Britain, peace, piety and
true religion. In this it was in accordance with the rest of the pageantry
on this occasion. But as opposed to the other triumphal arches erected
in 1603–04 the Dutch included a couple of mementos for the newly
crowned King taken from the Old Testament as well as history. First,
there were the scenes from the life of Solomon already mentioned, but
of greater significance was the painting of the two Old Testament kings,
David and Josiah, the former 'the first godly King of the Jews' and a
great warrior, and the latter, 'the restorer of the decayed religion of
Israel' with the inscription *Nascitur in nostro Regum par nobile Rege,
Alter Iseades, alter Amoniades* which created a link to Isaiah, the Old
Testament prophet, who had preached strongly against religious hypoc-
risy, and Amos, the first literary prophet of the Old Testament, who had
condemned the corrupting results of peace and prosperity in Israel.[36] It
was a strong reminder to James that peace and plenty might be obtained at too high a price. It might well be a subtle criticism by the
Dutch community of James's unwillingness to continue the war with
Spain and of the peace negotiations between the two countries which
resulted in the Treaty of London in August 1604. The Dutch community in England was far from happy with the peace treaty, as can be seen
from the commentaries of its minister Simon Ruytinck in his history of
the community, where he states that the government 'in spite of having
been warned of the inconveniences of peace still went ahead with the
treaty'.[37]

Combined with the pendant painting of Lucius, 'the first Christian
King in Britain who had brought the Christian faith to the country', and
Edward VI, who 'had reformed the false teachings' of the English
Church this picture together with the inscription: *Lucius ante alios,*

Edwardus et inde Jacobus Sextus et hic sanxit, sanxit et ille fidem might also serve to emphasize the need for a further reformation of the Church of England.[38] It was quite an audacious allusion to a delicate subject by the Dutch community, especially coming as it did in the wake of the Hampton Court Conference of January 1604.[39] The fact that Simon Ruytinck spent ten pages of his history of the Dutch community covering the Hampton Court Conference is in itself indicative of the importance the community attached to this event. As one would expect, Ruytinck's sympathy lies with the Puritan side in the debate, even if he admits that the way several Puritan ministers had tackled the issue was unfortunate as well as inconsiderate, whereby 'a good cause had not been treated with sufficient delicacy and uniformity'. Instead it had only served to embitter most of those who had supported the Elizabethan church settlement. Likewise, Ruytinck deplores the result of the Conference, especially the dismissal of a considerable number of Puritan ministers with tender consciences 'to the affliction of many good Christians'.[40]

The back of the arch demonstrated the profitability of God's providence to England, that is, the importance of the Dutch community to the English nation in general and the City of London in particular. If the front of the triumphal arch served to promote the Dutch community's relations with the Crown, then the back aimed at doing the same *vis-à-vis* the local authorities and host population.

That contemporaries were impressed by the Dutch arch is evident from a tract written by G. Dugdale, *Time Triumphant, in King James his happy coming to the Crown of England*, published in London in 1604:

> Along Cornhill, they trooped with great majesty. But His Highness, being right over against the Exchange, smiled looking toward it; belike, remembering his last being there, the grace of the merchants, and the rudeness of the multitude: and casting his eye up to the third Trophy or Pageant, admired it greatly; it was so goodly, top and top many stories, and so high as it seemed to fall forward.
>
> On the top, you might behold the sea dolphins as dropping from the clouds on the earth, or looking to behold the King; pictures of great art, cost, and glory, as a double ship that being two, was so cunningly made as it seemed but one, which figured Scotland and England in one, with the arms of both in one escutcheon, sailing on two seas at once.
>
> Here, was a speech of wonder delivered too. But the glory of this Show was in my eye as a dream, pleasing to the affection, gorgeous and full of joy: and so full of joy and variety, that when I held down my head, as wearied with looking so high, methought it was grief to me to awaken so soon. But thus the Dutch and French spared for no cost to gratify our King.[41]

Apart from the description of the arch, the architect, Conraet Jansen, also provides interesting information about the royal procession. According to him it set out from the Tower of London at ten in the morning. Fences had been erected on both sides of the street. On the right, behind a rail covered in blue cloth, benches had been erected for members of the 26 Livery Companies who stood or sat with their company colours, wearing long black gowns with hoods, half red, half black, hanging on their shoulders. On the left, a fence had been erected in order to keep the public under control. When the King approached the Dutch triumphal arch he was greeted by music from the trumpeters, drummers and flautists in the gallery. Next to the arch was an enclosure where 50 to 60 of the leading members of the Dutch community were gathered, quite likely supplemented with some of those from the Walloon/French community who had contributed to the arch, in order to greet the King. Here a podium had been erected from where a young Dutch scholar, Samuel Beerens, dressed in white and wearing a laurel wreath round his head, delivered a Latin speech in verse which explained the meaning of the arch to the King.[42] Having listened to this speech, James and his retinue rode through the Dutch arch while the musicians in the gallery continued to play. The music continued throughout the day and would, according to Dutch custom, have continued all night, but for the fear of fire. This fear, however, did not stop the Dutch from having torches and braziers placed in the evening to illuminate the coats of arms of the 17 provinces on the stage; young girls had sat holding them while the King rode through. Likewise, lamps were placed within the obelisks on top of the arch (Figures 8.1 and 8.2). Holes in the obelisks were covered with coloured glass which provided a spectacular light and sight and caused crowds of people to gather around the arch, not only that evening but also for the next couple of days.[43] Evidently, the Dutch community and Conraet Jansen took great delight in the London population's appreciation of their efforts. That Jansen took the trouble to record the reaction of the citizens demonstrates the double aim of this triumphal arch. At the same time as it payed homage to the King, it emphasized the community's value to the City of London. For the Dutch the royal entry offered an opportunity to show, with considerable pride, the importance and wealth of their community to the new King as well as to their local community.

Charles I's coronation entry

The stranger communities reacted swiftly when James died in 1625. They did not want 'to be among the last' to congratulate the new ruler.

When James had succeeded Elizabeth in 1603 their deputies had greeted him as early as 23 May 1603 when he had just arrived at Greenwich. Then the learned minister to the French/Walloon church, Robert de la Maçon, sieur de la Fontaine, had requested the King to renew the privileges of the foreign churches. On 30 April 1625 they sent a deputation of ministers and elders to Charles to perform the same duty. This time their spokesman was another minister to the French/Walloon church, Gilbert Primrose, who had good royal connections. As had been the case in 1603 they also elicited a positive response from the new monarch.[44]

The planned marriage of Charles to Henrietta Maria of France caused the Dutch to plan another triumphal arch, this time apparently in co-operation with the other stranger communities, such as the Italian and French/Walloon. The leading spirit behind this initiative might well have been the merchant-poet, Jacob Cool, who had written some of the poetry for the Dutch pageant at James's coronation entry into London. The description of this planned arch, with Cool's annotations, seems to indicate it never got much further than an early planning stage.[45] According to the Venetian ambassador a celebration of Henrietta Maria's arrival was still intended by the City authorities by late May: 'Everything is prepared for the entry into this city, although they will delay the time in order to perfect the apparatus they are making which will be very costly, both publicly and privately'.[46] Due to the plague, Henrietta Maria and Charles, who had joined his bride in Dover, eventually entered the City by boat on 24 June.[47] Accordingly the preparations the Venetian ambassador was alluding to in May might well have been those the Lord Mayor and Aldermen had already ordered in April in connection with the royal entry which was to follow the coronation.[48] Consequently, the stranger communities' plans for a triumphal arch celebrating the royal marriage and Henrietta Maria's arrival were modified. The representation of Charles as a warrior King on horseback accompanied by some of his ancestors was discarded; so was the planned portrait of Charles in parliamentary dress being given the sceptre by God, with the addition of two inscriptions from Psalm 72, v. 1: 'Give the king thy justice, O God' and v. 4: 'May he crush the oppressor'. The representation of the strangers residing in England dressed according to their national customs and performing their trades and crafts were dropped as were other inscriptions from the Bible, such as Psalm 85 v. 11 and Psalm 1.[49] As in 1604 the plans for this arch indicate that it would have involved professional builders, painters and architects and 'amateur' poets from within the foreign community. Some of these concepts were eventually incorporated in the triumphal arch which the Dutch community erected on its own in connection with Charles's

planned royal entry into London, such as the representation of Henrietta
Maria's father, Henri IV, the Huguenot warrior King, and the allegory
of flowers – lilies and roses.

The Dutch community having learned from experience and the rush
in 1603–04 were not slow in taking notice of the Lord Mayor and
Aldermen's decision to celebrate Charles's coronation. On 28 April the
consistory of the Dutch church in London decided in principle that the
community should build a triumphal arch. Part of the arch should be
built in the churchyard next to the church in Austin Friars and in a
separate section of the church. Likewise, it was agreed that Charles
should be greeted by all the ministers of the church and two elders,
Seger Corselis and David Clinckenberg.[50] The former was a merchant
of considerable wealth, born in Roeselare in Flanders, who had made
his money in the linen trade; having been made a denizen in March
1616 he had served the church as an elder since 1601.[51] The latter, who
was also a merchant, had arrived in London from Aachen and had
served the community as an elder since 1604.[52]

The following day another meeting of the consistory took place; this
time it included the deacons, who were regularly called in to help take
responsibility for major decisions. The meeting decided to go ahead with
the arch and accept the request of the Lord Mayor that members of their
community who were naturalized should be excluded – presumably the
magistracy wanted these members to contribute to the arches which were
to be built by the City and the Livery Companies. The arch should be
erected in the name of the members of the Dutch church solely and
members of the French church who wanted to contribute under this title
should be welcomed. A committee consisting of four elders, David
Clinckenberg, Joos Godschalck, Cornelius Godfrey and Abraham Beck,
along with two deacons, Dirick Hoste and Hendric Pauwels, was elected
to supervise the work. Another two leading members of the community,
the merchant-poet Jacob Cool and the wealthy merchant-banker Philip
Jacobs, were elected 'to pay attention to the design of the arch' – in other
words to decide on the architecture, decoration and poetry to be commissioned in connection with the Dutch pageant. Cool would appear to have
been an obvious choice. His involvement in the 1604 arch and the plans
for the abandoned arch to celebrate the arrival of Henrietta Maria, not to
mention his great classical learning and interest in such matters, made
him indispensable. Philip Jacobs's claim to expertise in this connection is,
however, more difficult to determine, and would appear to have been of a
purely financial nature.[53]

The committee met on 29 April in order to take the necessary decisions, and some members of the committee crossed the Thames to
Southwark the next day in order to hire workers, while others started to

raise money for the enterprise under the guidance of the treasurer, Joos Godschalck. The first collection within the community raised a little over £500. Among the main contributors were Philip Jacobs and Jacob Cool, each giving £10. Their contributions were only surpassed by those of Sir Pieter von Loor and Sir William Courten, who each contributed £20, John de Moncy who contributed £15 and Lucas Corselis £12. These men numbered among the wealthiest merchants/bankers in the City.[54] Evidently, the Dutch community must have decided to ignore the Lord Mayor's request to exclude naturalized members from contributing to their arch, since both Van Loor and Courten were naturalized subjects.

The work and the expenses on the triumphal arch accelerated during May. On 2 May £20 was paid towards the cost of paint, while another 1s. 6d. was spent on mugs for the workmen and a boat was hired to go to Ratcliffe to buy timber and wood. On the same day the first official meeting between committee members and leading craftsmen and artists involved in the building of the Dutch triumphal arch took place. Eleven shillings were spent on a meal for the participants. Among the most prominent were the architect Bernard Jansen and the poet Ben Jonson.[55] The former was an experienced surveyor and architect who had worked extensively for the Howard family. Jansen had been involved in the building of Northumberland House in the Strand for Henry Howard, Earl of Northampton, and between 1605 and 1614 he had played a significant part in the construction of one of the greatest Jacobean Houses in England, Audley End in Essex.[56] The latter, apart from being one of the best known poets of the day, had already established his credentials in this particular field when he had designed the drama which took place at the first and last arches in James's coronation entry in March 1604.[57] The Dutch were evidently going for the best money could buy in London and for the first time the community decided not to rely on the poetic abilities of members in connection with the tableaux to be performed at their arch – the need for something more imaginative than a simple monologue had clearly been recognized – and the decision to hire Jonson made accordingly. Presumably, this would also have meant a change of language from Latin to English.

Most of the work on the triumphal arch appears to have been done in the three months from May to July. By far the largest amounts in salaries to workmen and for materials were paid during these months.[58] A number of lunch and dinner meetings between committee members, especially Jacob Cool (who appears to have been the leading spirit within the committee with regard to design) and the leading designers Bernard Jansen and Ben Jonson, also took place in this period.[59] By the end of July, however, plague had halted all work on the Dutch triumphal arch and the Dutch community had hired a watchman to guard what had so far been erected in Gracechurch Street.[60]

In July the Dutch church recorded its first payment to the leading painter of pictures for the arch, Francis Cleyn. On 25 July Cleyn's servant was given £6 for his master. This payment was followed by another two in August totalling £37. He was, however, not the first of the impressive creative troika of Jansen, Jonson and Cleyn, to be remunerated by the Dutch committee. That honour fell to the poet Ben Jonson, who had received a book worth 12s. three days earlier. The architect and surveyor Bernard Jansen, on the other hand, had to wait until 10 October before receiving his first payment of £15. Retrospectively, the late payment to Jansen might well be seen as indicative of his problematic relations with his compatriot employers, which eventually forced him to petition the Lord Chief Justice, Sir Randolph Crew, for assistance in getting paid in full in June 1626.[61]

The employment of Francis Cleyn as the ornamental painter for the arch is a further indication that the Dutch community wanted to employ the best money could buy. Cleyn, who had been born in Rostock in 1582, had originally been in the service of Charles I's uncle, King Christian IV of Denmark. While residing in Denmark he had painted several portraits and decorative paintings for Christian IV's pleasure-castle near Copenhagen, Rosenborg. Cleyn, who had studied in Rome and Venice, was spoken of as a second Titian by contemporaries and must have been recommended to Charles I by the English ambassador to Venice, Sir Henry Wotton, whom he had met in 1616, and Wotton's colleague in Denmark, Sir Robert Anstruther.[62] After a brief visit to England in 1623, Cleyn had returned on a permanent basis in 1625 to take charge of the designs for the new tapestry manufactory in Mortlake which had been started by Sir Francis Crane in 1621. On 18 May 1625 Cleyn was made a denizen. Charles I granted him a pension for life of £100 and built him a residence in Mortlake.[63] On his arrival in England Cleyn appears to have become an ally and collaborator of the Surveyor-General, Inigo Jones. He was paid £11 in 1625 for 'all manner of drawings for ye Arch Triumphall' produced under the supervision of 'Mr Survaior', that is, Inigo Jones. Likewise, it must have been Jones's patronage which secured Cleyn the engagement as decorator of the Royal residences, Somerset House and Wimbledon House.[64]

Cleyn's appointment to Mortlake brought him into direct contact with the Dutch church in London under whose aegis the community of Dutch tapestry weavers had been established and on whose consistory the small community in Mortlake depended.[65] When Charles I bought the Mortlake manufactory from Sir Francis Crane in 1637 Cleyn's involvement in the tapestry production might well have increased, since Charles granted him an annual salary of £250.[66]

While the design and building of the triumphal arch went according to schedule, the treasurer, Joos Godschalck, was faced with considerable difficulties in collecting the necessary funds. The wealthier members of the Dutch community had indicated their willingness to underwrite the arch in May 1625.[67] By February 1626 Joos Godschalck had to inform the consistory that he found it increasingly difficult to collect the sums promised for the arch and when he submitted his first accounts they showed a deficit of over £160.[68] Consequently, Godschalck was promised assistance from the deacons and the 'political men'; but their help seems to have been of little avail.[69] Eventually, members of the consistory were each forced to lay out £25 and wealthy members such as Sir William Courten and Sir Thomas Cotteel were requested to do the same.[70] They were probably never reimbursed. When Jacob Cool died in 1628 he made the following additional bequest in his will: 'The 25 li. disbursed by me for the Duch pagiante I give to the reparation of the Duch Churche called Jesus Temple'.[71] Even if the Earl of Pembroke did not inform the Lord Mayor of London until 25 May 1626 that Charles had decided to cancel his royal entry into the City altogether, rumours might well have been ripe before that date within the traditionally well-informed Dutch merchant community that the King had no intention of fulfilling his obligations in this respect. Such rumours would help explain the difficulties Godschalck was faced with in collecting the funds and the consistory's decision in June to provide a loan to the treasurer from the 'kerk-penninge'.[72]

Work on the Dutch arch had been resumed in January 1626, after the plague had died down, and had continued through February and March. On 28 March Ben Jonson received his payment of £10 through Jacob Cool. That Cool should have been the committee's contact with Jonson should not surprise us. Apart from their shared literary and historical interests they would have had a mutual reference point in the historian William Camden. Camden had been Ben Jonson's schoolmaster at Westminster and was a friend of Jacob Cool and his uncles, Emanuel van Meteren and Abraham Ortelius.[73] Jacob Cool also appears to have been close to Francis Cleyn since he paid him the amount still outstanding in July 1626.[74] By July close to £1000 had been spent by the Dutch community on a triumphal arch which was never to be fully finished nor used because of Charles's cancellation. As in 1604 the Dutch community's willingness to build an impressive arch and sponsor the pageantry in 1625 compares well with the overall expenditure of the City which spent £4,300 on its arches and pageants designed by Gerard Christmas and Thomas Middelton.[75]

However, further expenses had to be paid in 1627 when the Dutch community was ordered to pay the architect/surveyor Bernard Jansen £7 9s. 2d. on the admonition of the Lord Chief Justice, Sir Randolph Crew, and the arbitration of 12 men.[76] Obviously, hand in hand with the inability to secure contributions from the community towards what turned out to be a non-event went a measure of unwillingness to pay the bills in full. The cancellation of the coronation entry after huge sums had been spent on the pageants did not endear Charles I to his subjects. The London population had been cheated of a grand and popular entertainment which they considered theirs by right and the Dutch merchant community had spent a considerable sum on public relations with nothing to show for it. The canvas paintings for the arch remained in the Dutch church until June 1628 when, after an inspection by the consistory 'on a dry and sunny day', they were sold at a public auction in order to recover some of the expenses for the abortive pageant.[77] The only memento of this unfortunate investment was a model of the triumphal arch which, according to Cesar Calandrini who continued Simon Ruytinck's history of the London Dutch community, was kept in the church's library.

Fortunately Calandrini provides us with a description of the arch erected in 1625–26. Like its predecessor in 1604 it had three gates. Above the central gate were placed two paintings, one on top of the other. The top picture portrayed Britannia carrying a banner with the English cross in her right hand and a buckler in her left, while in the sea stretching out in front of her the figure of Neptune was seen riding a seahorse with his trident. The inscription: *Oceana Securo meo* was inserted above. Below this picture was a much larger painting showing Hymen sitting among clouds and angels and handing a rose to Henrietta Maria and a lily to Charles I respectively, with several inscriptions inserted below and above the painting. At the feet of Henrietta Maria and Charles more angels were spreading roses and lilies across the ground. On Charles's side, standing on a pedestal, was a portrait of James I dressed in his parliamentary clothes with a sceptre in his hand, and on Henrietta Maria's side a matching portrait of her father, Henri IV, with a sword in his hand. Above the side-gates were another two paintings. Next to James was a portrait of Minerva with Saron below her; next to Henri IV there were pictures of Mars and Vulcan.

Cesar Calandrini informs us that this was 'a nice congratulation on the King's wedding expressed in poetical terms'. He adds that it was supplemented by the representations of both the bride and groom's famous fathers, Henri IV and James I. The former, 'a bellicose hero', was accompanied by Mars, the 'president of war' and Vulcan, the maker of weaponry. The latter, a man of piety, peace and wisdom, was supported by Minerva, 'the president of learning', and Saron, 'the president of maritime law'. The smaller painting, inserted above, was in praise of Britain – a country which had no need to fear her enemies, being protected by the sea.[78]

The back of the arch was dominated by a large painting of Sapientia placed over the central gate. It showed her as a princess sitting in the sun between two pillars with curtains drawn back by two angels. Above the painting was the inscription: *Consilium regni*. Immediately below Sapientia were three maidens – Horæ, according to Hesiod the daughters of Justice – here given the names 'Legum, Iustitiæ and Pacis'. Finally, at the bottom of this picture was a representation of three sisters – Parcæ, 'presidents of life and death', supplemented by an inscription expressing the hope that Charles would continue the privileges granted the exiled Dutch community in London by his predecessors Edward VI, Elizabeth and James.

A smaller painting immediately above this central piece showed Religio, represented by a winged maiden leaning against a cross with an open Bible in her lap and with Death under her feet, with the inscription *Summi filia patris*. Above the two side-gates were paintings of Mercurius holding a money bag, and Janus, supplemented by two smaller paintings of the Penates – the household gods.

According to Calandrini, this, on the one hand, indicated the devoutness which flourished in the country – through the promotion of true religion (thanks to the wisdom of the Privy Council) and good laws and the exercise of justice and peace, which in turn served to guarantee the enduring and blissful existence of the King's subjects. On the other hand, the paintings of Mercurius, 'the president of art and wealth', and Janus inserted over the side-gates served to emphasize the value of the strangers who had enriched England with their manufactures, while the two smaller paintings of the Penates, pointed to the fact that the Dutch immigrants had fled persecution in order to preserve their Reformed religion.[79]

In other words, a considerable development had taken place since the Dutch community in London had erected its first triumphal arch in 1603–04. Gone were all the biblical allusions and the Protestant allegories. By 1625–26 they had been replaced by purely classical and rather bland statements of the importance of maintaining true religion. Henrietta Maria's Catholicism and Charles's dislike of strict Calvinism would have made this change politic. Likewise, the emphasis from 1603–04 on the community's roots and contacts in the Netherlands, then represented by the paintings of Dutch ships and fishing vessels along the English coast and the harbour of Middelburg, not to mention the pictures of the crafts and arts where the Dutch made their main contributions to the English economy, had disappeared or been made totally anodyne in 1625–26. The only references to the Dutch community were the anonymous paintings of Mercurius, Janus and the Penates. Evidently, the Dutch community realized that Anglo-Dutch relations had seen a considerable change since 1604 because of the growing mercantile competition between the two nations. Memories still lingered in the City of Alderman Cockayne's project for an English export trade of dressed and dyed cloth which had finally collapsed in December 1617, not least thanks to the efforts of the Dutch. Similarly, a growing confrontation between the Dutch and English East India Companies had led to clashes in the Moluccas which had culminated in the massacre of the English at Amboyna in 1623. These developments had served to fuel anti-Dutch sentiments, especially in London where the East India Company was actively promoting popular xeonophobia towards the Dutch as late as February 1966.[80] In this climate the Dutch community had no wish to draw attention to either their Dutchness, which was already weakening at a time when most of its members had been born in England, or their Reformed religion.

Charles II's coronation entry

Charles II's coronation entry into the City of London in April 1661 was to be the last of its kind. It was organized in the same way as its Elizabethan and Stuart precursors with pageants and triumphal arches. By 17 February the Dutch community in London had realized that the magistracy expected it to adhere to the established tradition and erect its own triumphal arch. A consistory meeting in Austin Friars felt compelled to decide that it was in the community's best interest to inform the Lord Mayor and Aldermen that they were willing to make their traditional contribution to the festivities. The consistory, however, decided not to take any action in this matter until they had been officially approached by the magistracy. Memories of the considerable sums which had been squandered in connection with Charles I's abandoned entry may well have remained fresh within the community. It is evident from the debate within the consistory, that they hoped to be able to avoid having to pay the considerable expenses involved in building a triumphal arch. It turned out to be a short respite. Five days later they received a letter from the recently established committee of Aldermen and common councilmen:

> And finding by our Records that the straingers residing within this
> Citty were desirous at their owne charges to make some shewes
> and devises against the tyme of the like Cor and to that end did

make their umble suite to the Lord Mayor and the then Committee who were at their good discretion to take such ordour with the said Straingers for and concerning the doeing and performance thereof in such sort as the said Commitee should thinke most meet and convenient. Wee haue thought fitt hereby to give you this freindly and tymely notice thereof, to the end you may take this opportunity to expresse your affections to the honour of his Majesty in such a way as shall seeme best vnto you and soe desireinge speedily to know your resolucions herein for the better ordering the rest of our preparacions ... .[81]

When the ministers, elders and deacons of the church met two days later, they resolved that it would be too difficult to find the money for this enterprise. They deputized three of their colleagues to approach the City's committee and inform it that they only expected to be able to collect what they described as 'a reasonable sum' which they promised to hand over to the committee. Their proposal was accepted with thanks.[82] Having adopted this plan, however, the consistory found that it was opposed by a majority of the merchant members of the church. This was particularly problematic since these men were expected to provide most of the cash. The merchants wanted something to show for their money and insisted that the Dutch community together with their French/Walloon friends should attempt to erect its own triumphal arch. The Dutch consistory acknowledged the importance of these members and obliged them. Accordingly a meeting took place on 7 March with representatives from the French/Walloon church. The French informed their Dutch brethren that they expected to be able to raise £175 for this purpose from among their members while the leadership of Austin Friars calculated that they would be able to raise £389. It was agreed that this total was enough to go ahead with the plans for a triumphal arch.

However, before representatives from the two churches approached the City's committee an agreement had to be hammered out between them. The French promised to raise a minimum of £200 for the arch. The Dutch were to have six representatives on the committee while the French would have only three. Initially the Dutch insisted on keeping all the materials which were used for the arch for the sole benefit of the Dutch community, but eventually they gave in to French demands that they be given a third for the deacons of their community.[83] Thus the two communities were able to make a joint approach to the City's committee in the second week of March. But with only five weeks to go before the entry was to take place they had obviously been sitting on the fence for too long. The committee had already made its plan for the royal entry and started the construction of the triumphal arches. The Dutch and French deputies were told that the committee was unable to assign them a place for an arch without spoiling what had already been initiated. Instead, it was suggested that the two stranger communities take over and finish one of the triumphal arches on which the City had already started construction. This suggestion was rejected by the Dutch and French who continued to lobby the committee to be allowed to build their own arch. It was, however, to no avail. The deputies from the two congregations were told in no uncertain terms that they were expected to collect a 'good sum' of money to be spent on the arches which were under construction and 'in case the congregations were unwilling to consent to this idea they had better remember what power they (the committee) had'. This admonition had the desired effect and the stranger churches agreed to 'collect as much as possible' from their members and hand it over to the commitee.[84] On 22 April, the day of Charles II's entry into the City, the Dutch and French paid the committee £400 towards the cost of the pageantry.[85] Obviously, members of the two communities were far from happy, having been forced to contribute to the City's scheme. They had all along wanted their own arch in order to have something to show for their investment. Not surprisingly the £400 finally paid to the committee constitutes only a little over two-thirds of what members of the two communities had been willing to contribute towards an arch of their own. Furthermore, it would appear that the Dutch deputies had encountered some difficulties in collecting their share of the £400.[86]

Thus the Dutch community made no artistic and creative contribution to Charles II's entry on 22 April 1661. According to the Venetian ambassador the City 'was decorated in the most delightful manner, a number of triumphal arches being set up in the streets at which they have laboured for many months, and in which his Majesty was entertained on his passage by music, discourses and other recreations at the cost of the city companies of London and of private individuals who have left nothing undone to show their zeal and love for their sovereign. The day ended with bonfires in every corner of the city and the most abundant evidence of rejoicing and consolation'.[87]

Having been excluded from paying their customary tribute to the new monarch, not least because of their initial hesitation, the Dutch community was nevertheless in some way indirectly associated with the four triumphal arches which the City erected for Charles II. These arches were partly designed by one of their close associates, Sir Balthazar Gerbier, architect, painter, military engineer and diplomat, born in Middelburg in Zeeland, who had arrived in England in 1616 in the retinue of the Dutch ambassador, Sir Noel de Caron, a leading member of the Dutch church in Austin Friars. Shortly after his arrival, Gerbier married Deborah the daughter of the jeweller and engraver William Kip, who had made the engravings for Stephen Harrison's *Arches of*

Triumph in 1604. In 1617 Gerbier was registered as living with his father-in-law in Coleman Street. He probably attended service in the Dutch church in London together with his in-laws who were members of the church. Trained as a calligraphic artist, Gerbier is said to have painted the ten commandments in Austin Friars.[88]

Gerbier might well have been inspired by the design of his friend Rubens of the street decorations and triumphal arches for the entry of Ferdinand of Austria, the new governor of the Spanish Netherlands, into Antwerp in 1635. This event took place while Gerbier was based in Brussels as Charles I's agent. Gerbier described the event in a letter to Secretary Coke of 20 April 1935:

> On the 7th April 1635 Prince Ferdinand Governor of the Nether-lands, and brother to Philip II King of Spain made his public entry into Antwerp. The triumphal arches eleven in number, through which he passed, were, at the solicitation of the magistrates of the city designed by Rubens.[89]

The celebration of Charles II's coronation in London was a more modest affair than the Antwerp entry of Ferdinand 25 years earlier. According to John Ogilby who wrote the poetry for the occasion and published an elaborate folio volume with engravings of the entry, only four triumphal arches were erected in 1661. One was in Leadenhall Street near Lime Street representing Rebellion and Confusion. The second was a Naval arch near the Exchange in Cornhill. The third was the Temple of Concord near Wood Street, while the fourth was the Garden of Plenty in Fleet Street near White Friars.[90] The magnitude of the Stuart coronation entries had evidently contracted by the Restoration: James had been given seven arches in 1604, and five, according to the Venetian ambassador, had been erected for Charles's planned entry in 1626, as opposed to the four offered to Charles II in 1661.

Thus the Dutch community made no direct contribution to the festivities surrounding either the first or the last of the royal coronation entries into London. At Elizabeth's accession they had not yet returned from exile on the Continent while the reticence of the consistory of Austin Friars in 1661, attempting to spare the community unnecessary expense, guaranteed that the Dutch had no other option than to contribute financially to the scheme already initiated by the City. Thus they missed a significant opportunity to pay tribute to the new monarch and to stress the importance of their community to the nation in general and the City of London in particular. However, by the Restoration, the London Dutch community was no longer as financially and politically influential and self-assured as it had been at the turn of the century. Furthermore, by then the community had become increasingly anglicized while its leaders had lost much of the religious zeal and evangelical commitment which had characterized their predecessors within the consistory. After more than a century in exile the time had finally come for what was now an Anglo-Dutch community to integrate itself into the City which had offered it refuge for all these years.

Notes

I should like to thank Jeremy Maule of Trinity College, Cambridge, for advice about Ben Jonson and Jonson's interest in pageantry.

1. The charter is reprinted in J. Lindeboom, *History of the Dutch Reformed Church in London 1550–1950*, The Hague 1950, 198–203. See also A. Pettegree, *Foreign Protestant Communities in Sixteenth-Century London*, 1986, 23–45.
2. See O. P. Grell, *Dutch Calvinists in Early Stuart London*, Leiden 1989, 86–8.
3. For this pageantry, see R. Strong, *Art and Power. Renaissance Festivals, 1450–1650*, Woodbridge 1984.
4. D. M. Bergeron, *English Civic Pageantry 1558–1642*, London 1971, 78. See also S. Anglo, *Spectacle, Pageantry and Early Tudor Policy*, Oxford 1969.
5. Bergeron, *English Pageantry*, 73.
6. De Steur, a merchant, donated a couple of books to the library of the Dutch Church in London in 1609, see Guildhall Library MS 20.185/4, f. 11. For this arch, see G. Hood, 'A Netherlandic Triumphal Arch for James I', in S. Roach (ed.), *Across the Narrow Seas. Studies in the History and Bibliography of Britain and the Low Countries*. London 1991, 67–82, for De Steur, see especially note 23.
7. J. J. van Toorenenbergen (ed.), *Geschiedenissen ende Handlingen die voornemelick angaen de Nederduytsche Natie ende Gemeynten woende in Engeland ende bysonder tot London*, Utrecht 1873, 178 and 190.
8. For Jacob Cool, see J. van Dorsten's, introduction to Jacob Cool, *Den Staet van London in hare Groote Peste*, eds J. van Dorsten and K. Schaap, Leiden 1962 and J. van Dorsten, 'I.C.O.': The Rediscovery of a Modest Dutchman in London' in *The Anglo-Dutch Renaissance. Seven Essays*, Leiden 1988, 8–20; for Cool's correspondence, see J. H. Hessels, *Ecclesiae Londino-Batavae Archivum*, 3 vols, 4 parts, Cambridge 1887–97, especially vol. 1; for the unpublished work by Cool, see Cambridge University Library MS Gg-6-9. Cool may well have re-edited this work in 1627.
9. See R. W. Innes Smith, *English Speaking Students of Medicine at the University of Leyden*, Edinburgh 1932, 223 and J. J. Keevil, *Hamey the Stranger*, London 1952, 85–6, 142, 173; A. Wood, *Athenae Oxoniensis*, ed. Philip Bliss, 4 vols, London 1813–20, 2, 378–9.
10. *Epicedia in Obitum. Reverendi Clarissimi Doctissimij Viri D. Simionis Rutingi ... ,* Leiden 1622.
11. British Library, Sloane MS 1768, ff. 38v–39r.
12. For a detailed descripton of this work, see G. Hood, 'Triumphal Arch', 69–79.
13. Croft-Murray refers to this pamphlet as a broadsheet giving the names of the painters and other leading craftsmen on the arch, see E. Croft-Murray,

Decorative Painting in England 1537–1837, vol. 1, London 1962, 213; for Jonson, Dekker and Harrison, see Bergeron, *English Pageantry*, 71.

14. Hood, 'Triumphal Arch', 73.

15. See Emanual van Meteren, *Commentarien Ofte Memorien Vanden Nederlandtschen Staet, Handel Oorloghen ende Gheschiedenissen van onsen Tyden*, London 1610, f. 96r–v.

16. C. Jansen, *Beschryvinghe vande Herlycke Arcvs Trivmphal ofte Eerepoorte vande Nederlantsche Natie opgherecht in London*, Middelburg 1604/05, A2; apart from Joos Otger they were Ian Weylant and Bartholomeus Paul; for Otger see W. J. C. Moens (ed.), *The Marriage, Baptismal and Burial Registers*, Lymington 1884, 211; for the others, see I. Scouloudi (ed.), *Returns of Strangers in the Metropolis 1593, 1627, 1635, 1639*, Publications of the Huguenot Society of London, London 1985, nos 878 and 1161.

17. Jansen, *Beschryvinghe*, B4.

18. Croft-Murray, *Decorative Painting*, 213, points out that 'Jansen also speaks of Italians as having been employed on the other arches'. This must be due to a misunderstanding of the Dutch text – 'dewyle de beste Wercklieden van d'Engelsche ende Italianen al besproken waren', see Jansen, *Beschryvinghe*, A2v.

19. Jansen, *Beschryvinghe*, A2; A. M. Hind, *Engravings in England in the Sixteenth and Seventeenth Centuries*, 3 vols, Cambridge 1952–64. 2, 341–3. Little is known about Adriaen van Sond, see E. Croft-Murray, *Decorative Painting*, 215 and Hood, 'Triumphal Arch', 82, note 38. See also L. Cust, 'Foreign Artists of the Reformed Religion Working in London from about 1560 to 1660', *Proceedings of the Huguenot Society*, 7, 1903, 60–2 and I. Scouloudi, *Returns of Strangers*, no. 409.

20. For Kip, see Hind, *Engravintgs*, 2, 210–11, Cust, 68 and above, Chapter 6 'From Persecution to Integration: The Decline of the Anglo-Dutch Communities in England, 1648–1702'.

21. See A. von Würzbach, *Niederländisches Künstler-Lexikon*, Wien 1910, 2, 820–21; for the archduke of Austria's triumphal entry into Antwerp and the work of Marten de Vos and his family, see Antoinette Doutrepont, 'Martin de Vos et l'Entrée triomphale de l'Archiduc Ernest d'Autriche à Anvers en 1594', *Bulletin de L'Institut Historique Belge de Rome*, 1937, 125–97; see also J. Bochius, *Descriptio publicae gratulationis spectaculorum et ludorum, in adventu Sereniss. Principis Ernesti Archiducis Austria ...* Antwerp 1595. For the Duke of Anjou's entry, see *Joyeuse et magnifique Entrée de Monseigneur François fils de France ... en sa trés renommée ville d'Anwers*, Antwerp 1582. For the painter Pauwels van Overbeke, see Croft-Murray, *Decorative Painting*, 214 and P. Rombauts and T. van Lerius, *De Liggeren en andere Historische Archieven der Antwerpsche Sint Lucasgilde*, Antwerp 1872, 249 and 652.

22. Hessels, *Ecclesiae*, 1, nos 330–31. Marten de Vos appears to have been actively involved in the Reformed, anti-Catholic propaganda which was produced in the Netherlands in the 1580s, see *Antwerpen, verhall van een metropool 16de–17de eeuw*, Ghent 1993, 275.

23. Jansen, *Beschryvinghe*, A2v; see also Croft-Murray, *Decorative Painting*, 194 and 214.

24. See E. Auerbach, *Paintings and Sculpture at Hatfield House*, London 1971, 103–105.

25. For Cool's remarks, see *Den Staet van London*, 27–8. Bergeron's statement that the arches were taken down thus appears to be mistaken, see *English Pageantry*, 72.

26. For the Venetian ambassador's view, see *C.S.P. Venetian*, 1603–07, no. 201, 26 March 1604, see also Bergeron, *English Pageants*, 78; for Emanual van Meteren, see *Commentarien Ofte Memorien van-den Nederlandtschen Staet, Handel, Oorloghen ende Gheschiedenissen*, f. 96r–v.

27. Jansen, *Beschryvinghe*, B4.

28. Emanuel van Meteren gives the figure of 10,000 Guilders, see *Commentarien Ofte Memorien*, f. 96r–v. For the sum raised by the City, see Bergeron, *English Pageantry*, 73.

29. For recent descriptions depending on Thomas Dekker and Stephen Harrison, see Bergeron, *English Pageants*, 78–80 and G. Parry, *The Golden Age Restor'd*, Manchester 1981, 10. The only exception being Hood, 'Triumphal Arch' 74–9.

30. Jansen, *Beschryvinghe*, A3r and Toorenenbergen, *Gheschiedenissen*, 190. Parry is mistaken when claiming that the dolphins (described by him as two great fish) are symbols of the important Dutch fishing trade, see Parry, *Golden Age*, 10.

31. Jansen, *Beschryvinghe*, B1r, Bergeron relying on Harrison and Dekker has been unable to identify these figures, see *English Pageantry*, 79.

32. Jansen, *Beschryvinghe*, B3r.

33. Parry, *Golden Age*, 21. In their address and petition to James at Greenwich on 23 May 1603 the exiled Reformed communities in London had compared James with Solomon, see Toorenenbergen, *Gheschiedenissen*, 175.

34. Jansen, *Beschryvinghe*, B2r and v (my translation).

35. Jansen, *Beschryvinghe*, B2v.

36. Thus, the Dutch triumphal arch does not fit Parry's general description of James's royal entry; 'Stylistically the Entertainment had demonstrated a sophisticated handling of classical mythology and displayed a notable inclination to cast moral and political wisdom in classical moulds. Biblical material was scarcely employed at all, in contrast with Elizabeth's entry when the purity of Reformed religion was a dominant theme.' See Parry, *Golden Age*, 20. See also Bergeron, *English Pageantry*, 89.

37. Toorenenbergen, *Gheschiedenissen*, 200; see also G. Davies, *The Early Stuarts 1603–1660*, Oxford 1976, 47–51.

38. Jansen, *Beschryvinghe*, A4v–Bv, and Toorenenbergen, *Gheschiedenissen*, 191.

39. For a recent treatment of the Hampton Court Conference, see N. Tyacke, *Anti-Calvinists. The Rise of English Arminianism c. 1590–1640*, Oxford 1987, 9–28.

40. See Toorenenbergen *Gheschiedenissen*, 179–89, especially 179 and 187.

41. Dugdale's pamphlet is reprinted in C. H. Firth (ed.), *Stuart Tracts 1603–1693*, Westminster, 79.

42. Jansen, *Beschryvinghe*, B3r; see also Emanuel van Meteren, *Commentarien Ofte Memorien*, f. 96v, who is more specific, claiming that it was the principal Dutch merchants who stood within this enclosure. The dramatic form chosen by the Dutch on this occasion, a monologue given by a child, appears to have been more in line with what happened at Elizabeth's entry than with the rest of the 1604-pageant where dramatic dialogue had come to dominate, see Bergeron, *English Pageantry*, 89.

43. Jansen, *Beschryvinghe*, B4r.
44. Toorenenbergen, *Gheschiedenissen*, 172–7 and 473–9.
45. Hessels, *Ecclesiae*, 1, 369.
46. *C.S.P. Venetian*, 1625–26, no. 73, 51.
47. *C.S.P. Venetian*, 1625–26, no. 125, 87.
48. Bergeron, *English Pageantry*, 106–107 and D. M. Bergeron, Charles I's Royal Entries into London', *Guildhall Miscellany*, 3, 1970, 91–2.
49. See Hessels, *Ecclesiae*, 1, 369.
50. Guildhall Library MS 7397/7, f. 124r.
51. Grell, *Dutch Calvinists*, 161, 260; see also W. Page (ed.), *Letters of Denization and Acts of Naturalization for Aliens in England, 1603–1700*, Publications of the Huguenot Society, Lymington 1893, 23, and J. Briels, *Zuid-Nederlanders in de Republiek 1572–1630*, Sint-Niklaas, 1985, 41.
52. Grell, *Dutch Calvinists*, 259, 272.
53. Guildhall Library MS 7397/7, f. 124r (29 April 1625). For Philip Jacobs, see Grell, *Dutch Calvinists*, 4, 46, 150, 167, 263.
54. Guildhall Library MS 7390/1, ff. 227–31; for these wealthy contributors see Grell, *Dutch Calvinists*, and R. Ashton, *The Crown and the Money Market, 1603–1643*, Oxford 1968.
55. Guildhall Library MS 7390/1, f. 232 (2 May 1625); see also Hessels, *Ecclesiae*, 3, no. 1852, where Bernard Jansen specifically refers to the payment of 'the Poett'.
56. H. Colvin, *A Biographical Dictionary of British Architects 1600–1840*, London 1978, 455.
57. Bergeron, *English Pageantry*, 71.
58. Guildhall Library MS 7390/1, ff. 232–42.
59. Guildhall Library MS 7390/1, ff. 232–42: 3 May with Bernard Jansen and Ben Jonson; 24 May with Bernard Jansen; 17 June with Bernard Jansen and Ben Jonson; 20 June with Bernard Jansen, Ben Jonson and Jacob Cool; 29 June with Ben Jonson and Bernard Jansen; 9 July with Bernard Jansen; 22 July with Bernard Jansen and Jacob Cool.
60. Guildhall Library MS 7390/1, ff. 232–42; the watchman was paid 8s. on 27 February 1626 for 8 months' work; for the plague of 1625 and the Dutch community, see below, Chapter 10, 'Plague in Elizabethan and Stuart London: The Dutch Response'.
61. Guildhall Library MS 7390/1, ff. 232–42 (10 October 1625); for Jansen's petiton, see Hessels, *Ecclesiae*, 3, no. 1852.
62. For Cleyn's work in Denmark, see F. Beckett, *Kristian IV og Malerkunsten*, Copenhagen 1937 and M. Stein, *Christian den Fjerdes Billedverden*, Copenhagen 1987, especially pp. 141–5.
63. W. Page, *Letters of Denization*, 38 and *DNB*.
64. Croft-Murray, *Decorative Painting*, 1, 196 and Peter Thornton and Maurice Tomlin, 'Franz Cleyn at Ham House', *National Trust Studies*, 1980, 21–34 especially 23–4.
65. For Archbishop Abbot's permission to establish a Dutch church in Mortlake, see Hessels, *Ecclesiae*, 3, no. 1807.
66. See Croft-Murray, *Decorative Painting*, 1, 196; for the problems the Mortlake community faced during the Civil War, see above, Chapter 6, 'From Persecution to Toleration: The Decline of the Anglo–Dutch Communities in England, 1642–1702'.
67. Guildhall Library MS 7397/7, ff. 124r–v.

68. Guildhall Library MS 7397/7, ff. 131r and 132r; for the deficit, see Guildhall Library MS 7390/1, ff. 232–42.
69. For Godschalck's problems in collecting the money, see Guildhall Library MS 7397/7, ff. 134r and 135v; for the 'political men', see Grell, *Dutch Calvinists*, 86–7.
70. Guildhall Library MS 7397/7, ff. 136v–137r.
71. Hessels, *Ecclesiae*, 1, LXI.
72. Guildhall Library MS 7397/7, f. 137v; for Charles's cancellation, see Bergeron, *English Pageantry*, 107–108.
73. Guildhall Library MS 7390/1, ff. 232–42; for Camden's friendship with Cool, Ortelius and Van Meteren, see Hessels, *Ecclesiae*, 1, nos 162, 262 and 286; for Ben Jonson and Camden, see *Aubrey's 'Brief Lives', 1669–1696*, ed. A. Clark, Oxford 1898, 2 vols, 2, 11–17.
74. Guildhall Library MS 7397/7, f. 137r (8 June 1626); Cool was instructed to use his contribution of £25 to pay 'Franciscus Cleyn, Schilder'; Cleyn was paid 3 July, see Guildhall Library MS 7390/1, f. 242.
75. See Bergeron, *English Pageantry*, 108–109 and his 'Royal Entries', 93; for the Dutch expenses, see Guildhall Library MS 7390/1, ff. 232–42.
76. See Hessels, *Ecclesiae*, 3, no. 1852; and Guildhall Library MS 7397/7, ff. 137r and 148v–149r and Guildhall Library MS 7390/1, f. 260.
77. Guildhall Library MS 7397/7, ff. 191r–v. The City of London also auctioned off such artefacts in order to recoup some of its expenses, see Bergeron, *English Pageantry*, 73.
78. Toorenenbergen, *Gheschiedenissen*, 480–82.
79. Toorenenbergen, *Gheschiedenissen*, 482–3.
80. Grell, *Dutch Calvinists*, 149–53.
81. Hessels, *Ecclesiae*, 3, no. 3533. This letter was addressed to a group of merchant strangers of whom the overwhelming majority were elders of the Dutch church in London.
82. Guildhall Library MS 7397/8, f. 258r (24 and 28 February 1661).
83. Guildhall Library MS 7397/8, ff. 258r–v; for the list of the Dutch contributors, see ff. 260r–v.
84. Guildhall Library MS 7397/8, ff. 258v–59r.
85. Hessels, *Ecclesiae*, 3, no. 3536, see also nos 3534–5.
86. Guildhall Library MS 7397/8, f. 268v (5 December 1661).
87. *C.S.P. Venetian*, 1659–61, no. 340, 286.
88. Gerbier designed the triumphal arches together with Peter Mills, see Croft-Murray, *Decorative Painting*, 1, 202; see also *DNB* and above, Chapter 6, 'From Persecution to Integration: The Decline of the Anglo-Dutch Communities in England, 1642–1702'.
89. W. N. Sainsbury (ed.), *Original Unpublished Papers Illustrative of the Life of Sir Peter Paul Rubens, as an Artist and a Diplomatist*, London 1859, 187. For Rubens's design, see J. R. Martin, *The Decorations for the Pompa Introitus Ferdinandi*, London 1972.
90. J. Ogilby, *The Entertainment of his Most Excellent Majestie Charles II, in his Passage through the City of London to his Coronation*, London 1662; see also E. Halfpenny, 'The Citie's Loyalty Display'd', *Guildhall Miscellany*, 10, 1959, 19–35.

CHAPTER NINE

Calvinist *Agape* or Godly dining club?

Among the rich and fascinating documents relating to the history of the Dutch church, Austin Friars, in London, which are preserved in the Guildhall Library, is a volume containing an odd collection of rules, regulations and customs which were in use within the London Dutch community during the early Stuart period. Nearly all of the volume is in the handwriting of Simon Ruytinck, who served the church as a minister for 20 years, between 1601 and 1621. In this volume we find the following, extraordinary document, concerning the introduction of a quarterly *agape* or 'Maeltyd der Liefde' among the ministers and elders of the London church and a few approved guests:

'Acte Aengaende de *Maeltyden* der Liefde die voortaen onder de dienaren des woords ende d'ouderlinghen der Gemeinte Christi tot London sullen ghehouden werden tot meerder bevestnynge van t'onderlinghe broederschap.

Oud gebruyck

Het is een *oud* ende *Lofluck* ghebruck under Godes volck, tot gedenckenisse Godes Zeghen ende bevestinghe van ouderlinghen *Liefde Maeltyden to houden*. Dat is, aen haere Tafel vrienden t'onthalen met Spyse ende Dranck, goede propoosten ende vriendeluck ghelaet.

Richtsnoer

Het richtsnoer devan Lesen wy, Actoren 2. 45 46.

Wie

Want daer word vns verthoont wie se zyn die met elckanderen brod behooren te eten, namelyck de geloouige die eerst discipulen ende sub Christenen ghenemt werden: De kinderen Jobs aten met elckanderen. Joseph vhthaelde zyn broeders ende d'Egyptenaers en saten niet aen. Philon dien philosooph en wilde nergens ter maeltyd gaen of hy en kende eerste de ghenoodde, vp dat de byencomste niet en wierde verstoort door eenige vremd, ergerlick ende ongeschickt gheselschap.

Waer

Dese Maeltyden wierden gehouden inde huysen der gheluowgen,
het en sticht niet wel en t'is costeluck zulcx in herbergen aenterichten.

Hoe

Dese discipulen aten t'samen met *Vreught* ende *Matigheyd*.

Vreught

Daer moet Vreught zyn inde *Nooder*, want God heeft Lief den
blymoedigen gever: ende die de gunste *entfanghen* moeten vort
blyde zyn om datse tsamen ghenieten ende smaken, datde heere
den arbeyd haere handen zeghent. Ende hun vergunt brood om
t'licham te stercken, ende wyn om t'herte te verheugen. Psal. 104.
Dese wottende Vreught word zeer geheylight indien de Speyse ende
Dranck tot Sausce heeft goede ende stichtende propoosten: de
geluowge inde Apostolische tyden spraken van aenwas van Christi
rycke, hun verheugende over de bekeerynghe der heydenen. Ten
tyden Tertulianus werden inde maeltyden eenige redenen voorgestelt
onderwysinge ende verheuginghe vande ghenoodde: Onse voorfaders
onder t'Cruyce hadden daer vor vermaerk in: Luthers discipulen
hebben ons nagelaten zyn disch-redenen. Ende hoe en souden de
Christenen sulx niet doen ghemerckt dat de heydenen sulx niet
versuymt en hebben.

Matigheyt

Dese vreught was vergeselschapt met Matigheyt want het besluyt
van maeltyden was danckbaerheyt: Ende niet vergetentheyt zynder
gauen, het blyckt ooc dat t'menschen watme haeft is versadigheid,
maer niet zyn beggerlicheyt. Inden de maeltyden der Lacedeimoniers
werden ghenemt Scholen der Matigheyd, hoe veel te meer de
Maeltyden der Christenen.
 Na de mate van der rechtsnoer zo worden neergestelt dese
naevolgende *Wetten*.

I

Tyd

Dese maeltyden sullen aengherecht worden Vier-mael t'jaers,
namelyck den eersten dynsdagh s'avonds van October, Januarius,
Aprilis ende Julius.

II

Aenrichters

De persoonen die deselue sullen aenrichten zyn.
In October (names added in another hand) Abraham van Delden, Seger Corselis, David Clinckenberg.
In Januario Samuel de Visscher, Cornelis Godfrey, Daniel Haringhoeck.
In Aprili Geraert Cossyns, Johan Luce, Carolus Liebaert.
In Julio Joos Godschalck, Johan Moncy, Adam Boddens.

III

Genoodde

De persoonen die up dese maeltyden sullen verschynen zyn, de Domini ende ouderlungen ende noch twee ofte dry andere, die de nooders na t'goedvinden van vergaderinge, daerby sullen mogen bringen.

IV

Plaetse

De plaetse sal zyn der de nooders bequaemst zullen vinden.

V

Spyse

De spyse die bereydt wordt en zal niet moghen smaken noch te riecken na ouerdadigheyt.

VI

Propoosten

De propoosten sullen stichtende wesen ende tot dien eynde sal eenige nutte ende ghemackende vraghe voorgestelt worden door ymand van de Leeraers by gheheurte, up dat eenyder het zyne daertoe zegghe, mits dat de voorsaghde vraghe, des Sondaeghs te vooren in die Vergaderinghe, bekent ghemaeckt werde.

VII

Men zal vergaderen ter bestemder plaets voor den seven vren, ende scheyden voor den thueren. Die op den bestemden tyd niet en verschynen zullen verbeuren voor den armen.[1]

The man who took down this document, Simon Ruytinck, son of the former Secretary of Ghent, Jan Ruytinck, who had fled to Norwich in England in 1573, had in 1594 commenced his career as an alumnus of Austin Friars and had studied in Geneva before he was appointed minister to the congregation in 1601.[2] The fact that the document is in Ruytinck's hand, except for the later addition of the names of the 12 elders, some of whom are known to have been appointed after Ruytinck's death on 3 January 1621, indicates that the document was written towards the end of Ruytinck's life. Likewise, Ruytinck's use of the word 'voortaen' in his introduction to the guidelines of the *agape* clearly indicates that it was a scheme for the future which had yet to be initiated.[3] That the names of the elders, who were supposed to organize the quarterly *agapae*, have been added to Ruytinck's draft would indicate that the scheme was realized. A closer scrutiny of the names of the elders provides an indication of when the new practice might have been introduced. Abraham van Delden served Austin Friars as an elder between 1599 and 1624, Segar Corselis served between 1601 and 1626, David Clinckenberg between 1604 and 1626, Samuel de Visscher between 1610 and 1623, Cornelis Godfrey between 1611 and 1636, Daniel Haringhoeck between 1612 and 1626, Geraert Cossyns between 1612 and 1626, John Luce between 1616 and 1636, Carolus Liebaert between 1617 and 1626, Joos Godschalck between 1617 and 1642, Johan Moncy between 1621 and 1632 and Adam Boddens between 1621 and 1628.[4] The first of these elders to leave the consistory was Samuel de Visscher who stepped down sometime during November/ December 1623. This provides us with a date *ante quem* the *agape* must have been in use. The last two elders on the list were appointed on 22 April 1621, thus supplying a date *post quem* for the 'Liefde Maeltyd'.[5] Within the two and a half years between April 1621 and November 1623 this early Christian tradition was probably revived among the leadership of the Dutch community in London. A qualified guess could probably narrow the starting date further, to sometime during spring or early summer of 1621, bearing in mind that the initiative originally seems to have emanated from Ruytinck, which would support the theory of a date not too distant from his death. That no later addition to the list of elders was made would indicate that the tradition was shortlived and might have been discontinued before Samuel de Visscher retired from the consistory in November/December 1623.

   The manuscript falls in two separate sections, each divided into seven paragraphs. The first section is a historical and Scriptural justification of the *agape*. The second consists of the rules which were to guide the *agape* or 'Maeltyd der Liefde' within the Dutch community in London.

The historical guideline starts by pointing to the *agape* as an ancient and justifiable tradition among the 'people of God' before, in the second paragraph, referring to Acts. II, 45, 46 as the central Scriptural foundation for this tradition. V 45 emphasizes the social care and charity of the participants in the *agape*. V 46 simply describes the practice that they, 'breaking bread from house to house, did eat their meat with gladness and singleness of heart'. In the third paragraph of this section Ruytinck discusses who took part in the *agape*. He, of course, mentions the Disciples, but then refers to two Old Testament cases, the children of Job and Joseph who entertained his brothers in Egypt, before finally pointing to a non-Christian source, the Judaic-Hellenistic philosopher, Philon. Regarding the Old Testament references, Ruytinck must have had Job 42.11 and Gen. 43.32–34 in mind. Concerning Philon, he probably thought of Philon's *De Vita Contemplativa* where the philosopher describes the practice of the meals of the 'Therapeutæ'. Ruytinck would have had a copy of Philon's work at hand in the library of the Dutch church in London, as one such had been donated to the church by his colleague, the minister Johannes Regius.[6]

It is emphasized in the first section, paragraph four, that these *agapae* should take place in private houses and that inns were not only too expensive, but also improper. Ruytinck then turns his attention to the form and spirit of these gatherings. The 'Liefde Maeltyd' should take place with 'gladness and singleness, meaning temperance ('Matigheyd'), of heart'. It was obviously important for Ruytinck to evade misunderstandings on this issue and he accordingly devoted the remaining three sections of the historical justification of the *agape* to this aspect. We are told that gladness ('vreught') through the 'eating of bread and drinking of wine' serves to produce edifying conversation among the guests. Here Ruytinck refers us to Psalm 104, where he must have had v. 15 in mind: 'And wine that maketh glad the heart of man, and oil to make his face shine, and bread which strengthenth man's heart'. In discussing the godly conversation which should take place during the *agapae*, Ruytinck mentions Tertullian and, surprisingly for a Calvinist divine of the early seventeenth century, when the confessional lines were hardening, Luther's Tabletalks. The text by Tertullian he refers to is obviously '*Apologeticus*', Chapter 39, where the following passage concerning the proper godly conversation can be found: 'We meet to call one another to remembrance of the Scripture, if the aspect of affairs requires us either to be forewarned or to be reminded of anything. In any case we feed our belief on holy words, we raise our hope, we strengthen our confidence, we clinch the teaching none the less by driving home precepts. There too are pronounced exhortations, corrections and godly judgements.'

As in the case of the above-mentioned work by Philon, Ruytinck would also have been able to consult this book in the church's library.[7]

The second section is concerned with the rules which should guide the planned *agapae* within the London Dutch church. The first paragraph specifies that they should take place four times a year, on the first Tuesday in October, January, April and July. The seventh and last paragraph adds that the gatherings should commence at seven in the evening and that late-comers would forfeit an unspecified sum for the benefit of the congregation's poor. Three elders were responsible for organizing each quarterly meal at a place chosen at their discretion. In effect, this meant that one of the three elders must have hosted the *agape*, assuming that the instructions in the historical guidelines, which expressly excluded inns as acceptable venues for these meetings, were being taken seriously. The participants were the church's three ministers and 12 elders plus two or three guests invited by the organizers, but vetted by the whole consistory. Concerning the meals, the rules simply stated that they should not taste nor savour of luxuriousness. That the 'Maeltyden der Liefde' should not be excessive, appears to indicate a deliberate lack of emphasis on simplicity as practised by the 'Therapeutae', according to Philon. It would also seem to disregard Calvin's commentary on the Acts of the Apostles, where he writes about II.46: 'that they used to eat together and do so frugally. For those who make sumptuous banquets do not enjoy such fellowship together in their meal. Again, Luke adds, in singleness of heart, which is also an indication of temperance. In brief, this meaning is that their method of life together was brotherly and sober.'[8]

One is certainly left with the feeling that the governors of Austin Friars expected something slightly more elaborate on these occasions than just a simple meal of bread and wine. This perception is reinforced when it is borne in mind that the Dutch community had traditionally displayed a taste for banqueting. This issue had been discussed during the Colloquium of the Dutch churches in England in 1609. It had been decided that it was a 'terrible sin' to take part in 'groote maeltijden ende Bruyloften' on the Sabbath which prevented the participants from attending the service. However, the action taken by the Colloquium could hardly be said to correspond with what might have been considered an appropriate remedy against a 'terrible sin'. Members were only requested to avoid needless meals which might interfere with church attendance.[9] This appeal, however, had hardly any effect. Five years later, in 1614, it was pointed out to the Dutch consistory by the French/Walloon church during one of the monthly Coetus meetings of the alien congregations in London, that the expensive and elaborate meals which took place among the Dutch were the cause of considerable vexation among the English. When the matter was discussed again during the Colloquium of 1615 it was evident that the offended party among the English were Puritans:

> *Neffens dien de groote ergernisse die de Godtvruchtighe ende Welgeneghene Engelschen rechtveerdichlyck over sulx nemen, waer door sy dickmael veroorsaeckt worden te versuchten, dat onse Gemeinten die de in-landeren souden behoiren als exemplairen ende voorbeelden der Godsaliheit vooren te gaen, soodanighe grote abuysen alsnoch onder hen behouden, als daer is een dadelycke ontheyliginghe van den Sabbath'.*[10]

It was primarily the Colloquium's concern for the exile communities' standing among 'welgeneghene', English Puritans, which appears to have conditioned its advice to the individual congregations not to lay on luxurious dinners on the Sabbath. However, no trace of a negative attitude to lavish meals or banqueting in general, which was much in evidence among English Puritans during this period, can be found within the Dutch community. Accordingly, the Colloquium only reiterated its plea of 1609, asking members to refrain from putting on banquets which might prevent members attending service.[11] This ambivalent attitude to banqueting in general, combined with the vague rules for the 'Maeltyd der Liefde' in particular, should not automatically lead us to assume that the *agapae* organized by the leadership of the Dutch church were in effect only a dining club, with an added godly gloss to make them acceptable. Admittedly, they appear to have been far removed from the Spartan ideal, as referred to by Ruytinck in his paragraph on temperance ('Matigheyt'). Still, they certainly aspired, at least in the spirit and the discussion which was expected to be conducted over and after the meals, to be in accordance with the early Christian *agapae* as described by Tertullian: 'When worthy, when good men come together, when the pious and pure are gathered together, it is to be called not a club, but a council chamber'.[12] This aspect was emphasized in the last paragraph of the rules governing the *agapae* among the Dutch in London. One of the three ministers of Austin Friars, in turn, was expected to commence the godly discussion by giving a short talk on a 'useful and practical' godly question which had been previously announced in the consistory. The participants were then expected to contribute to the subsequent discussion.

The most interesting question, however, is how the enterprise came about within a solidly Calvinist community. In other words, who might the originator(s) have been and what possible lines of tradition and inspiration might they have drawn upon?

I would suspect that the driving force behind the *agapae* was the minister, Simon Ruytinck. As opposed to his colleagues within the ministry of the church, Johannes Regius and Ambrosius Regemorter, he was an industrious scholar in his own right. His history of the church which was later continued by his successors, Cesar Calandrini and Aemilius van Culenburg, provides us with the picture of a man who was well-read in the classical literature and the Fathers of the Church. This image, of a theologian of considerable learning, is further in evidence in his attack on the Catholic Church, *Gulden Legende van de Roomsche Kercke*, published in London in 1612.[13] He would, accordingly, have been the person most likely to have been acquainted with the works of Tertullian and Philon and the early Christian tradition of the *agapae*. Furthermore, he might have seen this idea as a chance of reviving and reforming a tradition from the days of the establishment of the stranger churches under Edward VI which appears to have fallen into disuse before the beginning of the seventeenth century. During the reign of Edward VI the consistory of Austin Friars had met quarterly, on the second Thursday in September, December, March and June, in order to 'inspect and discuss' the teaching and lives of the congregation's ministers.[14]

Inspiration might also have come from other sources. The Dutch community had by then abandoned another of its original traditions. In Ruytinck's days, the congregation took the Communion either standing or seated according to personal choice, only kneeling was expressly excluded in *The Corpus Disciplinae* of 1609. This had not been the case in the 1550s when members had taken the Communion seated round a table in as close as possible a re-enactment of the Last Supper.[15] Together with Ruytinck's reading, especially of Tertullian, this would appear to have been the most obvious tradition which might have influenced him. However, he might also have drawn some inspiration from the growing number of household seminars which were introduced during the early Stuart period by many of his godly, English colleagues. The Puritan divine, Herbert Palmer, with whom the leadership of Austin Friars was later on friendly terms, ran a household seminar when he was a minister in Ashwell in Hertfordshire. Other and more famous seminars were those of Richard Blackerby and Thomas Gataker who both could count future ministers to Austin Friars among their pupils. Jonas Proost, who originally served the Dutch church in Colchester until, in 1644, he was appointed minister to the Dutch church in London, attended Blackerby's seminar. Wilhelm Thilenius, who became Ruytinck's successor in London in 1624, was a pupil in Thomas Gataker's 'academy' in Surrey.[16] Godly Englishmen like Blackerby and Gataker, might well have been the type of guests whom Ruytinck had envisaged attending the *agapae* of the Dutch church, especially since we find no indication that the two or three guests allowed to participate should be members or in any way connected with the congregation.

However, how and why these highly unorthodox plans for quarterly *agapae* materialized within the Dutch community in London will remain within the domain of speculation. The later addition of the names of 12 elders in the document would indicate that the meals were in fact introduced, at least for a brief period; yet the lack of any further reference to them in other sources to the history of the church would indicate that the tradition was shortlived.

Notes

1. Guildhall Library MS 10.055, ff. 132r–134r.
2. For Simon Ruytinck, see *Nieuw Nederlandsch Biografisch Woodenboeck*.
3. See above note 1.
4. See O. P. Grell, *Dutch Calvinists in Early Stuart England*, Leiden 1989, Appendix I.
5. Ibid.
6. Guildhall Library MS 20.185/4 (Catalogus Benefactorum Bibliothecæ Londino-Belgicæ), f. 3. For Philon, see also J. F. Keating, *The Agape and the Eucharist in the Early Church*, London 1901, pp. 24–8.
7. Guildhall Library MS 20.185/4, f. 6. Donated by Dominicus ab Heyla or Verheyl in 1606. See also Q. Septimi Florentis Tertulliani, *Apologeticus*, ed. J. E. B. Mayor, Cambridge 1917, pp. 110–17, especially pp. 110–12.
8. See *Calvin's Commentaries; The Acts of the Apostles 1–13*, eds, D. W. Torrance and T. F. Torrance, London 1965, p. 89.
9. J. J. van Toorenenbergen (ed.), *Acten van de Colloquia der Nederlandsche gemeenten in Engeland, 1575–1609* (Werken der Marnix-Vereeniging, Serie II – Deel I), Utrecht 1872, p. 124 (Acten van de Colloquia).
10. Guildhall Library MS 7397/7, f. 51v (1614); for 1615, see Guildhall Library MS 7411/2, f. 21v.
11. Ibid.
12. See Q. Septimi Florentis Tertulliani, op. cit., p. 117.
13. J. J. van Toorenenbergen, *Gheschiedenissen ende Handelingen die voornemelick aangaan de Nederduytsche Natie ende Gemeynten wonende in Engeland ende in bysonder tot London* (Werken der Marnix-Vereeniging, Serie III–Deel I.), Utrecht 1873. An excellent example is Ruytinck's letter to the consistory in connection with the church's decision to start a library in 1606, see pp. 224–8. See also Simon Ruytinck, *Gulden Legende van de Roomsche Kercke: mitsgaders hare Heylichdommen ende Aflaten aan den Toetsteen der Warheyt beproeft*, London 1612, especially the dedication and introduction.
14. Marten Micron, *De Christlicke Ordinancien der Nederlantscher Ghemeinten te Londen* (1554), ed. W. F. Dankbaar, The Hague 1956, pp. 137–9.
15. Ibid., pp. 100–101 and *Acten van de Colloquia*, p. 146. See also Andrew Pettegree, *Foreign Protestant Communities in Sixteenth-Century London*, Oxford 1986, p. 60.
16. For Wilhelm Thilenius, see Samuel Clarke, *A Collection of the Lives of Ten Eminent Divines, Famous in their Generations for Learning, Pru-*

dence, Piety and Painfullness in the Work of the Ministry, London 1662, p. 146. For Jonas Proost, see Samuel Clarke, *The Lives of Sundry Eminent Persons in this Later Age*, London 1683, p. 58. See also John Morgan, *Godly Learning, Puritan attitudes towards Reason, Learning and Education, 1560–1640*, Cambridge 1986, pp. 292–300. For Herbert Palmer, see *DNB*; for his close relations with Austin Friars, see above Chapter 4, 'From Uniformity to Tolerance: The effects on the Dutch church in London of reverse patterns in English church policy, 1634–1647'. For Richard Blackerby and Thomas Gataker, see *DNB*.

CHAPTER TEN

Plague in Elizabethan and Stuart London: the Dutch response

Plague was, without doubt, the most devastating disease that could hit an urban community in the early modern period. It was a regular visitor to London for three centuries from the Black Death of 1348 until its last outbreak in 1665. Its most terrifying impact was obviously felt when major epidemics occurred in the City – as they did in 1563, 1593, 1603, 1625, 1636 and finally in 1665. Nearly a quarter of London's inhabitants died in 1563 and more than 80,000 in the last epidemic in the metropolis in 1665 – almost 20 per cent of the City's population. Apart from these major outbreaks, plague persisted in London during most of the intervening years in a milder, more endemic form. Between 1563 and 1665 – the first period for which we have reasonable data, thanks to the Bills of Mortality – it was only absent from the City from 1616 to 1624 and again from 1650 to 1664.[1]

I will concern myself with the social response to plague within the Dutch community in London, whose provision for and care of infected members has been held up as 'an example of foreign civility close to home' by Paul Slack in his recent study on the impact of plague in Tudor and Stuart England. I hope not only to expand this verdict but also to modify it substantially. Accordingly, I shall attempt to demonstrate how and why this exceptional system, introduced by the London Dutch church during the plague of 1563 for the care and relief of plague-ridden members, was allowed to decay under the early Stuarts. Likewise, I shall try to show how this collapse of solidarity among the Dutch in London was accompanied, if not directly caused, by a gradual decline in religious commitment, that is, secularization, loss of Dutch identity, and growing anglicization; and where possible compare it with the changing response of their English hosts. However, before taking a closer look at the Dutch community, it will be useful to make a brief assessment of the impact of the disease, and the reactions to it, within the metropolis.

Plague struck in fearful concentration. Most of the major epidemics appear to have run their course within a few months. In 1625, for instance, plague did not break out until the beginning of June and was petering out by November, having killed over 20,000 people out of a population of more than 200,000. Thus more than a tenth of London's population perished in less than six months – small wonder that local as well as central government found itself under tremendous pressure in times of plague. Paul Slack has demonstrated how outbreaks of plague gradually became more concentrated in London, both topographically and socially, during the early Stuart period. The reason for this change is to be found in London's colossal growth in the previous century, from around 85,000 in 1563 to 459,000 in 1665. This happened in spite of more than a sixth of the population being killed by plague at irregular intervals. It must have been a staggering task for the Lord Mayor and Aldermen just to keep the City going under normal conditions, not to mention during the havoc wrought by major epidemics.

The population explosion led to overcrowding and bad health among the poor, who could only afford to live in the most dilapidated tenements as pressure on the housing market grew. During the plague of 1563 there was hardly any difference in mortality between the different parishes in the City. By 1665 the mortality rates in the poorer parishes and suburbs to the south and northeast of the City were double those in the centre. In the early seventeenth century, plague began to show a clearer social bias, as the poor found themselves squeezed together in sheds, cellars and subdivided tenements on the outskirts of London. A contributive factor to the improved mortality rate of the richer, central parishes during the early Stuart period should also be sought in the growing tendency among the richer citizens to flee the City.[2]

England was much slower than most European countries in introducing public precautions and regulations against plague. Not until 1518 had the first tentative steps been taken towards marking infected households. But the country had to wait until 1578 before it received its first plague orders and London did not receive any regulations until May 1583. Issued by the Privy Council, the plague orders are evidence of government intent rather than expressions of practical policy. Most of the regulations, such as certification of deaths, appointment of searchers and watchmen, control of times of burial, and the fundamental policy of household segregation, were similar to those already in force in a number of continental cities. In two respects the English regulations differed from their continental prototypes: they introduced taxation to support the sick, and the isolation of the infected was unusually strict. This strictness was reinforced in 1604, when the government provided penal sanctions to support the policy of isolation. Watchmen were given the right to use force to keep people shut up, and anyone with plague sores found wandering outside their homes in the company of others might be hanged. Alongside the penal measures were more positive attempts to provide for care: the orders of 1583 provided for a number of plague officers in each parish and when they were revised in 1609, they also included orders for the appointment of six surgeons who should supervise medical aid in the City. The 1609 edition of the plague orders was reprinted without major alterations in 1630, 1646 and 1665.

The implementation of the orders, however, left much to be desired. It turned out to be difficult to recruit people for the jobs of searchers, nurses, watchmen, and so on, in most parishes. The financial limitations of several parishes made the employment of extra personnel difficult; only few candidates could be found for such dangerous jobs, and those who did come forward were often unreliable. What parish relief there was tended to break down in the greater epidemics. During the plague of 1625 the London Aldermen initially allowed one member of each infected household to go out for provisions, but by the middle of August even this 'softer' approach to segregation had broken down totally – a development that repeated itself in 1665.[3]

In spite of these shortcomings, the responses to the crises from the Lord Mayor and Aldermen and the Privy Council eventually bore some fruit. A pesthouse was started in St Giles Cripplegate in 1594, although it was far from sufficient for a city the size of London. Small and unfinished as it may have been in 1603 – only 135 people are listed as having died there while the outbreak peaked from the beginning of July until the end of December – the London-based Dutch merchant and writer Jacob Cool, nevertheless considered it extremely useful for the City during the plague in 1603. Cool, an eye-witness who remained in London throughout the plague, informs us that carts drove through the City at midnight to collect the sick and bring them to the pesthouse. It would appear, however, that this service was primarily for the benefit of the poor or used by masters and householders who forced their sick and often unwilling servants into the carts.[4]

By the end of the sixteenth century a number of parishes had begun to employ at least a couple of searchers and nurses. Segregation of infected households was attempted in most parishes from 1625 onwards and only appears to have folded completely in the midst of major outbreaks. Not until the epidemic of 1636, however, were extra taxes collected in London, even if the City had benefited from a national collection in 1625, ordered by Parliament while it met in Oxford. During the outbreak of 1625 the City fathers employed for the first time two doctors to look after plague victims, and they paid out nearly £300 in medical expenses. Admittedly, the responses to plague were slow in materializing in the metropolis and when adopted were often less than efficient, but the Stuart period especially bears witness to a gradual, albeit modest, improvement in the attempts to control and regulate the epidemics.[5]

The efforts of the Dutch congregation in London certainly outstripped those of its English host community during the plague of 1563. Apart from marking infected houses and some attempts by the Lord Mayor and Aldermen towards segregation of infected households, very little was achieved by local government in London. By contrast, the Dutch church in Austin Friars, which then had around 1,600 members spread around the City, took immediate action when the epidemic started to accelerate in July. The consistory decided to employ one surgeon and secure the services of another, if need arose, to look after the poorer members of the community in particular. The surgeon was given a lump sum of 16 shillings and promised a salary of five shillings a week for looking after the poor. The elders used the opportunity to stipulate who was included under this heading: only those who received alms from the congregation! The richer members were expected to pay the surgeon for his services. Names were also taken down by the consistory of members who were willing to serve as watchers and nurses. A few days later, the community appointed two deacons as visitors of the sick to assist the ministers in attending the infected.[6] The visitors were charged with appointing watchers and nurses, helping the sick in drawing up their wills, and providing consolation and admonition. They were expected to cover both the spiritual and medical domains, but a clear emphasis was placed on pastoral care. Like the surgeon, they were offered a respectable salary. The Dutch consistory was careful when employing people to look after its plague victims. Thus rumours to the effect that the Walloon-French community's surgeon was attending the sick in the company of a whore, made the ministers and elders of Austin Friars refuse to recommend him to their members.

The Dutch community in London may well have taken the lead among the Dutch Reformed churches in exile, as well as in the Netherlands, by creating these positions. They should be seen as an early example of community medicine with their emphasis on care and consolation for the sick. M. J. van Lieburg has indicated that the visitors of the sick employed by the Reformed Church in Rotterdam in the early seventeenth century paid increasing attention to the medical aspects of their job during epidemics. Whether or not that was true for the visitors in Austin Friars by the turn of the century remains an open question.[7]

Originally Austin Friars appears to have intended to inform its members of the Lord Mayor's order for the isolation of infected households – allowing only one member per household out for provisions. Then they changed their minds and struck out the order previously entered in the minutes of the consistory. Evidently it did not fit the community's policy of allowing healthy members from infected households to attend service in Austin Friars together with those who were involved in looking after the sick. The church took the precaution, however, of requesting these members to sit separately in the church in order not to worry the 'weaker brethren' and 'pregnant sisters'. Likewise, those members who had recovered from the disease were requested to be certified as healthy by the surgeon or 'such people who have experience of plague' before they started to attend service. The community also demonstrated its enlightened attitude by debating whether or not plague was contagious, but in spite of the debate being 'intelligently conducted', it appears to have caused considerable anxiety among the less well-educated members.[8]

The three-tiered structure of the Dutch community, comprising ministers, elders and deacons, held up well in this crisis. Consistory meetings continued throughout the summer and, while the infection spread, the officers of the community did their best to tackle the effects of the disease. There was, however, a price to be paid for this unlimited solidarity within the community – the two most senior ministers died within a couple of days of each other in September and the church's finances were in disarray well into the 1570s.[9]

In noting the vigour of this collective action, however, we should not forget that the epidemic of 1563 happened only three years after the Dutch community had been re-founded under Elizabeth after years of exile during the reign of Mary. Obviously a strong sense of community and solidarity prevailed within the congregation. The church was still in its apostolic age, regularly sending ministers and elders to the Netherlands to assist 'the churches under the cross', and its officers were highly committed Protestants rooted in the Second Reformation. The community was, in other words, extremely well equipped to tackle this crisis.[10]

No records covering the community's response to the plague in 1593 have survived. Only the minister Simon Ruytinck's short note in his *History* confirms that the epidemic in 1593 was less serious than in 1563, stating that 'because the Godly humbled themselves before the Lord his punishing hand was removed'.[11] Ten years later, in 1603, London was faced with another serious outbreak of plague. This outbreak took a severe toll among the Dutch community. We can safely assume that the mortality rate among the Dutch was at least as high as among the English, which would mean that around one-fifth of the community died. Simon Ruytinck, who served Austin Friars as a minister from 1601 to 1621, wrote that 370 Dutch households were affected by the plague and that some 670 people died. Once more the community lost a minister in the epidemic. Assuerus Regemorter, the most experienced of the church's three ministers, died in September. With nearly three-quarters of all the congregation's households infected, it is

not surprising that the ministers were exposed.[12] The gap in the minutes
of the consistory, due to the loss of a consistory book, makes it difficult
to assess what measures the community introduced in 1603.

Fortunately, the already mentioned merchant-writer and later elder to
Austin Friars, Jacob Cool, offers some assistance. In his narrative poem,
Den Staet van London in hare Groote Peste (The State of London
during the Great Plague), written in 1604 immediately after the plague
had subsided and published in Middelburg two years later, Cool informs us that 'the brave Dutch shepherds and others did not fail to go
in God's name to see those who wanted their assistance'. The church
also appointed two visitors of the sick 'who without fear served under
the ministers'; it was therefore the same arrangement and number of
visitors as in 1563.

Jacob Cool, a self-taught classicist, a learned collector of Greek and
Roman coins and medals, a herbalist, and above all a staunch Calvinist,
remained in London throughout the plague. He admitted to having
been terrified, but his faith came to his assistance and stopped him from
fleeing the City. This, however, did not lead him to rely passively on
Providence. He took good care of himself in accordance with the advice
of his physician, who might well have been another Dutch exile, Dr
Baldwin Hamey, who had settled in London in 1598. Cool informs us
that he 'carried something in his hand and something in his mouth'
when he ventured out, avoiding the sick and those who frequented
infected houses. Evidently he believed in traditional remedies prescribed
in times of plague and would have had angelica in his mouth and
carried something to sniff while walking the streets. In spite of being
scared, he felt that 'reason and necessity' obliged him where possible to
make himself useful to the afflicted. Cool's exemplary behaviour caused
his friend Johannes Radermacher, a former elder to Austin Friars then
living in Middelburg, to write: 'I must praise you for having faced the
dangers of the plague rather than abandon your people and I have no
doubt that God rewarded you by sparing your family and restoring
your kinswoman to health'.[13.]

Besides providing us with these glimpses of a rich and well-educated
Dutchman's reaction to plague, Cool's poem also provides some interesting observations about the social conditions in London during the
epidemic of 1603 and in particular offers two important correctives to
the accepted view of plague in London during this period. First, he
claimed that the longer the plague lasted in 1603, the more people's fear
of it diminished. One of the consequences was that the increasing
number of poor people who found themselves out of work made it
much easier for the parishes to find enough 'strong and brave people' to
look after the sick, thus solving the difficulties of recruiting reliable

nurses, watchmen and searchers. Second, Cool confirms the well-known fact that the impact of the 1603 outbreak was much graver in the suburbs than the inner City, because of overcrowding and the miserable housing conditions in those areas. But he adds another important reason for the high mortality in the suburbs. He pointed to the fact that several well-to-do citizens in London owned small 'garden- or pleasure-houses' in these areas, where they chose to send members of their households who caught the plague, thus adding to the number of suburban casualities.[14]

The elders in London might well have gratefully accepted the suggestion of the Dutch congregation in Sandwich:

> As we hear that the Lord Chastises London with the plague against which there is no better remedy than praying and a sincere repentance, combined with means granted by him, as skilful Doctors, one of our brethren, a devout man, who has faithfully served us formerly as *pestemeester* in times of epidemic, offers you his services now.[15]

This statement, together with Jacob Cool's reaction, demonstrates the practical and activist attitude to plague which prevailed among the Dutch churches in England. That God was seen as chastising the communities with this terrible disease did not lead to its passive reception. The strong, Counter-Remonstrant Calvinism of the Anglo-Dutch congregations, with its emphasis on Providence, did not generate anything akin to apathy; rather, in accordance with Calvin's *Institutes*, it guaranteed that the churches considered it part of their Christian obligation to try to preserve human life, through the means God had placed at their disposal, that is, care and medical remedies. And the advice from the church in Sandwich echoes the writings of such leading hardline Zeeland Calvinists or Pietists as Willem Teellinck, a friend and correspondent of Jacob Cool, and Godfrid Udemans. Teellinck's argument in his pamphlet *Zion's Trumpet*, for the medical treatment of plague victims, as being 'part of God's advice which we must follow', provided the theological rationale for the Sandwich congregation's letter.[16]

Some form of self-imposed household isolation appears to have become standard practice among the Dutch in London at the time of James I's accession, assuming that the example of Hadrianus Damman, the Ambassador of the States General to Scotland, who had accompanied James to England in 1603, is typical. Writing to the consistory of Austin Friars from Edinburgh in January 1605, Damman apologized for not having thanked the consistory in person before returning to Scotland. His son-in-law and niece had died from the plague in the house he had rented in London after the whole family had taken communion in Austin Friars. He and his wife had then returned to

Edinburgh 'after having patiently waited for a month for the Lord in prayers'.[17]

With or without assistance from the former *pestemeester* from Sandwich, the visitor of the sick, Francoys vanden Broecke, managed to get through the epidemic of 1603. He is included in the earliest list of salaried personnel in the church from 1606. The experience in 1603 had probably convinced the leadership in Austin Friars of the need to employ him on a permanent basis. Being a married man without offspring, he was well-suited for the job. He was a silk weaver by training, but unlike his predecessors in 1563 he was never considered for a deaconship – his humble position as a craftsman would probably have excluded him, since the end of the sixteenth century elders and deacons were almost all recruited from among the merchants, the upper social category within the congregation. Vanden Broecke's normal salary as visitor of the sick was £8 p.a., but during periods of plague he received extra payments from the church. In 1608 the consistory offered him a gift of £3 for his efforts on behalf of plague-stricken members, and from 1612 Vanden Broecke combined his position as visitor with that of *voorleser* ('reader') and consequently received a higher salary of £12 p.a.[18]

Not until London was hit by another surge of infection in 1625 does a more detailed picture of how Austin Friars responded to epidemics in the early seventeenth century materialize. By now the original, committed front-line efforts of several of the church's ministers and deacons appear to have been replaced by those of lower-ranking officials like Francoys vanden Broecke. The consistory, in fact, went a step further in 1625. The ministers and elders decided in June that Vanden Broecke should be spared from visiting those members who had caught the plague. Instead the community wanted to hire a temporary visitor of the plague-stricken to look after the growing number of victims. The attempt to employ a certain Steven Schier failed and the consistory found it necessary to request Vanden Broecke to look after infected members for another three or four weeks until an extraordinary visitor of the sick could be appointed. A consistory meeting on 10 July decided to employ Jan Schram as a temporary *siecken-trooster*. He was given a lump sum of 15 shillings and promised 9 shillings a week for looking after plague-stricken members. Schram was only employed after a thorough examination by consistory members. He was a silk weaver like his colleague, but was considerably younger than Vanden Broecke, and the father of at least four children. He was also substantially poorer. Unlike Vanden Broecke, who lived in Duke's Place within the walls of the City and whose moderated rent was assessed to £5 in 1638, Schram lived in Southwark and was listed under the category of members of Austin

Friars who in 1617 were described as 'householders the most part very poor'.[19]

> Our brother, Joos Godschalck, has informed us that he has talked to the wife of Jan Schram asking her firstly whether she consented to her husband occupying the position of extraordinary visitor of the sick; to this she replied in all frankness that she had prayed to the Lord, together with her husband, for this to happen and that she approved. Secondly, our brother Godschalck asked her whether her husband had not left her for a period going abroad without her knowledge or consent. In denying this she swore fervently and added that those who claimed this did her and her husband great injustice. Jan Schram appeared before the brethren after certain brethren had negotiated with him; he was informed that according to his request we would now call and employ him as a visitor of the sick in these difficult times; and that the brethren once and for all, would make him a present of fifteen shillings and promised to pay him nine shillings a week as long as the plague may last; and when we do not need his services any longer he will be given two months notice (by the time the Lord decides to remove his punishing hand from us). He accepted this and accordingly counted his fifteen shillings in our presence.[20]

The consistory took great pains in making sure that Jan Schram's marital and domestic situation was in reasonably good order and that his wife consented to his employment in an obviously risky job. The ministers and elders had to assure themselves that no serious doubt could be raised about his moral integrity. After all, Schram was to be entrusted with the life and property of members who were seriously ill and dying, helping them in drawing up their wills. Any irregularities in this respect would reflect badly on the consistory members, who were ultimately responsible.

Dealing with the casualties of the plague was only part of the duties of the ministers and elders during epidemics. They also had to calm and console those members who were not infected but who lived in constant fear of contracting the disease. In July members were told that services in Austin Friars would be continued on Sundays as well as weekdays. A month later some members complained to the consistory that they were anxious about people appearing in church 'with open sores'. The consistory decided to request these people, obviously convalescing from plague, either to stay away from the services, or if they insisted on attending, to remain segregated from the rest of the community in a separate section of the church.[21] This decision was not totally dissimilar to the one reached by their predecessors in 1563, despite the fact that by 1625 considerations for the healthy appear to have taken precedence over care for those who had been struck by the disease.

The Dutch congregation probably suffered as much as the English parishes during the outbreak of 1625, but this time at least it lost none of its ministers. The ministers and elders appear to have fulfilled their obligations towards the church and the weekly consistory meetings continued throughout the crisis, except for a couple of interruptions in September. By December the infection was on the wane and the consistory decided it was time to discharge its extraordinary visitor of the sick, Jan Schram. On top of his salary, Schram was given a gift of £2 for his services to the community, while the permanent visitor, Francoys vanden Broecke, was awarded £10 for his efforts during the plague. Vanden Broecke and Schram's salaries and awards were generous compared with what the City fathers paid their employees. The keeper of the pesthouse in St Giles Cripplegate received £5 p.a. in 1612 and during the plague of 1625 the resident surgeon in the pesthouse was given a salary of £30; both these gentlemen were offered a gift of £5 as a 'reward for their care and pain'.

Francoys vanden Broecke retired five years later, in January 1630, having served the community as its sick-visitor for more than a quarter of a century. His retirement, however, turned out to be brief. In July he agreed to look after plague-stricken members of the community for half a year, for which he was paid a salary of £6.[22] But an era had come to an end within Austin Friars and the church had begun to retrench in earnest on its social commitments. The congregation was never again to employ a permanent visitor of the sick. Some attempts were made to reintroduce the position in 1641, but eventually the consistory only employed Jan Schram for two years at £10 p.a. – 'if God gives him health to perform this duty', as one of the ministers added in the minutes. It was specified on this occasion that, under ordinary conditions, Schram was obliged to look after all the community's sick, but in times of plague he should concentrate on the infected.[23]

Thus, when another major epidemic hit London in 1636, the congregation in Austin Friars was as unprepared as it had been back in 1563, while it had to face the new outbreak at a time when the original sense of community and solidarity within the church was disappearing. The church decided to re-employ its former extraordinary *siecken-trooster*, Jan Schram, in early May, but at a considerably lower salary than in 1625 – 3 shillings a week, as opposed to the 9 shillings he had received originally. Neither was Schram offered any terms of notice in 1636; instead the minutes simply stated that 'he will be bound to us but we not to him'. This meaner attitude on the part of the church's leadership coincided with its efforts to bring Austin Friars's alms expenditure under control, while the new Archbishop William Laud's drive for religious uniformity from 1634 can only have caused

the ministers and elders to show great care in their financial administration.[24]

By 1636 the Privy Council and the Lord Mayor and Aldermen sought
to enforce household segregation more rigorously than before. The
consistory in Austin Friars must have received information about the
stricter policies, since in May it discussed how far and where the temporary visitor of the sick, Jan Schram, would be allowed to go during the
plague. It was decided to contact the French consistory to learn what
information it might have received from the Lord Mayor and Aldermen. At the following week's consistory meeting in Austin Friars, the
ministers and elders were of the opinion that in future they should be in
touch with Schram before he went to see new plague casualties within
the community.[25] The activities of the visitors from the Dutch and
French churches did not go unnoticed by the English authorities. On 7
June the Privy Council enjoined the Lord Mayor to stop the visitors of
the Dutch and Walloon-French congregations from criss-crossing the
City and moving freely between the infected and the healthy and to
guarantee the maintenance of household segregation among the foreign
communities. The Lord Mayor was ordered,

> to send to the French and Dutch churches to charge them to take
> order that the houses of such of their congregations as are infected
> be presently shut up, that there be no such visits made where the
> plague is, and if they will not forbear, he is to take care that such
> consolators be shut up in the houses infected.[26]

If this order was passed on to the Dutch church, the ministers and
elders chose to ignore it. On 16 June the consistory decided that concerning the undertakings of the *pest-siecken-trooster* the church would
act 'in accordance with God'. This was a clear indication that the
leaders of the community had every intention of continuing to send
their visitor to assist members who caught the disease. In the spiritual
field, however, the community joined hands with its hosts. It decided in
October to obey the Royal Proclamation and institute a weekly day of
fasting and praying on Wednesdays, with two sermons, one in the
morning and one in the afternoon, at the same time cancelling its
normal services on Tuesdays and Thursdays.[27]

While the number of casualties grew during the summer and the
pressure on the church's finances increased, the ministers, and most of
the elders and deacons, continued to honour their responsibilities. The
consistory met regularly throughout 1636, often together with the deacons, to deal with matters small and great. The schoolmaster, Abraham
de Cerf, whose school recruited most of its pupils from the congregation, informed the church in July that the plague had brought a halt to
his activities. Evidently, most of his fee-paying pupils had stopped

attending his school because of fear of infection, well in advance of the City-fathers' decision to close all schools. De Cerf was recommended to the charity of the deacons. His predicament, however, is the first indication in the minutes of the church that the richer members of the community, like their English counterparts, had started taking to their heels, leaving London for the safety of the countryside.[28] That this was the case is confirmed by the minutes from October and November, when the three officers decided that a special collection was needed within the community in order to reinstate the poor-box after its colossal outlay over the summer for the plague stricken. After a lengthy debate in October, the ministers and those elders and deacons who had not fled the City decided to write to their absent colleagues, requesting them to attend the following week's consistory meeting. Their presence was needed in order to determine whether or not it was advisable to start a general collection for the poor 'at this time of the plague when the wealthier members have taken up their residences in the countryside'. Accordingly, the next consistory meeting took the decision to launch a collection: 'The members who are residing in the country this summer because of the plague or for other reasons, should receive letters if they are not able to appear in person, in order that they may write and inform us of their benevolence.'[29]

The church's poor-box was in a lamentable state towards the end of 1636. The crisis had seen expenditure soar from £1,530 the previous year to £2,680 in 1636 – £925 more than the deacons had managed to collect. During May and June the deacons had paid out more than £700, as opposed to between £100 and £200 under normal conditions. The general collection that took place from November to December netted the community an extra and much needed £803, which restored some balance to the accounts. The £2,680 Austin Friars spent on its poor is an impressive example of Calvinist charity, especially when compared with the total of £2,532 that the City had spent on poor relief during the previous outbreak of plague in 1625.[30]

The temporary *pest-siecken-trooster*, Jan Schram, remained in the church's employment until June 1638, when it was decided to pay him off since the plague 'with God's assistance' had disappeared. Schram, who after two years' employment had hoped for the position to become permanent, was paid a salary until the end of the year in recognition of his services.[31]

We can conclude that the early Stuart period witnessed a gradual decline in the social care and commitment shown by the Dutch church during outbreaks of plague, compared with its efforts in 1563. However, in spite of the decline, the church fared considerably better than most London parishes. In times of crisis the congregation could still rely on its ministers and a nucleus of committed elders and deacons to keep the community together and provide care for the afflicted, assisted by at least one *pest-siecken-trooster*.

After the epidemic of 1563, Austin Friars does not appear to have employed any physicians or surgeons during the following outbreaks of plague. We can, however, assume that the Leiden-educated, Anglo-Dutch poet and physician Raphael Thorius, a member of the College of Physicians and a close friend of the minister to Austin Friars, Simon Ruytinck, attended infected members of the community during the epidemics of 1603 and 1625. Thorius, who eventually died of the infection during the summer of 1625, appears to have offered his services unflinchingly during outbreaks of plague, acting 'more for the publick (by exposing his person too much) than his most dear concern'.[32] The services of Thorius, or for that matter other foreign doctors practising in London, such as the Royal physician, Theodore de Mayerne, Johannes Brovaert, and the Baldwin Hameys, Senior and Junior, would not have been restricted to the richer members of the church. That members of modest means, assisted by the deacons, were able to consult these gentlemen can be seen from the case of the Austin Friars's verger who in June 1649 was advised by Theodore de Mayerne to seek cure at a water resort.[33]

The earlier example of Raphael Thorius did not inspire those physicians who were members of the Dutch church at the time of the plague of 1665. It would appear that Dr Johannes Rhegius, or John King, as he was known in the College of Physicians, had fled the City like many of his colleagues from the College. That would explain why the minister to Austin Friars, Philip Op de Beck, was able to consult him while 'convalescing' in Barnes in September 1665, at a time when Dr King's expertise on fevers must have been badly needed in the City.[34]

In 1665 – five years after the Restoration – the provisions offered by Austin Friars in times of plague saw a further decline. Now the church could not even manage to employ a temporary sick visitor and its governing body, the consistory, appears for the first time in the community's existence to have been unable to cope with the crisis. It only managed to meet twice while the infection peaked during the summer months, and there is no record of meetings between 15 June and 28 September. Those officers of the church who remained in the City and did their duty had great difficulty in convincing their less stalwart colleagues to return. The wealthy merchant and deacon to Austin Friars, Joas Evensen, was not tempted to obey the call of the minister, Jonas Proost, and return from Oxford. He excused himself with urgent business obligations and added:

On the 12th of October my partner's house was attacked by the
plague, and one of our servants died while another died of it within
three weeks, while my maid-servant, who remained with my servant in my house near Founder's Hall, was attacked by many ulcers
in the beginning of November. My servant writes to me that she is
now better, but I, who have been now for nearly three months in
the open air, could not go at once to my house without great
danger.

And the rot did not stop there – for the first time one of the ministers
failed the community during an epidemic. In May, Philip Op de Beck,
the youngest of the congregation's three ministers, claimed that his
health did not allow him to stay on in London. He pointed out to his
colleagues that several doctors had advised him to go to the countryside
to convalesce. The consistory accepted his excuses and released him
temporarily from his duties.[35] The other two ministers appear to have
soldiered on until Cesar Calandrini, who had served the church since
1639 and who was by then close to 70, informed the consistory on 21
September that one of his maids had caught the plague.

Mr Apothecary Upton, son of the plague-master, has her in hand
and hopes to cure her. This is the reason why I have not been at the
service for two days. I have separated my room and study from the
sick room as far as my small house would allow me, and have
taken a woman in the house to wait on me, who has not been near
the invalid, whom my other servant has undertaken to nurse. I
should have left the house if I had known where to go, not for fear
of myself, but in order not to be prevented from our public services.

Calandrini was temporarily allowed to use the house of his colleague
Philip Op de Beck, while the latter 'convalesced' in Barnes. Unfortunately Calandrini's move came too late. He died only five days later, on
26 September, having been ill for four days, and was buried the following day in the presence of a few leading members of the Dutch and
French communities, since, as the minutes added, larger gatherings
were prohibited by the City authorities 'in this time of general infection
of the plague'.[36]

Consequently the consistory found it necessary to request Op de Beck
to return from Barnes to assist the minister, Jonas Proost. The church
received a pathetic letter from Op de Beck, who claimed to suffer not
only from 'weakness in his head' but to have contracted a fever. This
made it impossible for him to join the community in London, but in
spite of his excuses, he was unable to hide his true motives.

Moreover, even if I were strong enough to discharge my duty, I
should not dare to go so soon to my house from which our late
brother Calendryn has been so recently carried away. Brother Proost

writes that it is certain that brother Calandryn did not die of the plague; but it is difficult to be certain of this, as he wrote to me that his maidservant had the plague, and he went from his infected house into mine, in which he died after an illness of a few days. It is sufficiently known that in times of plague, all fevers are, to say the least, subject to suspicion so that brother Calandryn's fever might create an impression calculated to bring me and my family into difficulty.[37]

Conditions had, in other words, changed dramatically within the Dutch community in London between 1563 and 1665. A letter like Op de Beck's would never have been written in the Elizabethan period, when the religious zeal of the congregation's leaders would have excluded the possibility.

The Dutch community might have been 'an example of foreign civility close to home' in 1563, but by 1665 it had nothing of which to be proud. While the local authorities in London gradually managed to introduce some measure of improvement in the ways plague was tackled, in spite of all the difficulties presented by the population explosion, a decreasing Dutch community let an admirable system fall into decay before it finally folded in 1665.

Two factors appear to have been at play. First, the religious zeal and commitment of the founding fathers of Austin Friars was fading rapidly among their successors in the early Stuart period, when the effects of a growing secularization were making themselves felt. Second, in conjunction with this development, the community had become increasingly anglicized towards the middle of the seventeenth century. It was by then more than 60 years since the community had had a significant influx of new refugees from the Continent and most of its leaders belonged to either the first or the second generation born in England. During the 1640s an increasing number of members from the upper echelons of the congregation became active within local government rather than within the leadership of the church. This development is exemplified by the roles played by Alderman, Sir John Frederick and the Lord Mayor, Sir John Lawrence, during the great plague of 1665. At a time when most other people in authority had taken to their heels, both stayed in London throughout the epidemic and honoured their civic duties. It is significant for the change which had taken place within the congregation in Austin Friars, that in spite of both men's membership of the church and their regular and generous contributions to collections, neither ever served the community as an elder or a deacon. This is even more remarkable when we bear in mind that both had married daughters of elders in Austin Friars. John Frederick married Mary, daughter of the merchant Thomas Rous, or Ruys, who served the Dutch church as a deacon from 1630 and as an elder from 1636; and

John Lawrence, who was a nephew of the elder Adam Lawrence, married Abigail, daughter of the merchant Abraham van Ceulen, or Cullen, who served the congregation as a deacon from 1641 and then as an elder from 1653.[38] Before the Civil Wars, such powerful men would have felt obliged to serve the Dutch community as elders. After the Restoration they chose instead to serve the wider community in London. Their careers and civic leadership illustrate and emphasize that the Dutch community's loss eventually became London's gain.

Notes

I should like to thank Professor M. J. van Lieburg, Professor J. van den Berg, Dr P. Hoftijzer, Dr A. Cunningham, and an anonymous referee for their comments and kind suggestions.

1. See F. P. Wilson, *The Plague in Shakespeare's London*, Oxford 1927; W. G. Bell, *The Great Plague in London 1665*, London 1951; P. Slack, 'Metropolitan Government in Crisis: the Response to Plague', in *London 1500–1700. The Making of the Metropolis*, ed. A. L. Beier and R. Finlay, London 1986, pp. 60–81, and P. Slack, *The Impact of Plague in Tudor and Stuart England*, London 1985, especially pp. 144–72.

2. For the example of the Dutch community, see ibid., pp. 205–206; see especially pp. 153 and 166 for changes in the patterns of disease.

3. Ibid., pp. 202 ff., 213–23; see also Slack, 'Metropolitan Government', op. cit., note 1 above.

4. See Jacob Cool, *Den Staet van London in hare Groote Peste*, ed. J. A. van Dorsten and K. Schaap, Leiden 1962, p. 32. For Jacob Cool, see also J. A. van Dorsten, '"I.C.O.": the rediscovery of a modest Dutchman in London', in *The Anglo-Dutch Renaissance. Seven essays*, Leiden 1988, pp. 8–20.

5. Slack, 'Metropolitan Government', op. cit., note 1 above, pp. 65–72. For the attempts to control epidemics in London during the 1630s and the co-operation between the College of Physicians and the Privy Council, see Harold J. Cook, 'Policing the Health of London: the College of Physicians and the Early Stuart Monarchy', *Soc. Hist. Med.*, 1989, 2: 1–33.

6. See A. Pettegree, *Foreign Protestant Communities in Sixteenth Century London*, Oxford 1986, pp. 207–208; see also Slack, *Impact of Plague*, op. cit., note 1 above, p. 272. The minutes of the Dutch church from 1563 would indicate that the two visitors of the sick were employed to assist ministers in their house visits, not to replace them, as suggested by Pettegree and Slack; see *Kerkeraads-Protocollen der Nederduitsche Vluchtelingen-Kerk te London 1560–1563*, ed. A. A. van Schelven, Amsterdam 1921, pp. 432–3, henceforth *Kerkeraads–Protocollen*.

7. *Kerkeraads-Protocollen*, p. 434. For the example of Rotterdam, see M. J. van Lieburg, 'Geneeskundige zorg als kerkelijke taak. De situatie in de gereformeerde kerk van Rotterdam in de zeventiende eeuw', in *De Zeventiende eeuw*, 1989, 5(1): 162–71, especially p. 165. For visitors of the sick in general in The Netherlands, see the forthcoming book by F. A. van Lieburg and M. J. van Lieburg, *De ziekentrooster in de gereformeerde*

kerk tijdens de Republiek. Een studie over de pastorale geneeskunde te Rotterdam.

8. *Kerkeraads-Protocollen*, pp. 435–6. See also *Gheschiedenissen ende Handelingen die voornemelick aengaen de Nederduytsche Natie ende Gemeynten wonende in Engeland ende in bysonder tot London*, ed. J. J. van Toorenenbergen, Werken der Marnix-Vereeniging, Serie III – Deel I, Utrecht, 1873, p. 59, henceforth *Gheschiedenissen.*

9. Pettegree, op. cit., note 6 above, pp. 208–209.

10. See O. P. Grell, *Dutch Calvinists in Early Stuart London*, Leiden 1989, especially chapters 1 and 3.

11. *Gheschiedenissen*, p. 154.

12. Grell, op. cit., note 10 above, p. 101, notes 198, 199.

13. See Cool, op. cit., note 4 above, pp. 31, 48–9. For Johannes Radermacher's letter, see *Ecclesiae Londino-Batavae Archivum*, ed. J. H. Hessels, 3 vols in 4 parts, Cambridge, 1889–97, vol. 1, no. 334, henceforth Hessels. The 'Dr "Anneus", the physician', whom Johannes Wouerius from Antwerp asked Cool to salute in November 1603, adding that he hoped that 'they are all well and have survived the mortality', can only refer to Baldwin Hamey or Hameus, see Hessels, vol. 1, no. 332. Dr Hamey stayed in London throughout the plague of 1603 and again in 1625; see J. J. Keevil, *Hamey the Stranger*, London 1952, pp. 95, 142–3.

14. See Cool, op. cit., note 4 above, pp. 31, 33.

15. Hessels, vol. 3, no. 1575.

16. For Willem Teellinck and Godfrid Udemans, see M. J. van Lieburg, 'Zeeuwse Piëtisten en de Geneeskunde in de eerste helft van de 17e eeuw', in *Worstelende Wetenschap. Aspecten van wetenschapsbeoefening in Zeeland van de zestiende tot de negentiende eeuw*, Archief Medelingen van het Koninklijk Zeeuwsch Genootschap der Wetenschappen, Middelburg 1987, pp. 63–86. The opposite view of orthodox Calvinism, as encouraging passivity and apathy, has recently been argued rather unconvincingly by L. Noordegraaf and G. Valk, *De Gave Gods. De Pest in Holland vanaf de late Middeleeuwen*, Bergen 1988, especially pp. 124–31. For *Zion's Trumpet*, see W. Teellinck, *Zions Basayne. Aenstecken uit de woorden van Psalm 7: 13 en 14.*, Middelburg 1621. Jacob Cool and Willem Teellinck not only corresponded and exchanged books, Teellinck also dedicated one of his books to Cool (*Sleutel der Devotie*, Amsterdam 1624): see *Documentieblad Nadere Reformatie*, 1989, 13(1), pp. 3–4; and Hessels, vol. 1, no. 371.

17. See Hessels, vol. 3, no. 1640; for Hadrianus Damman, see *Nieuw Nederlandsch Biografisch Woordenboek.*

18. Guildhall Library MS 7390/1, ff. 12, 27.

19. *Returns of Aliens Dwelling in the City and Suburbs of London*, eds R. E. G. and E. F. Kirk, Huguenot Society Publications 10, 4 vols, London 1900–08. For Jan Schram, see vol. 3, pp. 142, 157, 168. For Francoys vanden Broecke, see ibid., pp. 142, 156, 175; and *Returns of Strangers in the Metropolis 1593, 1627, 1635, 1639*, ed. I. Scouloudi, Huguenot Society Publications 57, London 1985, p. 345, no. 2666.

20. Guildhall Library MS 7397/7, f. 127r.

21. Ibid., f. 127v.

22. Ibid., ff. 130r, 217r, 222r; see also Scouloudi (ed.), op. cit., note 19 above, p. 345, no. 2666. Vanden Broecke appears to have returned to

taffeta-weaving in 1635 when he was well over 60. He left £100 at 6 per cent p.a. in the hands of the consistory of Austin Friars, when he finally retired. See above, Chapter 4, 'From Uniformity to Tolerance: the Effects on the Dutch Church in London of Reverse Patterns in English Church Policy, 1634–1647'. For the salaries paid employees of the City, see Wilson, op. cit., note 1 above, p. 83.

23. Guildhall Library MS 7397/7, f. 103v.
24. Guildhall Library MS 7397/8, f. 42v. See also Grell, op. cit., note 10 above, pp. 94–104.
25. Ibid.
26. *C.S.P. Dom Charles I*, vol. 325, no. 69. The Dutch and Walloon churches in Norwich also employed visitors of the sick during outbreaks of plague in the early seventeenth century, but their activities appear to have been strictly controlled by the magistracy. They were ordered to retire from company, and not to go out after 'candle lighting except on absolute necessity and always to carry a red wand a yard and a half long, their wives and family also to do the same'. See W. J. C. Moens, *The Walloons and their Church at Norwich*, Lymington 1887/8, p. 82.
27. Guildhall Library MS 7397/8, ff. 45r, 45v, 46r. It would appear that the Dutch community shared its opposition to these public health measures with English Puritans: see Slack, *Impact of Plague*, op. cit., note 1 above, p. 231.
28. Guildhall Library MS 7397/8, ff. 45r, 45v, 46r; and Wilson, op. cit., note 1 above, pp. 94, 100, 134.
29. Guildhall Library MS 7397/8, f. 45r.
30. For the London figures, see Wilson, op. cit., note 1 above, pp. 166–8. For Dutch community figures, see Grell, op. cit., note 10 above, chapter 2, section 4.
31. Ibid., pp. 103–104.
32. A number of ministers in the Dutch Reformed churches in the Netherlands appear to have hesitated or even refused to visit plague-stricken members of their communities in the 1570s. The National Synod of Dort in 1574 emphasized ministers' obligation not to make any distinction between plague and other diseases, but to visit all sick members, at the same time underlining that ministers should not undertake any unnecessary risks. The Synod's decision is to say the least ambiguous, see *Acta van de Nederlandsche Synoden der zestiende eeuw*, ed. F. L. Rutgers, Werken der Marnix-Vereening, Serie II – Deel II, Utrecht 1889, p. 159; see also Noordegraf and Valk, op. cit., note 16 above, p. 124. The Synod of the Dutch and Walloon-French churches in England, which met in London in May 1644, emphasized that it was 'the duty of a Minister at all convenient times to visit the sick, that are under his charge, when he is called thereunto', in spite of the claim of the Dutch representatives to the Synod that the ministers in the Netherlands were under no such obligation, see *Acten van de Colloquia der Nederlandsche Gemeenten in Engeland 1575–1609. Aanhangsel. Uittreksels uit de Acten der volgende Colloquia 1627–1706*, ed. J. J. van Toorenenbergen, Werken der Marnix-Vereening, Serie II – Deel I, Utrecht 1872, p. 333. For Thorius, see Anthony Wood, *Athenae Oxonienses*, ed. Philip Bliss, 4 vols, London 1813–20, vol. 2, p. 380; and *Gheschiedenissen*, pp. 190, 395. For Hamey, see Keevil, op. cit., note 13 above, especially pp. 142–3; for Johannes

Brovaert, see A. G. H. Bachrach, *Sir Constantine Huygens and Britain 1596–1619*, Leiden 1962, pp. 71, 120.
33. Guildhall Library MS 7397/8, f. 192v. The consistory of Austin Friars, however, decided that the verger should first try the cheaper treatments available in the baths within the City before seeking cure at a water resort. This was not the first time the church paid for medical advice to one of its members. In 1612 the consistory had requested the Royal Surgeon, Christopher Frederick, a Dutchman, but not a member of the church, to provide medical advice for a certain Abraham Willemsen, see Guildhall Library MS 7397/7, f. 32r (22 October 1612). For Christopher Frederick, father of Sir John Frederick who became a member of Austin Friars, see A. T. Young, *The Annals of the Barber-Surgeons of London*, London 1890, pp. 550–3.
34. W. Birken, 'Dr John King (1614–1681) and Dr Assuerus Regemorter (1615–1650)', *Med. Hist.*, 1976, 20: 276–95, pp. 292–3.
35. For Joas Evensen's letter, see Hessels, vol. 3, no. 3683. For Op de Beck, see Guildhall Library MS 7397/8, f. 272v.
36. Hessels, vol. 3, no. 3676; see also Guildhall Library MS 7397/8, f. 273v; for the plague-master, Nathaniel Upton, see Wilson, op. cit., note 1 above, p. 89.
37. Hessels, vol. 3, no. 3680. The sum Austin Friars spent on poor relief during the plague of 1665 was smaller than in 1636. £2,511 was collected and £2,279 spent. The crisis inspired members to extra contributions of over £1,000 as compared with the immediately preceding collections, for instance in 1664, when the deacons collected £1,185 and spent £1,523, see Guildhall Library MS 7408, under 1664 and 1665.
38. Bell, op. cit., note 1 above, pp. 82–4, 277–8. For their membership of Austin Friars, see for instance Guildhall Library MS 7397/8, f. 255v (collection for the repair of the church in 1659; Alderman Jan Frederick £5 and Alderman Jan Laurens, jun., £5). John Frederick's engagement to Mary Ruys is registered in the minutes of Austin Friars in December 1636, see Guildhall Library MS 7397/8, f. 46r. Frederick was a lukewarm supporter of the Restoration and an anti-Court MP. He was worth £2,000 p.a. in 1660 and left £42,000 in his will. Lawrence married Abigail van Cuelen in 1643; Abraham van Cuelen became an elder in Austin Friars in 1653, see Hessels, vol. 3, no. 3241. Lawrence was also worth £2,000 p.a. and a leading City Whig. For both see J. R. Woodhead, *The Rulers of London 1660–1689. A Biographical Record of the Aldermen and Common Councilmen of the City of London*, London, London and Middlesex Archeological Society, 1966. There were, no doubt, a few exceptions to this picture of a community in decay. The Dutch church was still able to benefit from the dedicated service of at least one of its elders, the wealthy merchant Willem de Visscher, who had served the congregation from 1632, first as a deacon and then as an elder, see Grell, op. cit., note 10 above, p. 268. Visscher, however, was by then an unusual member of the church's consistory, being one of the few surviving leaders who had been born abroad. John Aubrey, who included Visscher in his *Brief Lives*, informs us that 'he stayed in London during the whole time of the Plague, and had all the time not one sick in his family. He was a temperate man, and had his house very cleanly kept', see *Aubrey's Brief Lives*. Harmondsworth 1978, pp. 466–7. It is interesting to see that Aubrey

considered cleanliness, one of the standard attributes of the Dutch nation, a significant factor in explaining why Visscher and his household avoided catching the disease. Cleanliness among the Dutch does not, however, appear to have made any difference within the London community, which suffered as much as its English hosts.

CHAPTER ELEVEN

The attraction of Leiden University for English students of medicine and theology, 1590–1642

'No one, I believe has so far properly investigated the extent to which Englishmen dissatisfied with Oxford and Cambridge sent their sons to Leiden University, or what Leiden's influence on English thought was.' This statement can be found in Christopher Hill's pioneering work, *Intellectual Origins of the English Revolution*, published more than a quarter of a century ago.[1] Sadly, or fortunately, depending on one's point of view, no one has yet found it worthwhile to research this area. Thus Leiden University hardly figures in Charles Webster's important book, *The Great Instauration*, or in Hugh Kearney's *Scholars and Gentlemen*, while the few references to English students at Leiden in the large jubilee volume, *Leiden University in the Seventeenth Century*, add little to our knowledge.[2] Instead, we are left with the Victorian compilations of Edward Peacock, based on the *Album Studiosorum Academiae Lugduno Batavae*, published in 1875, which are, to say the least, insufficient. Peacock made the unfortunate mistake of promoting all matriculated English students to graduate status, when in fact only a minority obtained a degree from Leiden. Reliable information about English students at Leiden University will, in other words, have to be obtained from the *Album Studiosorum*, supplemented by information to be found in P. C. Molhuysen's *Bronnen tot de geschiedenis der Leidsche Universiteit*, not to mention the manuscript department of the University Library in Leiden. In the case of medical students we are on considerably firmer ground thanks to R. W. Innes Smith's *English-Speaking Students of Medicine at the University of Leyden*, published in 1932. But none of these works amounts to much more than a source-publication, and no attempt has been made to put the attraction of Leiden University to English students into any historical context.[3]

In what follows I shall make a modest attempt to remedy this situation, at least as far as English students of medicine and theology are concerned. There are good reasons for focusing on these particular subjects, rather than on other fields of study, such as law and philosophy, since theology and medicine were generally studied with careers in mind. They were among the first academic 'professions' to establish themselves in early modern society. Their practitioners shared similar values and aspirations, being part of the same social stratum, and close social and intellectual links existed between doctors and clergymen. Many held degrees in theology, as well as medicine, including the considerable number of ministers who practised in both fields.

First of all there is the basic question to be answered: why should English students of medicine and theology have wanted to attend Leiden University rather than their own more venerable institutions in Oxford and Cambridge or any of the other older, continental seats of learning? After all, in 1590 the University of Leiden was still a new and in many ways untested institution, having been founded as a Protestant university on 8 February 1575 only 15 years earlier. Furthermore, it was the first university to be founded in the rebellious United Provinces, even if others were to be established shortly afterwards, in Franeker (1585), Groningen (1614) and Utrecht (1636).

But in some respects the foundation of Leiden University could hardly have happened at a more opportune moment. The leading Protestant universities in northern Europe – such as Wittenberg, Heidelberg and the Academy in Geneva – had started to show serious signs of decay towards the late 1570s, thereby causing Protestant students of theology, willing and able to travel, to look for alternative places of education. At the same time the famous medical schools at the Italian Universities of Bologna and Padua, which had been much favoured by English students, had begun to feel the effects of the Counter-Reformation, making it difficult for them to retain and recruit the best teachers, while Protestant medical students from northern Europe found it an increasingly dangerous business to matriculate there.

Established at a time when the effects of the Counter-Reformation were being felt all over Europe and confessional border-lines were hardening, Leiden University appears to have been unique in espousing truly humanist and tolerant ideals. From its foundation it was a Protestant university, but a remarkably tolerant one, not least thanks to several of its founding fathers, among whom Janus Dousa played a particularly important role. His influence was considerable as President of the Board of Curators during the first 29 years of the university's existence; for instance, it was largely due to his efforts that the great humanist scholars, Justus Lipsius and Joseph Scaliger, became professors at Leiden.[4] The Board consisted of three Curators, appointed by the States of Holland for life, and the four annually elected burgomasters of Leiden.[5] The humanist interests of the former and the tolerant and generally anti-clerical attitudes of the latter managed to prevent the university from coming under the control of the Dutch Reformed Church. In 1582 the burgomasters of Leiden even went so far as to declare that they would oppose 'the Genevan Inquisition as resolutely as the Spanish Inquisition'.[6]

This did not, however, prevent a constant power struggle within the university between adherents of a strict, orthodox Calvinism on one hand, and those who represented a more liberal, humanist and latitudinarian Reformed tradition on the other. The University Statutes of 2 June 1575 had stated that all students had to swear an oath of allegiance to the university, promising not to profess any other religious doctrines than those that were taught within the university as long as they remained there as students.[7] This was a much milder requirement than at the neighbouring, Catholic University of Louvain, where a 'Declaratio Fidei' was needed. Nevertheless the oath appears to have been enough to cause concern among a number of foreign students who consequently decided to leave Leiden in 1577. Not surprisingly, the Curators showed great sensitivity to the problem, since foreign students constituted nearly half of the student population in Leiden. It was obviously a question of finance – the prospective loss of a considerable number of fee-paying foreigners was enough to alarm a money-conscious magistracy – but academic reputation was also at stake. With the authority of the States of Holland the oath was rescinded the following year and from March 1578 it was possible to matriculate in Leiden 'without having to swear any oath of allegiance to the religion adhered to there', apart from divinity students, for whom the oath remained obligatory.[8] This, however, was the only concession given to the Reformed Church which was otherwise denied any direct influence, even in the Faculty of Divinity. The meek request of the Synod of the Reformed Churches, that Curators who were well disposed towards the Reformed faith should be nominated, and that professors of theology at least should be 'adherents of the doctrine and confession of our Churches' only serves to emphasize the feeble position of the Dutch Reformed church vis-à-vis the University of Leiden.[9]

It was hardly a coincidence that in 1578 Justus Lipsius became a professor in Leiden, for during these years the humanist liberal wing was in the ascendancy within the university and a number of internationally renowned professors were given chairs, such as Bonaventura Vulcanius, Thomas Sosius and Rembert Dodonaeus, who were not exactly the staunchest Calvinists.[10] Simultaneously, however, political pressure from orthodox Calvinists was building up outside the university, in spite of support for the tolerant 'liberal' wing from William of Orange. The years following the Pacification of Ghent (1576) had seen an aggressive Calvinist minority take over several of the cities in the Southern Netherlands, such as Ghent, Bruges and Courtrai, often encouraged by immigrant co-religionists in Holland, Zeeland and England.[11]

The 'liberals', however, managed to maintain the upper hand within the university, even during the Earl of Leicester's governor-generalship in the Netherlands between 1586 to 1588, which augmented the political clout of the Calvinist 'precisians'.[12] The success of the liberal policies pursued by both the university and the magistracy of Leiden undoubtedly encouraged the famous Antwerp printer Christopher Plantin to set up his Officina Plantiniana in the city in 1583. Plantin, who stayed in Leiden between 1583 and 1585, found the university a tolerant oasis, where nobody was forced to relinquish their faith, not even Roman Catholics, informing us that students and teachers were only obliged to show obedience to the magistracy in civil affairs. Plantin was the first of a number of distinguished printers, such as Franciscus Raphelengius and his sons and Louis Elzevier and sons, not to mention the English printers, Thomas Basson and Thomas Brewer, to establish themselves in Leiden, thereby helping to publicize Leiden's leading role in humanist scholarship to the rest of Europe.[13]

Although liberal humanism served to encourage scholarship in the arts and medicine, it created problems for the new university within theology, since the Curators found it difficult to recruit professors of divinity. Thus the former Lady Margaret Professor in Cambridge, Thomas Cartwright, who had lost his post in 1570 because of his Presbyterianism, declined a chair in Leiden ten years later because of the religious quarrels between the Dutch Reformed Church and the Leiden magistracy.[14] A similar conflict made the theology professor, Lambert Danaeus, leave Leiden in 1582 after less than a year's service to the university. Danaeus, a Huguenot, who had been recruited from the Academy of Geneva, was highly regarded within the international world of Calvinism. When he moved from Leiden to the newly established theological academy in Ghent in 1582, the three students sponsored by the Dutch church in London, Samuel Ashe, Peter Regemorter and Peter Lambert, on the instructions of the elders, accompanied him.[15]

It proved difficult to establish the Faculty of Theology on a firm footing. One professor, Johannes Holmannus Secundus, died within four years of his appointment; another, Adrian Saravia, fled Leiden for England with his co-conspirator, Adolf van Meetkercke, after having been involved in the Earl of Leicester's failed *coup d'état* in 1587.[16] Only after Saravia's departure did the faculty achieve any form of stability. That year the Curators appointed the minister to the Walloon church in Leiden, Lucas Trelcatius, and five years later the Huguenot, Franciscus Junius, was given a chair. Both men were orthodox, but more importantly, eirenic Calvinists, who managed to secure a measure of consensus and toleration within the faculty.

Meanwhile, the political and religious equilibrium in the United Provinces was changing rapidly. The considerable immigration from the Southern Netherlands which had begun after the Duke of Alva's attempt to repress the rebellion against Spain in the late 1560s, and accelerated during the 1570s until it peaked in the wake of the Spanish recapture of Antwerp in 1585, was putting the 'liberals' under pressure. These refugees were predominantly hardline Calvinists, strongly opposed to Spain and Catholicism, who had suffered for their beliefs. Their arrival helped to strengthen militant Calvinists in the North, whose cause was further advanced when a considerable number of wealthy Calvinist merchants, originating from the southern Netherlands, began to immigrate from Germany in particular. They were attracted by the sudden amelioration in the Republic's economic and political fortune by 1590, when Philip II, intervening in the civil war in France, suddenly changed his strategy towards the United Provinces from the offensive to the defensive and lifted his embargo against the Republic.[17]

By 1591 the influence of the hardliners was felt within the States of Holland, when a committee suggested that no one should be appointed to the University of Leiden who did not adhere to 'the true religion'. Even if this suggestion was never endorsed, it had practical consequences and made the Board of Curators tread a more conservative path. It was undoubtedly this growing intolerance which led Justus Lipsius to resign in 1591 and take up a position at the Catholic University of Louvain. In June Lipsius informed his friend, the geographer, Abraham Ortelius, in Antwerp:

> It is likely (but keep this to yourself) that I shall not return to the Hollanders, though they are friends to me and kind. But you will easily see my reasons. I have never been, and my nature prevents me from being, factious or favourable to parties.[18]

The following year, in order to reinforce the Faculty of Theology which had failed to develop into the important training centre for ministers as the Dutch Reformed Church originally hoped, the States College, modelled on the Collegium Sapientiae in Heidelberg, was inaugurated in Leiden. Fifteen years later this college was supplemented by a Walloon College, founded especially for the furthering of the French-speaking Calvinist ministry. As opposed to the States College, which until the Synod of Dort and Vossius's dismissal was dominated by Arminian theologians, the Regency of the Walloon College attracted such leading orthodox Calvinist theologians as Daniel Colonius and Louis de Dieu.[19]

It is worth noting that during the first 15 years of the university's existence the professorships within the Faculty of Divinity were occupied by Frenchmen, Germans and Southern Netherlanders, while only one Northern Netherlander was appointed, and he only acquired his chair because of the lack of qualified candidates. Later, in the early seventeenth century, the only two Northerners to be appointed were the Remonstrants, Jacob Arminius and his pupil, Simon Episcopius; and it was not by chance that they, born and bred in the humanist climate of Holland, came to represent the 'liberal', latitudinarian Reformed theology that would later be known as Arminianism. The appointment of Arminius as Junius's successor in 1603 had clearly been intended by the Curators to balance the earlier appointment of the hardliner Franciscus Gomarus: therefore, it must be seen as an attempt by the university to continue its traditional 'liberal' line. In spite of the quarrels which ensued between Arminius and Gomarus about predestination, which caused reverberations within international Calvinism, when appointing a successor to Arminius, who had died in 1609, the Curators of Leiden University still intended to fill his chair with another Arminian theologian, the German, Conrad Vorstius. By now, however, Arminianism had become a matter of international debate, not least because of James I's antipathy towards Vorstius, and the German was never able to take up his position.[20] It is remarkable that the Curators, having been under considerable pressure over the Vorstius-affair, continued to fight for the university's humanist values; so in 1611, the year Gomarus resigned, they appointed the orthodox, but conciliatory Calvinist, Johannes Polyander, who promised the Curators to tolerate Arminian colleagues. Whether or not the Curators still hoped to retain Vorstius, whom they allowed to keep the title of professor plus his salary until he was finally dismissed in the wake of the Synod of Dort, is doubtful but they may well have contemplated another Arminian appointment. The following year they appointed Simon Episcopius, who was to defend the Arminian position at the Synod of Dort.[21] This theological conflict finally came to a head at the Synod itself in 1619, but by then the confrontation between Remonstrants and Counter-Remonstrants had become totally enmeshed in politics, and the outcome – victory for the anti-Spanish, hardline Calvinists, the Counter-Remonstrants, supported by the Stadtholder, Maurice of Nassau – was a foregone conclusion.

There was no way the university could avoid the effects of the Synod, and not only did the Arminian spokesman, Episcopius, lose his chair; others outside the Faculty of Theology, such as the Professor of Hebrew, Wilhelm Coddaeus, and the Arminian Regent of the States College, Gerard Vossius, were also deprived of their positions. Even one of the Curators, Cornelius van der Myle, was sacked. But even then, the Curators demonstrated that they were not totally cowed. They continued to pay Vossius's salary, finally making him Professor of Rhetoric in

1622, and they decided not to recall the militant Calvinist, Gomarus.[22] The experiences of 1619, however, forced the university authorities to promote peace and concord within the Faculty of Divinity, acknowledging that a minimum of orthodoxy was needed. Consequently, only theologians who were not unacceptable to the Synods and assemblies of the Dutch Reformed Church were appointed to the chairs in theology for the rest of the period here under consideration.

The strength and attraction of Theology in Leiden undoubtedly lay in its solid foundation in critical, Scriptural theology and biblical exegesis. This scholarship escaped most of the negative effects of the Synod of Dort. The faculty also benefited from the presence at the university of some of the leading philological experts of the time, such as Bonaventura Vulcanius, Louis de Dieu, Joseph Scaliger, Lipsius's successor, and Daniel Heinsius. During this period neither Oxford nor Cambridge could muster a similarly impressive group of teachers. For many English students of theology who, in order to matriculate and obtain a degree from Oxford and Cambridge, had to subscribe to the creed of the Church of England and the Thirty-Nine Articles, the diversity and quality of the teaching in Leiden must have been appealing. That this avenue was pursued primarily by a small number of Puritan dissenters is hardly surprising, for the option available to English physicians of having their foreign degrees incorporated at either Oxford or Cambridge was not automatically available to those who had received their degrees in theology at a continental university. Thus, the number of English theology students at Leiden remained fairly modest and constant throughout this period.

In contrast to the Faculty of Divinity, most of the professors of medicine were recruited from within the United Provinces and they were predominantly solidly anchored within the humanist 'liberal' tradition. A similar outlook characterized those of their colleagues in the Medical Faculty who were of immigrant stock, from the southern Netherlands and France, such as Carolus Clusius, Aelius Everhardus Vorstius, Franciscus de la Boe Sylvius and Johannes Waleus, son of Anthonius Waleus, Professor of Theology at Leiden.

The Faculty of Medicine had been much slower off the mark than theology; and had to make do with only one professor during the first five years of its existence. Geraert de Bont had been appointed in 1575 but did not acquire any colleagues until Johannes Heurnius and Rembert Dodonaeus were given chairs in the early 1580s. The Curators appear to have wanted to recruit 'the Dutch Hippocrates', the Delft-based physician Pieter van Foreest, and his colleague Laurens van Oorschot, in 1575, but nothing came of it probably because of the initial shortage of students.[23]

Johannes Heurnius, whose medical advice was widely sought in the United Provinces, even by the Stadtholders, William of Orange and Maurice of Nassau, demonstrated his and the faculty's humanism, when in 1594 he was instrumental in bringing about the rejection by the two faculties of medicine and philosophy of the water test in witch trials. In Rembert Dodonaeus, however, the Medical Faculty acquired its first teacher of international fame. He had served the Emperors Maximilian II and Rudolph II as Court physician and was the foremost botanist of the age, but unfortunately his influence on medicine at Leiden was to be minimal, since, dying in 1585, he only held his post for little over two years.[24] As Lindeboom claims, the tolerant climate which prevailed in Leiden proved particularly conducive to experimental research in the natural sciences, but teaching within the Medical Faculty remained traditional and theoretical, based on Hippocrates and Galen, until the arrival of Pieter Pauw in 1589.[25] It should, however, be mentioned that the University Statutes of 1575 also recommended that besides the theoretical teaching to be given to medical students, they should also receive proper practical training by accompanying a qualified physician on his visits to patients.[26]

A botanic garden had already been established in Leiden in 1587, two years before Pauw's arrival, which apart from a garden in Leipzig (1580) was to be the first university botanic garden north of the Alps (gardens had been established in Padua in 1545, in Pisa in 1547 and in Bologna in 1568).[27] Geraerd de Bont became the first Professor of Botany in 1587, but it was not until Pauw was made Professor *Ordinarius* in 1592 and charged with supervising the new garden, with the special task of expanding the collection, that botany became a serious subject in Leiden. The same year the Curators were able to employ yet another leading European academic when Carolus Clusius, the Protestant physician in ordinary to Emperor Maximilian II in Vienna while supervising the Emperor's botanical garden, was appointed Professor *Honorarius* in Botany. The already elderly Clusius was evidently not appointed for teaching purposes but in order to add further glory to the university. He was given a high salary, exempted from any obligation to lecture and only required to be present an hour a day to conduct research in the botanic garden – terms which present-day academics can only dream about. The fame of Leiden and its botanic garden must have spread quickly across northern Europe, since nearly all botanist/physicians of the age corresponded with Clusius.[28]

By 1598 De Bont was sharing the teaching of botany with Pauw, who, after the deaths of De Bont in 1599 and Clusius in 1609, took full charge of the botanic garden as well as the teaching of botany. It was due to Pauw's efforts that the Curators agreed to have a gallery built at the south end of the garden for the preservation of foreign plants during winter. Likewise, it was Pauw who in 1601 published in Leiden a catalogue of all the plants in the garden (*Hortus Publicus Acad. Lugduno-Batavae, eius ichonographia, descriptio, usus ...*), which went through further editions in 1603, 1617 and 1629. After Pauw's death in 1617 the responsibility for the garden fell to Aelius Everhardus Vorstius, who had become Professor *Extraordinarius* in Natural Philosophy in 1598, succeeding De Bont as full Professor of Medicine the following year. After the death of Vorstius, the professorship of botany was taken over by his son Adolph, who continued Pauw's work publishing catalogues of plants in the university garden (*Catalogus plantarum horti academiae Lugduno-Batavae*, Leiden, 1633, 1636, 1649, 1658).[29]

Professorial dynasty-building within the Medical Faculty was not a new phenomenon in Leiden when Adolph Vorstius succeeded his father in 1624. In 1606, Reinier de Bont, having been Professor *Extraordinarius* in Philosophy since 1599, had been able to follow in his father Geraert's footsteps.[30] In 1601, during the illness which led to his death, Johannes Heurnius had requested the Curators to elect his son, Otto, to be his successor. They obliged him posthumously. On 30 August 1601, 20 days after his father's death and only seven weeks after he had acquired his MD, they made Otto Heurnius Professor *Extraordinarius* of Medicine.[31]

Botany, however, was only one of the areas where Pieter Pauw proved a major innovator within Leiden University, for it was mainly due to his efforts that an anatomical theatre was opened in 1597. The teaching of anatomy in Leiden had begun ten years earlier when Geraert de Bont had not only started lecturing but during the winter months had begun to use corpses for anatomical demonstration. His colleague, Johannes Heurnius, may well have started to perform dissections privately at about the same time.[32] But public dissections were not performed until the arrival of Pauw, educated in Rostock and Paris, in 1589 – we know that Pauw, who had taught anatomy at Rostock University between 1585 and 1587, was performing dissections as part of his anatomy teaching by 1591.

Pauw performed more than 60 dissections on humans, not to mention numerous dissections and vivisections on animals during his Leiden years. But in spite of Pauw performing between three and four dissections in some years, public dissections remained unusual events in Leiden during Pauw's life, attracting considerable attention as social events. Consequently, the audience was by no means restricted to medical students and dissections were attended by the leading citizens of Leiden, such as the magistracy and professors from other faculties. Probably in order to control attendance, an entrance fee had to be paid. The significance of the event is illustrated by the fact that while the dissection was being performed the Medical Faculty suspended normal teaching. In 1613, the potential entertainment value of these occasions was emphasized when the university considered adding music to the performance, using the flute players who played at graduations and inaugurations. As elsewhere in Europe, corpses used for dissections in Leiden were those of executed criminals. In 1593 the States of Holland issued an order which allowed the Medical Faculty to collect such corpses all over Holland, a task performed by the anatomy-servant accompanied by two medical students.[33] Not surprisingly, Pieter Pauw also founded the collection of anatomical and pathological specimens kept in the theatre. Thus, in 1614, he obtained from England the diseased bladder of the famous Huguenot historian, Isaac Casaubon. This collection of medical curiosities grew steadily: in 1620, for instance, a donation was received from Humfrey Bromley, an Englishman based in Amsterdam, who offered 'some monstrous, embalmed small children'.

At the time of Pauw's death in 1617, the university's appreciation of his efforts was clearly demonstrated by the constant increase of his salary, which had grown rapidly since 1592 when Pauw had been appointed full professor at a salary of 300 guilders, until 1615 when it reached its peak at 900 guilders per annum. Furthermore, in 1604 the Curators had given him a golden cup worth 100 guilders in appreciation of his teaching of anatomy. Evidently, by then the Curators had realized the value of anatomy and dissections to the university. Consequently, they quickly filled Pauw's chair with Johannes Heurnius, while appointing one of Pauw's pupils, Adrian van Valkenburg, lecturer of anatomy. Thus Van Valkenburg found himself performing dissections and teaching anatomy four years before he received his MD.[34]

Further attempts at modernizing the medical curriculum in Leiden were made by Johannes Heurnius and Geraert de Bont in the field of clinical medicine. Both had studied at Padua under Albertino Bottoni and Marco degli Oddi, who had revived Montanus's bedside teaching, and it was undoubtedly on their prompting that in 1591 the Medical Faculty suggested to the Curators that bedside instruction be introduced in Leiden. But the idea proved premature and the medical curriculum remained unchanged. Apart from the influence of Padua, inspiration for clinical teaching may well have developed out of the apprenticeship practice, which as we have seen had been encouraged in the University Statutes of 1575. Forty-five years later bedside teaching was finally added to the Leiden curriculum thanks to the efforts of Otto Heurnius and the need to catch up with the new medical school in Utrecht, which had introduced clinical teaching that year.[35] The Leiden emphasis on bedside instruction was later developed by the Huguenot immigrant Franciscus de la Boe Sylvius, who also gave lessons in Anatomy in Leiden from 1637 to 1644 but was not given a chair in medicine until 1658 after having practised in Amsterdam.[36]

The Curators were prepared to limit the teaching obligations of certain famous professors in order to attract them to Leiden, as we have already observed in the case of Clusius. The value of the glory they added to the young university is self-evident. Concerning teaching in general, however, the Curators conscientiously tried to make sure that professors fulfilled their teaching duties. A beadle was employed to check whether or not lectures were given in accordance with the lecture list, and a system of fines quickly introduced. Thus, in 1595, Geraert de Bont, while Rector Magnificus, was reprimanded and fined by the Curators, who told him to make a greater effort with his teaching in future.[37]

As we have seen, the success of the University of Leiden depended in no small measure on its 'liberal' and tolerant academic climate. How little the medical school was affected by the reactionary climate of the Synod of Dort can be seen from the example of Otto Heurnius. Shortly after Dort, he had the audacity to decorate the Theatrum Anatomicum with allegorical biblical prints, partly borrowed from the Sistine Chapel in Rome – hardly the actions of a man hampered by hardline Calvinism.[38] But perhaps more than anything else, leading academics were enticed to Leiden by the money and special benefits on offer. When Clusius was recruited in 1592 he was exempted from teaching but still given a salary of close to 700 guilders per annum. In that year Franciscus Junius was appointed at 1,200 guilders per annum, plus 200 guilders in moving expenses; and the following year Joseph Scaliger received the same annual salary and moving expenses as Junius, plus a honorarium of 800 guilders, while being offered fringe benefits such as liberty to print and freedom from lecturing.[39]

The success of the medical school in Leiden had been acknowledged early on by the Curators, who, in 1589, had proudly stated that the number of medical students in Leiden was already greater than it had been at the Catholic University of Louvain during its most flourishing period. A considerable proportion of the students came from abroad, enticed to Leiden not only by the tolerant atmosphere and excellent teaching on offer, but also by the city's famous print works and bookshops.

English students constituted the largest group among the foreign nationalities attracted to the medical school, and they had good reasons to seek a better education abroad. The medical schools in Oxford and Cambridge remained old-fashioned and undistinguished, still basing their purely theoretical curriculum on the texts of Hippocrates and

Galen.[40] Thus a botanical garden was not founded in Oxford until 1622 and not finished until the mid-1630s, while Cambridge had to wait until the 1660s and John Ray before the university could lay claim to any botanical credentials (a chair in botany was instituted in 1724). In Oxford the Tomlins Readership of Anatomy had been founded in 1624, but did not receive its permanent endowment until 1637 and was not given to an individual other than the Regius Professor of Physic until 1650. Cambridge, once more, had to wait until the early eighteenth century before acquiring a chair in anatomy. The situation was even worse in the field of clinical instruction. Bedside teaching never became part of the official medical curricula in Oxford and Cambridge during the seventeenth century. Instead, students appear to have relied on apprenticeships for their clinical training, but no official recommendation for such instruction, as prescribed in the Statutes of Leiden University of 1575, was given by either of the English universities.[41] The difference from Leiden could hardly have been more pronounced.

The economic boom in Holland and the accompanying Dutch hegemony over world trade which manifested itself in the years between 1590 and 1609, as recently demonstrated by Jonathan Israel, would have served to direct English attention to the Dutch Republic in general.[42] Leiden in particular, with its geographical proximity to England, not to mention its fast expanding economy and growing population – it more than doubled between 1581 and 1600, from around 12,000 to over 26,000 and had reached 50,000 in 1640 – would have attracted English students.[43] Furthermore, a number of ties already existed between England and Leiden. Since the late sixteenth century a growing number of Englishmen had settled in the city. An English Reformed church had been established in 1607 – two years later its membership consisted of 200 families – and a Separatist church had come into existence in 1609 with around a hundred members, growing to 300 in 1620 under the pastorship of the learned John Robinson, who had himself matriculated in theology at Leiden University in 1615. Until the exiled Scottish minister, Robert Dury, father of the famous John Dury, was elected minister to the English Reformed church in 1610, the congregation had depended on sermons given by the minister of nearby Oegstgeest, Jonas Volmar. He was bi-lingual, born to Dutch parents in Sandwich, Kent, and educated as an alumnus of the Dutch church in London at Leiden University on the recommendation of the former Leiden Professor of Theology, Adrian Saravia.[44] The English church in Leiden also benefited from occasional sermons given by the Leiden Professor of Theology, Franciscus Gomarus, who had studied at both Oxford and Cambridge during the early 1580s and among whose student-boarders in Leiden were alumni from the

Dutch church in London. Gomarus was an important spoke in the Anglo-Dutch wheel.[45]

When Dury died in 1616 the English church failed to recruit either the well-known Puritan Arthur Hildersam, a close friend of the influential Middelburg minister Willem Teellinck, because his wife was unwilling to move to Holland, or the exiled minister, Johannes Blanquius, who had matriculated at the University of Leiden at the mature age of 50. Eventually, in 1617, the church managed to employ another recently arrived theology student, Hugh Goodyear, who had acquired his MA from Emmanuel College, Cambridge the previous year. Goodyear had matriculated together with his travelling companions, John Bastwick and Alexander Leighton, with whom he also lodged in Leiden.[46] This Puritan troika, with its antagonism to the Church of England, was typical of a considerable proportion of English theology students at Leiden, but less so of medical students, even if the latter subject was chosen by both Bastwick and the minister, Alexander Leighton. Bastwick and Leighton are included among the 164 English medical students in Leiden listed in Table 11.1 below, a list which also includes a number of students who were not English nationals, but who spent most, or a considerable part, of their working lives in England, such as John Maculo, Raphael Thorius, Johannes Brovaert, Baldwin Hamey Senior, Theodore Diodati, Ludovicus du Moulin, Gerard and Arnold Boat, and Ludovicus Rosaeus.

Bastwick and Leighton, who acquired near martyr status among English Puritans after their Star Chamber sentences in the 1630s, were not the only Puritan medical students in Leiden during this period. Others were Robert Child, one of the early New England scientists, a friend of Samuel Hartlib and an associate of the founders of the Royal Society; the ejected minister John Burgess; John Milton's friend, Nathan Paget, who was a nephew to the minister of the English Reformed church in Amsterdam, John Paget; and finally John Pordage, who switched from caring for the body to caring for the soul, taking up the ministry in the 1640s and later becoming associated with the Ranters.[47]

The significance of Leiden for the development of English medicine is also evident from the fact that more than 15 per cent of the membership of the Royal College of Physicians under the early Stuarts had studied there.[48] Similarly, the significance of English students for the Medical Faculty in Leiden is obvious when we consider that more than 50 Englishmen studied there between 1580 and 1625, at a time when no more than 137 students graduated from that faculty. Thus, it was no coincidence that the first medical student to matriculate at Leiden was an Englishman, John James, who after graduating in 1581 became physician to the Earl of Leicester.[49] Close to a third of all the English

Table 11.1 English students matriculated at Leiden, 1590–1642

	1590–1600	1601–10	1611–20	1621–30	1631–42	Total
Medicine	12	7	24	22	97	162
Theology	21	12	14	10	15	72
Other	40	24	27	65	101	257
Total	73	43	65	97	213	491

Note: data compiled from *Album Studiosorum*, Molhuysen, and Innes Smith.

Table 11.2 English MDs from Leiden, 1590–1642

1590–1600	1601–10	1611–20	1621–30	1631–42	Total
3	3	10	13	26	55

Note: data compiled from Innes Smith.

medical students who matriculated at Leiden during this period also
graduated from the Medical Faculty, as can be seen from Table 11.2.
This is a significant number, especially when we bear in mind that
during the period 1620–40 Oxford only granted 1 MD per year while
the equivalent figure for Cambridge was 1.5.[50] In other words, Leiden's
output of English graduates was on a par with the total output of
medical graduates from Oxford and Cambridge during these decades.

English Puritans were even more strongly represented among the 69
English theology students. Among them were Samuel Wright, who matriculated in 1594 after having acquired his BD from Magdalen College,
Cambridge. He was a close friend of another leading Puritan, Richard
Rogers, and became the first Fellow and President of the new Puritan,
Cambridge college Sidney Sussex, in 1599.[51] In this connection, it is
notable that Sidney Sussex was the Cambridge college favoured by
students from the Dutch community in London.[52] Other Puritans, apart
from Hugh Goodyear and John Robinson already mentioned, were the
well-known William Ames, later Professor of Theology at the University of Franeker, and Christopher Preston, son of the renowned Calvinist divine John Preston.

As can be seen from Table 11.3 more than 50 per cent of the English
theology students in this period came from the Dutch/Walloon immigrant communities in England. A considerable proportion of these students were alumni of the stranger communities and later served them as
ministers. They often constituted near dynasties of ministers, stretching
over several generations, such as the Regius, Regemorter and Ruytinck
families who served the Dutch church in London, not to mention the
Elisons who served the Dutch church in Norwich. Even the French-
speaking Walloon communities appear to have favoured Leiden, rather
than one of the other Calvinist universities on the Continent. Ministers
to these communities, such as Abraham Aurelius (who served the
Walloon/French church in London and who was the offspring of the
minister to the Italian church in London, Jean Baptiste Aurelius), Peter
de Laune (a brother of James I's apothecary, Gideon, who served the
Walloon church in Norwich), John Bulteel, Charles Beauvais, Elie Delme
and Nathanael Marie (another minister's son, in this case from the
Walloon community in Norwich), all received their theological training
in Leiden. They were undoubtedly encouraged to seek their education
in Leiden through the presence of such leading Reformed theologians at
the Walloon College in Leiden as Daniel Colonius and Louis de Dieu;
the latter's father, Daniel, had been an alumnus of Austin Friars, the
Dutch church in London.[53]

The Dutch communities in England in particular maintained excellent relations with the theology professors in Leiden, placing several of

Table 11.3 Students from the Dutch/Walloon communities in England

	1590–1600	1601–10	1611–20	1621–30	1631–42	D/W total	Total % of all Eng. stud.
Medicine	2	2	1	8	1	14	9
Theology	15	9	4	7	3	38	53
Other	2	7	7	7	3	26	10
Total	19	18	12	22	7	78	16

Note: data compiled from *Album Studiosorum*; Innes Smith; F. de Schickler's *Les Eglises du refuge en Angleterre*, 3 vols, Paris 1892; *Ecclesiae Londino-Batavae Archivum*, ed. J. H. Hessels, 3 vols, Cambridge 1887–97; and Grell.

their students as boarders with Gomarus and Festus Hommius. Likewise, Austin Friars often consulted the former Professor of Theology at Leiden, Adrian Saravia, about academic matters and the appointment of future alumni. Thus, in 1612, Saravia was asked whether or not the son of his friend, Adolph Meetkercke, would accept a scholarship in theology from the London community. Edward Meetkercke, who later became Professor of Hebrew in Oxford, was unique in turning down the church's sponsorship.[54]

As can be seen from Table 11.3, the Dutch and Walloon communities were less well represented among English medical students. But their 9 per cent included some key figures in the English medical world of the period. Johannes Brouvaert, Theodore de Mayerne's assistant, was a member of the Dutch church in London, while Mayerne himself attended the French/Walloon congregation in Threadneedle Street. Other members of the Dutch church in Austin Friars were Raphael Thorius, Assuerus Regemorter and John King (Regius). Peter Chamberlen's sons, Nathanael and David, were also associated with the French/Walloon community. The two Baldwin Hameys, father and son, both members of the Dutch community, were to play an active and important role within the Royal College of Physicians.[55] Hamey Junior might well have studied theology instead of medicine and ended up as a minister to Austin Friars rather than a physician in London, since his father had approached the consistory of the Dutch church in London in 1614, suggesting that the church accept his son as an alumnus, promising to repay the church should young Hamey prove unsuitable for the ministry.[56]

Leiden was undoubtedly an attractive place for English students of medicine and theology during this period – the quality and fame of its teachers, the tolerant and humanist atmosphere of the university, and the existence of an economically and culturally affluent society were attractions in their own right – but the inspiration and role of the Dutch and Walloon communities in England in directing Englishmen to Leiden was important, as was the role of leading members of these communities in transmitting new ideas and generating an international republic of letters in England, thereby providing significant inspiration for what Charles Webster has re-labelled the 'Great Instauration'.

Notes

1. Christopher Hill, *Intellectual Origins of the English Revolution*, London 1972, 283.
2. Charles Webster, *The Great Instauration: Science, Medicine and Reform*

1626–1660, London 1975; H. Kearney, *Scholars and Gentlemen: University and Society in Pre-Industrial England, 1500–1700*, New York 1970; and *Leiden University in the Seventeenth Century: An Exchange of Learning*, eds T. H. Lunsingh Scheurleer and G. H. M. Posthumus Meyes, Leiden 1975. A similar lack of recognition of the growing importance of Leiden University for English students of Medicine from the end of the sixteenth century can be found in Gillian Lewis's recent essay on the Medical Faculty at Oxford during the sixteenth century in *The History of the University of Oxford*, ed. J. McConica, Oxford 1986, III, 255.

3. *Album Studiosorum Academiae Lugduno Batavae MDLXXV–MDCCCLXXV*, The Hague 1875; Edward Peacock, *Index to English-Speaking Students Who Have Graduated at Leyden University*, London 1883; R. W. Innes Smith, *English-Speaking Students of Medicine at the University of Leyden*, Edinburgh 1932; *Bronnen tot de geschiedenis der Leidsche Universiteit*, ed. P. C. Molhuysen, 7 vols, The Hague 1913–24.

4. J. A. van Dorsten, *Poets, Patrons, and Professors: Sir Phillip Sidney, Daniel Rogers, and the Leiden Humanists*, Leiden 1962, 1–8; and J. J. Woltjer, Introduction to *Leiden University in the Seventeenth Century*, 17 (see also C. S. M. Rademaker, *Life and Work of Gerardus Vossius, 1577–1649*, Assen, 1981, 41).

5. G. A. Lindeboom, 'Medical Education in the Netherlands 1575–1750', in *The History of Medical Education*, ed. C. D. O'Malley, London 1970, 202.

6. Woltjer, 1.

7. See *Resolutien van de Staten van Holland*, 289 vols, Amsterdam 1789–1814, 1575 ff. 349, Art. XVII.

8. J. E. Kroon, *Bijdragen tot de geschiedenis van het geneekundig onderwijs aan de Leidsche Universiteit 1575–1625*, Leiden 1911, 21; and A. G. H. Bachrach, *Sir Constantine Huygens and Britain 1596–1687*, Leiden 1962, 13.

9. O. Fatio, *Nihil Pulchrius Ordine*, Leiden 1971, 11–13; and Woltjer, 3.

10. Woltjer, 2–3.

11. See H. H. Rowen, *The Princes of Orange: The Stadtholders in the Dutch Republic*, Cambridge 1988, 10; Pieter Geyl, *The Revolt of the Netherlands 1555–1609*, rpt London 1988, 161–2; and Andrew Pettegree, *Foreign Protestant Communities in Sixteenth-Century London*, Oxford 1986, 215–61.

12. See Geyl, 209–17.

13. See J. K. Cameron, 'Humanism in the Low Countries', in *The Impact of Humanism on Western Europe*, eds A. Goodman and A. MacKay, London 1990, 151–63; and Paul R. Sellin, *Daniel Heinsius and Stuart England*, Leiden 1968, 9.

14. See Woltjer, 4; for Cartwright, see W. Haller, *The Rise of Puritanism*, rpt Philadelphia 1984, 5, 10–11.

15. Ole Peter Grell, *Dutch Calvinists in Early Stuart London*, Leiden 1989, 124–6 (see also Fatio, *passim*).

16. Geyl, 210–14 (see also W. Nijenhuis, *Adrianus Saravia (c. 1532–1613)*, Leiden 1984).

17. Jonathan I. Israel, *Dutch Primacy in World Trade 1585–1740*, Oxford 1989, 38–42.

18. *Ecclesiae Londino-Batavae Archivum*, ed. J. H. Hessels, Cambridge 1887, I, no. 198.
19. For the States College, see G. C. Kuyper and C. S. M. Rademaker, 'The Collegium Theologicum at Leiden in 1615; Correspondence between P. Bertius and G. J. Vossius the Resigning Regent and His Successor', *Lias*, 2/1 (1975), 125–73; for the Walloon College, see G. H. M. Posthumus Meyjes, *Geschiedenis van het Waalse College te Leiden 1606–1699*, Leiden 1975.
20. See F. Schriver, 'Orthodoxy and Diplomacy; James I and the Vorstius Affair', *English Historical Review*, 85 (1975), 449–74.
21. A. J. Lamping, *Johannes Polyander*, Leiden 1980, 41–54.
22. Woltjer, 5; and G. J. Hoenderdaal, 'The Debate about Armenius outside the Netherlands', in *Leiden University in the Seventeenth Century*, 149 (see also Sellin, 89).
23. Kroon, 89–91.
24. See Kroon, 22 and 93; for Dodonaeus, see G. A. Lindeboom, *Dutch Medical Biography: A Biographical Dictionary of Dutch Physicians and Surgeons 1475–1975*, Amsterdam, 1984, 453–54.
25. G. A. Lindeboom, 'Dog and Frog' – Physiological Experiments', in *Leiden University in the Seventeenth Century*, 279.
26. Kroon, 12–13.
27. Ibid., 69.
28. Ibid., 80–81 and 101 (see also *Dutch Medical Biography*, 347–9).
29. Ibid., 85–8 (and *Dutch Medical Biography*, 2088–91).
30. Ibid., 104–105.
31. Ibid., 93 and 107; and *Dutch Medical Biography*, 859–60.
32. Ibid., 47–8.
33. Ibid., Appendices IX and IXa.
34. Ibid., 47–68 and 97–8.
35. See Lindeboom, 'Medical Education', 204–205; and J. J. Keevil, *Hamey the Stranger*, London 1952, 19–20; also H. Beukers, 'Clinical Teaching in Leiden from Its Beginning until the End of the Eighteenth Century', *Clio Medica*, 21 (1987–88), 139–52.
36. 'Medical Education', 206 (see also A. Gubser, 'The *Positiones Variae Medicae* of Franciscus Sylvius', *Bulletin of the History of Medicine*, XL [1966]).
37. Kroon, 25–7.
38. Woltjer, 5.
39. Bachrach, 13; and Sellin, 17–18.
40. *The Great Instauration*, 120–21 (see also M. H. Curtis, *Oxford and Cambridge in Transition 1558–1642*, Oxford 1959, 152–5).
41. See R. G. Frank, 'Science, Medicine and the Universities of Early Modern England', Parts I and II, in *History of Science*, XI (1973), 211, 240 and 242–3; for anatomy specifically see A. Cunningham, 'The Kinds of Anatomy', in *Medical History*, 19 (1975), 1–19.
42. Israel, esp. 38–79.
43. Ibid., 35; and K. L. Sprunger, *Dutch Puritanism: A History of English and Scottish Churches of the Netherlands in the Sixteenth and Seventeenth Centuries*, Leiden 1982, 124.
44. See Sprunger, 125; and Grell, 132 and 136.
45. Grell, 135–6.

46. Sprunger, 126.
47. For Child, see Hill, 278; for Burgess, see *DNB* and Sprunger, 143–4; for Paget, see Christopher Hill, *Milton and the English Revolution*, London 1977, Appendix 3; and for Pordage, see Christopher Hill, *The World Turned Upside Down*, Harmondsworth 1976, 224–5.
48. See W. R. Munk, *The Roll of the Royal College of Physicians of London*, I, London 1878.
49. See Lindeboom, 'Medical Education', 203 and J. A. van Dorsten, 59 (see also M. Pelling and C. Webster, 'Medical Practitioners', in *Health, Medicine and Morality in the Sixteenth Century*, ed. C. Webster, Cambridge 1979, 190).
50. *The Great Instauration*, 121.
51. For Samuel Wright, see *Alumni Cantabrigiensis*, eds J. Venn and J. A. Venn, part 1, 4 vols, Cambridge 1922–24; and Samuel Wright, *Divers Godly and Learned Sermons*, London 1612, published by Richard Rogers in *Certaine Sermons Preached and Penned by Richard Rogers, Preacher of Weatherfield in Essex*, London 1612.
52. Grell, 135, 146 and 148.
53. Grell, 55–6, and 123–4.
54. Guildhall Library MS 7397/7, f. 33v; for Edward Meetkercke, see *DNB*.
55. See above, Chapter 10, 'Plague in Elizabethan and Stuart London: The Dutch Response', 435–6; and W. Birken, 'Dr John King (1614–1681) and Dr Assuerus Regemorter (1615–1650)', *Medical History*, 20 (1976), 292–3 (see also J. Keevil, 'The Hameys in the Netherlands, Russia, London and Chelsea 1568–1676', *Proceedings of the Huguenot Society*, XIX [1952–58], 27–55).
56. Guildhall Library MS 7397/7, f. 41v.

Index